# DOMESTIC SUBVERSIVE

## A FEMINIST'S TAKE ON THE LEFT
## 1960-1976

# Roberta Salper

ANAPHORA LITERARY PRESS

TUCSON, ARIZONA

Anaphora Literary Press
5755 E. River Rd., #2201
Tucson, AZ 85750
http://anaphoraliterary.com

Book design by Anna Faktorovich, Ph.D.

Copyright © 2014 by Roberta Salper

All rights reserved. No part of this book may be reproduced in any form or by any electronic or mechanical means, including information storage and retrieval systems, without permission in writing from Roberta Salper. Writers are welcome to quote brief passages in their critical studies, as American copyright law dictates.

**Cover Image:** Roberta Salper, Assistant Dean of College of Arts and Sciences, University of Pittsburgh. September 15, 1969. Credit: Dale Gleason, *Pittsburgh Press.*

Published in 2014 by Anaphora Literary Press

Domestic Subversive: A Feminist's Take on the Left 1960-1976
Roberta Salper—1st edition.

ISBN-13: 978-1-937536-67-1
ISBN-10: 1-937536-67-X

Library of Congress Control Number: 2014939989

# DOMESTIC SUBVERSIVE

---

## Roberta Salper

# CONTENTS

| | |
|---|---|
| *Introduction* | 9 |
| 1. Caldwell and Anti-Semitism | 14 |
| 2. New Jersey to Harvard to Spain | 32 |
| 3. Marriage and Fascism | 49 |
| 4. Madrid and Escape | 66 |
| 5. Women's Liberation and the New University Conference | 84 |
| 6. Cuba, 1969: A 'New Man' | 110 |
| 7. Pittsburgh's Feminist Dean | 133 |
| 8. San Diego State Women's Studies | 149 |
| 9. The Puerto Rican Socialist Party | 169 |
| 10. The Death of Orlando Letelier | 185 |
| *Epilogue* | 209 |
| *Acknowledgements* | 211 |
| *Endnotes* | 213 |
| *Bibliography* | 227 |

*To my grandchildren,
Isabelle and Maximillian,
future feminists.*

"A tendency to speculation though it may keep women quiet, as it does men, yet makes her sad. She discerns, it may be, such a hopeless task before her. As a first step, the whole system of society is to be torn down and built up anew. Then the very nature of the opposite sex, or its long legendary habit, which has become like nature, is to be essentially modified, before woman can be allowed to assume what seems a fair and suitable position."

—Nathaniel Hawthorne, The Scarlet Letter, 1850

# INTRODUCTION

From 1968 to 1973, I was under surveillance by the Federal Bureau of Investigation because they regarded me as a "domestic subversive," a category that includes subversion, extremism, sedition, treason, sabotage, certain bombings, violations of anti-riot laws, and protection of foreign officials. The FBI compiled 646 pages about me, their main goal being to determine if I should be put on the "Security Index," which had been recommended by the Pittsburgh field office in 1969 and the San Diego office in 1971. When I moved to New York, the second recommendation was updated to include my connection to the Puerto Rican Socialist Party and my second trip to Cuba. Fortunately, FBI Headquarters decided that inclusion of what they called "the subject" on the Index should be left to the discretion of the New York Division[1] and after a circuitous route, the recommendation was finally denied for insufficient evidence on April 12, 1973.

How did I become "the subject" in that period called the "sixties"? Born a Jew in the United States on the eve of World War II, my discovery of anti-Semitism in suburban 1950s America undermined the idea in Cold War ideology that America was the best country in the world. The fifth grade in Caldwell, New Jersey had only one non-gentile student, albeit one with red hair, blue eyes, freckles and a small nose, yet every morning she was a "dirty Jew girl," instead of Roberta Salper. I had no way of knowing that later I would recognize the value of being "different" and join the long list of Jewish Americans who have been a vibrant part of the left wing in the United States since the beginning of the 20th century. My sense of "difference" would propel me, as a young adult, to explore the multiple meanings and functions of "outsider" and "insider" within my immediate social circles and in the greater political arena.

I was a typical third-generation Jewish American: my Russian immigrant grandparents kept a kosher house and observed all the Jewish holidays. My paternal grandfather helped start the Jewish community in Caldwell New Jersey. My parents, the second generation, wanted to assimilate as much as possible and attended the synagogue only once or twice a year. I am a non-observant Jew, but grateful to have been born into that margin of society because the constant effort "to belong", and to feel like I was a first class citizen, led me to choose a life of political and personal risk-taking in the struggle for global social justice. Time and circumstances conspired to make the jump from small town New Jersey to revolutionary organizations, where I found that I shared with many thousands the idealistic belief that we could change the world.

In 1959, when I became a graduate student in the Department of Romance Languages and Literature at Harvard University, I hoped I was entering a world where ideas mattered and exciting, sophisticated people loved to talk about them. As it happens, I gained much from graduate studies but I learned more outside the university and found my true home among intellectually challenging political activists.

My political formation did not take place in Students for a Democratic Society and the civil rights movement in the United States, but rather in fascist Spain, guided paradoxically by upper middle class Marxist intellectuals who were all male. While the United States was experiencing "the sixties," Spain was still frozen in the past, in international isolation and poverty. Spain and neighboring Portugal were the last surviving redoubts of fascism in Western Europe, and the country was trapped economically and culturally in an all-consuming misogynist Catholic Nationalism. I lived under a fascist patriarchy where misogyny was integrated into the national agenda. Franco's society had its own strict laws and rules, overt and covert, to regulate the behavior and thoughts of women.

University students, restive under the autocratic rule of the General Francisco Franco, were a key element of the domestic ferment that was cautiously but resolutely laying the groundwork for a democratic Spain. Married to the scion of one of Madrid's prominent, anti-Francoist families, I was part of the anti-Franco movement from my arrival in Spain in 1961 until 1968, when I returned permanently to the United States, a bi-lingual feminist schooled in European socialism.

The feminism sparked in Madrid became political activism as I immediately joined the recently created New University Conference, a New Left organization for progressive academics. NUC led me to my next important political development: in the summer of 1969, I visited Cuba under their auspices. Learning more about feminism in a socialist state was my top priority. I had the opportunity to compare our American New Left definition of socialist feminism with the one constructed by the leaders of the then 10-year old socialist state. When we were in Cuba, Che Guevara's idea about creating the "New Man" (and Woman) who would, above all, work for the greater good of everyone was prominent throughout the island. The accomplishments of the revolution were impressive in many areas, but I found the creation of the 'New Woman' problematic. We came face to face with major differences in the meaning of socialist feminism for us in a developed capitalist country and for Cuban women.

Simultaneously, my career at the University of Pittsburgh started as Assistant Professor of Hispanic Literatures. I was the only woman in the department. The following year I became Assistant Dean of the College of Arts and Sciences, the only major female administrator at the university. I was in the right place at the right time. I plunged into organizing the start of the women's liberation movement in Pittsburgh and campaigning for, developing and teaching the first women's studies course at the University of Pittsburgh. My personal life was in turmoil as I underwent a crash course in public speaking, power dress codes, and learning how to further the agenda of the movement within the framework of an important research university. I was part of the first generation of Second Wave Feminists to recognize that, as educated women, our time had come.

In 1970 I went to San Diego State to help create a new institutional framework where different kinds of women — many of them previously denied access to the academy — would learn to produce scholarly knowledge and to make social change. Like other members of the New University Conference, I viewed institutes of higher learning as part of a larger complex of institutions that could be changed by progressive social activists. We called it "working toward socialism" and we meant it, even though no clear plan existed for what this socialism in the United States might look like.

Much of what we advocated has become standard fare: full-fledged women's studies programs across the nation, university-based daycare, and links to the community, important pedagogical reforms. What didn't endure was the vision we had; we didn't just want isolated (albeit important) reforms like equal pay for female faculty and access to administrative power; we wanted to change the structure in which education functioned. For that we had to campaign against corporate control of higher education and that fight was at the crux of the struggles that took place during the first year of the first women's studies program.

We were anti-imperialists. Some of us liked the idea of experimenting with a new kind of American socialism and some of us had even visited Cuba, a major crime, which set off bells at the FBI. Most of us in the New Left—female and male—believed that battles could be won against the expanding corporate control of America. The multinationals were just beginning their relentless forays into the third world; we believed that if more people, in the university and beyond, knew more about the "imperial" nature of our democracy, it could be combated or at least mitigated. This was the vision that formed the backdrop for all of my political work, particularly during these years.

Battle-scarred from the year at San Diego State, I returned east to earn my living at the Old Westbury campus of the State University of New York and to get involved in the struggle to free Puerto Rico from being a "colony" of the United States. Without abandoning any of my feminist convictions, I joined the Marxist-Leninist Puerto Rican Socialist Party (PSP) as soon as it formed a U.S branch and the Party platform became my political guide. The ultimate goal was independence for Puerto Rico and the establishment of Marxist socialism, based on the Cuban model, both in Puerto Rico and in the United States. Several months after I received the coveted status of "vanguard militant," the Party expelled me and I still do not understand why.

In 1974 I returned to a combination of scholarly research and political activism as a Fellow at the Institute for Policy Studies in Washington, DC, the nation's leading progressive think tank. There, I organized a monthly forum that hosted an impressive cross-section of policy makers from the Caribbean and Latin America. For two years, I worked on a daily basis with Orlando Letelier, who had been Foreign and Defense Minister and Ambassador to the United States under Chile's Marxist government led by Salvador Allende. Letelier was the single most effective organizer in the international struggle to combat Augusto Pinochet's military dictatorship in Chile.

My life was finally settling down and the time seemed right to have a baby. In the following pages I recount how I decided to become a professional single mother and navigated with dignity and financial and personal independence, the home birth of Ana Simone on November 9, 1974. Although virtually alone in this undertaking, with the idealism that characterized the time, I was determined to show Ana that girls could now have the world.

On September 21, 1976, my close friend and colleague Orlando Letelier was assassinated on the streets of Washington DC. His murder was considered the first act of foreign terrorism on US soil. For me, "the sixties" ended that day. One thing was clear: I would not be part of a socialist revolution in my lifetime. My daughter was two, and I had to figure out what life I would chart for her. It was time to reassess.

"Domestic Subversive" is my story, but also the story of an era, an extraordinary time. I believed then, as I do now, that women's liberation must come in conjunction with social and economic justice for all people. Capitalism's flagrant economic injustices are hard to reconcile with my idea of a just world. Our vision did not prevail. Could it have? Probably not. Was it worth the effort? Of course. Would I go through it all again?

Just tell me where and when.

In 1981, a friend suggested I take advantage of the Freedom of Information Act to see if I had a FBI file. James Lesar, an attorney specialized in litigating FOIA requests for journalists, authors, and academics, offered to do the paperwork. The process was agonizingly slow and arduous. After several years of correspondence, 351 pages were released, many with more than half the text blocked out in black ink. The reason given for "redacting" the material was the "national security" exemption of the Freedom of Information Act. The FBI regularly uses this exemption to hide information that actually has no bearing on national defense or foreign relations, but, instead shields evidence of the disruptive and frequently illegal activities and strategies taken by the FBI in its war against domestic advocates of political and social change.[2]

For me, 1968 to 73 had been years of professional distinction and social activism. I shed my private cocoon and learned to operate in the public sphere. For the FBI, they were years of wasting thousands of dollars of US taxpayers' money on an astounding repetition of documents and use of various agents to compile the same ultimately useless data. What did they prove in almost 700 pages? That I was a danger to national security by dissenting from mainstream politics?

I wrote this book for young women, and for everyone interested in the testimony of a struggle to become a feminist and political activist and to live like one. Countless female Americans were and remain political radicals, but their stories remain largely unknown. There are histories of the women's liberation movement and histories of the New Left. For many, the two are inextricably linked.[3] We need to hear more about how we found our political voice, and our impact on gender dynamics. This book is one effort to do so.

# CHAPTER 1

# CALDWELL AND ANTI-SEMITISM

I have been a feminist all my life. When I was six or seven, I told some of my relatives that I did not want just to have babies when I grew up because any animal could do that. They smiled with amused tolerance. A couple of months later, my father asked me what I wanted to do when I grew up. I said I did not care as long as I was famous. He smiled, too, but with pride and encouragement. I knew at that moment I had said the right thing, and an ambition was born that became characteristic of a large part of my life—the determination to be outstanding in everything I undertook.

In the mid 1950s, I went to high school in Caldwell, a small, all white, middle-class town, in northern New Jersey about 15 miles from New York City, where my father worked. My experience in grade school and high school was vanilla suburban. I won prizes for academic achievement, but acquired none of the savviness or sophistication of an urban kid—nor did I know anything about how the world really worked. My father and mother were liberals, albeit Jewish ones. Other than ensuring that I understood their abiding admiration for Franklin Roosevelt, their disgust with Joseph McCarthy, and their gratitude to Truman for having voted to recognize the State of Israel in 1948, they did not make politics part of the daily fare of my teen years. I knew about the Nazis, but not about trade unions, capitalism, socialism, social justice and other Big Issues. Without being rabid patriots, my mother and father made it very clear to me that I was lucky to be an American because the United States was the best country in the world. Although some people had more money than we did and some had less, we were all (with one exception) pretty much the same. It was important to be nice to, even go out of your way to help, the "Negroes" because they had a harder time than we did. That was because of the mistaken ideas of certain people, most of whom lived in the South.

This was pretty much the world-view I took with me when I went to live in Spain in 1961, where fascist dictator General Francisco Franco, who had triumphed in a brutal civil war (1936-39) ran the country. The most conservative Catholic Church in Europe dictated morality and ethics. The Church hierarchy had strongly supported Franco during the war and from 1939 on, Church and State were stalwart partners in an effort to resurrect the golden age of the "cross and the sword" reign of King Philip II in the 16$^{th}$ century when the Spanish empire ruled the Western world. It was a particularly bad time for women, who were legally infantilized — economically, intellectually, politically and socially dependent on fathers or husbands — and rendered unable to think or act for themselves.

Misogyny was widely internalized by Spanish women. The women's section of the Falange [the Spanish Fascist Party] worked in tandem with the Catholic Church to define, regulate and control every aspect of the public and private lives of Spanish women. As I was to learn, the subtle and not-so subtle reverberations of the overt legal restrictions were pernicious and all pervasive.

With a fellowship from Harvard to work on my doctorate in Romance Languages and Literatures, I moved into an apartment building at Lope de Vega 31, one of the narrow streets behind the Palace Hotel in an old, central section of Madrid. The Palace, still a luxury hotel today, is wedged between Cervantes and San Jerónimo Streets, about a half mile southeast of the Puerta del Sol, the historic epicenter of Madrid. This would be my neighborhood for a year.

Lope de Vega is part of a small network of narrow streets — some cobblestone and several with names from Spain's rich archive of literary figures like Cervantes, Echegaray and Lope de Vega — that have housed the capital's lower middle class since the end of the 16$^{th}$ century. Except for Echegaray Street, which boasted the highest concentration of *taperías* in Madrid (long before the 1990s when Spanish tapas became an international commodity), only an occasional beauty parlor, dry cleaner, bar, or small grocery interrupted the residential routine of grayish stucco four-story walk-up apartment buildings. Today, many residences still have the centuries-old massive dark wooden doors that open in the middle. When I lived on Lope de Vega, all of the buildings were tended by a *sereno*, a key man. This remained a custom in Madrid until relatively recently.

A *sereno* was in charge of the outdoor keys for a certain number of residential blocks. Each night he would lock the doors at 11:00 p.m. and unlock them at 6:00 or 7:00 a.m. The rest of the night he walked around "his blocks," occasionally sleeping on a doorstep; the *sereno* was not to come into any of the houses because he did not live there. I never knew where our *serreno* lived. If you got home later than 11:00, you had to clap your hands loudly and call for him to let you in. The inhabitants of a *serreno's* territory always knew his favorite doorsteps for napping. Our *serreno* knew the details of all of our comings and goings, for we rarely had use of an ancient six-inch metal outdoors key called *"La Llave."* This whole practice, in existence for decades, seemed rather senseless to me and I wondered why the custom existed. Why didn't the Spaniards just make copies of the front door key for the folks who lived in the building? It took me some time to understand that "key men" were part of the intricate web of "hidden unemployment" that helped maintain the precarious balance of the Spanish economy for years. On the fringe of Spain's wobbly market economy, a serreno did not have a proper job, but monthly tips from the inhabitants of his buildings allowed him to scrape together a minimal subsistence.

Manolita Roesset owned the apartment on the second floor of Lope de Vega 31 and rented rooms to two or three foreign students, all female. In her early fifties and separated from her husband (legal divorce did not exist in Spain until 1981), Manolita earned money in one of the few "decent" ways open to women—offering room and board to nice young women studying in Spain. I fit squarely into that category. A small, pleasant woman who went to mass every morning, Manolita scurried to conform to the definition of the ideal Spanish woman as laid out by her preceptors, the priests and the *Sección Feminina del Falange* [Women's Branch of the Spanish Fascist Party]. She was submissive to God and Government, happy and smiling and, above all, automatically obedient to male authority. Everything about Manolita was small and bird-like; she constantly fussed and bustled about arranging little objects and making plans for shopping, eating and repairing one thing or another. I never saw Manolita still and relaxed; she was intellectually passive and believed women were, by nature, submissive and obedient. Men were innately superior and it was a woman's duty to make life as pleasant and as easy as possible for her husband. It was a terrible shame that her husband had turned out to be a "scoundrel" (I never learned more details) but at least she had a son—and, she would add as an afterthought, a daughter too.

In tune with her social peers and, in fact, with the large majority of Spanish women, Manolita unquestioningly accepted the inextricable link between female sexual purity and male honor which was the bulwark of the patriarchal code of Spanish social mores. That is, the "good name" of a male is maintained by his ability to assure the chastity of all females related to him. In addition, like Franco Spain's official culture, Manolita lamented that the whole world was not Catholic, as Catholicism was the only path to salvation. The economic exigencies that dictated Manolita's daily life led to frequent contact with Protestants, even Jews. She knew I was Jewish, but this did not faze her; as long as the infidels were not home grown, her conscience was clear. Neither God nor Government could possibly fault her for this small transgression.

In the winter of 1962, after I had been in Madrid four or five months, Consuelo Vázquez de Parga invited me to *tomar una copa* [have a drink] with some of her university friends. Although only a few years older than me, Consuelo had been an instructor at *La Escuela Española* [Spanish Summer School] in Middlebury, Vermont, where I had been a student the summer before starting graduate school. We had corresponded sporadically since then, and I contacted her after arriving in Madrid. Consuelo had gone to the *Colegio Estudio* [then the sole private K-12 school supported by liberal anti-Francoists], and her circle of friends included a lot of *Colegio Estudio* graduates. Her parents were staunch anti-Francoists—in fact, many of the parents at the school had known each other for years and were part of a significant social network that passed from generation to generation.

One of the *Colegio Estudio* graduates Consuelo introduced me to in February 1962, in a little bar on Martinez Campos Street around the corner from the Colegio on Miguel Angel Street, was Gabriel Tortella. The Tortella and Vázquez de Parga families had been friends for decades. With Gabriel was his friend Gonzalo Anés. Both were students of economics and both were dedicated to the creation of a New Spain. Gabriel and I immediately began dating and saw each other daily for the rest of my stay in Madrid.

We embarked on an intense eight-month relationship that included trips to Paris to buy books and see movies banned in Spain and we also took clandestine trips to Gabriel's family's summer home in Pozuelo de Alarcón to get to know each other physically. We got married on October 2, 1962 in a civil ceremony in Gibraltar.

Gabriel came from the wealthy, educated, cultured Madrid bourgeoisie. He had princely tastes, Marxist intellectual leanings, and continental charm. He had a slight build, was slim, with narrow shoulders, about 5'9" tall. With compelling dark blue eyes and thick straight hair so black it was almost navy blue, Gabriel was handsome. His nose was rather thin and straight and his mouth well formed with very white teeth. One of his front teeth was slightly chipped, the result of a childhood jostle with his younger brother. At first glance, Gabriel resembled the French actor Alain Delon, but he had none of Delon's magnetic sexuality. Gabriel was intense, but gentle, and had a rather childlike quality that emanated sweet appeal but not sensuality. Later I would come to know and resent that childlike quality as a sign of weakness. Most of all, I was attracted by the fact that he belonged so solidly to a group that I had designated as 'interesting.' These were the Spanish intellectuals and technocrats, who read Marx and Lenin, never took off their spotless dark suits and ties, and had impeccably groomed wives who supervised households with two or three servants.

I was 23 when I married. It had already been a long, arduous journey that had wrested me from Caldwell, New Jersey, and the family baggage, and gotten me to Madrid, as a member of its cultured bourgeoisie.

Although I had unquestioningly imbibed the soft, unanalytical liberalism of my parents, a political vision typical of many Jews who were bringing up children during the Truman and Eisenhower administrations, I was never comfortable in Caldwell. My earliest memories are of feeling constrained by the reigning norms of behavior and thought. I became determined to find a way out of the life my parents led. Especially, I did not want to be boxed into a confined life like my mother.

My parents were eager to be "good neighbors" with everybody and defensive about their Jewishness. At an early age I felt their insecurity about their own dignity and worth and no amount of "rational" explanation about the superiority of the Jews ever convinced me that I was not in some way inferior. (Jesus was a Jew, you know. Jewish people never get drunk. Jewish men make the best husbands. Jews always send their children to college. Intellectual life is of prime importance to Jews. A Jewish army general? Roberta, don't be silly.)

In those years the knowledge that I, alone among all my friends, was a "Jew" confused and subtly isolated me from both my family and friends. I never shared my anxieties with anyone. I just wanted to close my eyes and make it all go away. What was the value of being Jewish? All it did was make me different at an age when one wants terribly to work out an identity similar to peers.

It would be many years before I learned to convert this "Jewish difference" I found in Caldwell into a strength that would empower me to become a skilled multifaceted institution builder in a quest for social justice. Being unique became an asset, but it made me vulnerable in my hybrid quest to bring about progressive change. I came to garner strength from never fully belonging anywhere in the way that everyone in Spain, in those days, knew how to be Spanish. Over the years I would carve out my own framework for being an American that I respected.

Although there was a small Jewish community in Caldwell (enough to support one synagogue), throughout grade school and high school I was the only Jewish person in my class. I hated being the only student who had to stay out of school on Jewish holidays. The troubling complexities of having to exist within the confines of an imposed ethnic identity form my earliest memories. In the early 1950s I was unaware that I was living in an affluent post World War II America that offered economic opportunities for middle-class women as never before or that I was to become a beneficiary of the flourishing economy in ways unknown to my mother. Historically, it was a moment that allowed women with financial and social profiles such as mine the economic space to break out of traditional constraints.

For too long I was under the sway of the low-keyed anti-Semitism that would flare up occasionally as part of the cultural mulch of that small northern New Jersey town. Essex Fells, the town next to Caldwell, was "restricted" — no Jews allowed. As early as kindergarten (where my five-year old peers frequently pointed out to me, "You people killed Jesus") I realized a lot of people didn't like Jews, particularly the Irish Catholics who lived on our street. Many students in my school were Catholic — of German or Irish descent — and several anti-Semitic encounters left indelible imprints on my formative years. From these experiences, I developed the sharpened sensibility and wakefulness of an outsider, but I was an involuntary outsider. Funny how cruelties and slights we receive as children live with us much more vividly than the blows of adulthood. It would be life under fascism; my Spanish apprenticeship in understanding, that was to empower me to overcome the constraints of minority status in the United States.

My parents were children of Russian Jewish immigrants. My paternal grandfather, Joe Schaltuper left Rogova, the same town near Vilna in Lithuania where Bakhtin was born, in the first years of the 20$^{th}$ century and moved to Johannesburg, South Africa. The Vilna-Johannesburg route was a common route of escape from the Russian anti-Semitic pogroms of the late 19$^{th}$ century. The economic base for the Jewish community in South Africa at that time was

Johannesburg's diamond trade—not mining, but refining, cutting, polishing, and by extension, the jewelry business. Joe was sent to South Africa to learn this craft and English before embarking for America. Some years ago, a cousin told me that Joe wanted his family to be "real Americans," so when passing through Ellis Island, he changed the last name to "Salper." I am not sure exactly when he and his brother Oscar came to New York's Lower East Side, but my father was born in 1911, in America.

Joe came to America with a wife already picked out for him; the Johannesburg/New York Jewish axis had arranged a marriage with Rose Stein. Rose's family had left Germany and Poland in the 1880s, and by the turn of the century her father had a successful wholesale jewelry business in Newark, New Jersey. The fact that her father didn't have a son and Rose was an American made her a desirable commodity in the new immigrant marriage business. Joe Salper/né Schaltuper was thus added to the Stein family, destined to take over the jewelry business, which he dutifully did. Joe always spoke English with a marked South African accent (Mommy, why does Pop speak such funny English?). In spare moments he wrote poetry in Hebrew and Yiddish as he used to do in Lithuania or he sat in a large upholstered armchair, silent for hours, thinking or brooding. I soon understood that he had very little interest in communicating with the women around him, namely his wife and my mother.

Even then, when I was seven or eight, I realized he was a man disappointed with the lot life had dealt him. It was about that time when he said to me, "It's a shame you are a girl, because you are smart." I didn't answer, but those words stuck. And over the years, those words have accompanied me like a Greek chorus in the background but always present and always powerful: You are a girl; that's a handicap; you are smart, but is that enough to overcome the handicap?

My father, Maurice (Murray) Salper, was a social worker at the American Jewish Congress in New York City. He took up this profession by default. Financially unable to get married without taking over the jewelry business my grandfather had made into a respectably profitable enterprise, my father, who was utterly uninterested in the business, had allowed it to sink into bankruptcy by 1948. Because he had a Masters Degree in Social Work from Columbia University, he was able to get a job with the American Jewish Congress working with Jewish European refugees. In spite of having close family living in Israel (paternal grandmother, aunt and her husband and two first cousins) my father was principally interested in the future of life as a Jew in the United States, not in Israel.

Because Joe's business had prospered, my father had not gone to tuition-free City College like many first generation New York Jews of Eastern European descent. He majored in French literature at a private institution, New York University. Our house in Caldwell had wall-to-wall bookcases lined with his books, mostly European and contemporary American literature and sociological studies documenting the wonders of the United States and its rapidly assimilating Jewish Americans. But the deep joy in his life came from music, from listening to Italian opera, playing the piano and composing popular songs. Shortly before the end of his life, he even had one song published, a homage to the Statue of Liberty entitled "I Love a Lovely Lady on an Island in the Bay." His idols were George Gershwin, Jerome Kern and Irving Berlin, hugely successful Jewish American creators of popular songs and musicals.

Of eight children, my mother, her oldest brother, and sister were the only three to go to college. (Her parents had immigrated to Boston from Odessa at the turn of the century.) It must have required perseverance to go to college during the Depression. She used to explain, "I had to sell stockings at Filene's to pay the tuition." But like many other women of her generation who were victims of unawareness, Louise Glaser tucked the hard-won B.A. in her purse, got married, and gave birth to me before her first wedding anniversary.

My earliest memories are of not wanting to be like my mother. Years later, Betty Friedan wrote with compassion about how women like my mother were trapped into *The Feminine Mystique*. But for most of my life I was incapable of seeing my mother in her own context. She never did anything that I wanted to do or that seemed the least bit interesting. Her days were filled with cooking, cleaning, waiting for my father to come home and generally being irritated. My mother spent hours talking on the telephone every morning to female friends. A "very important conversation that cannot be cut short" was the reason she gave for why she never had lunch ready at 11:30 when I came home for the hour lunch break during primary school. This became a point of contention for years. I would offer to make my own sandwich; she would say, "No, no, I'll do it; I'll be off the phone in a minute." But she invariably kept me waiting, hovering around the telephone for 15 or 20 minutes. My mother needed to be the center of attention constantly in order not to have her own wobbly sense of self-endangered. Her unconscious yearnings and unarticulated needs could never be fulfilled by the daily routine of being a mother and housewife.

Over the years, my mother became an expert in devising "attention getting mechanisms." The most destructive of these for family relations was her ceaseless talking, permitting no interruption. "Mom, listen to me!" became a litany in our house. Recognition and affirmation of another person, her daughters included, seemed to diminish or threaten her. She lived to be 91 but we never talked honestly with each other. I was always afraid her words would hurt me, and I was incapable of understanding her context: daughter of poor Eastern Europeans, a first generation American with ambitions and desires she was incapable of articulating. Her generation was trapped in silence and frustration, as Friedan explained.

But I did not know anyone else I wanted to be like. I thought my female schoolteachers led dull lives, as did the librarian, the secretaries, and the waitresses who constituted the only women I knew who were anything other than full-time mothers. Then one day my parents took me to see the Sadlers Wells Ballet in New York where I saw a beautiful woman who did something difficult well and was showered with thundering applause. I asked what she was and immediately announced that I too would become a prima ballerina. In first grade, I plunged headlong into a program to implement my goal. For the next five years I took tap, ballet, and acrobatic lessons three or four times a week. I out-danced everyone in my hometown classes, and the teacher suggested that I go to the American School of Ballet in New York City and take private lessons with Olga. A tall, regal middle-aged Russian lady with mounds of long grey hair piled on top of her head, Olga always wore a purple velvet tunic and carried an elegant walking stick that she used to emphasize her words and mark musical beats.

My father drove me into New York City for my dancing lessons every Sunday morning for three years. I knew my mother would have preferred for him to be home all day Sunday, and judging by the relieved expression on her face when at age fourteen, I announced I was giving up ballet, I realized that financing all this private instruction must have been a strain on the family. During the weekly drive to the ballet lessons in the old blue and white Pontiac, my father and I had long discussions about "life." As a result of these talks, I gleaned that he was a dissatisfied, insecure man who was devoting himself to making sure I would have a different lot in life than his. As a young girl of 11 or 12, I did not know how to deal with perceptions of my father that I would have rather not have had. I felt so bad for him and so impotent when I tried to think how to help him. About that time, people began to tell me that I never smiled. They said that I was such a "serious child," and frequently asked me if anything was the matter. I never answered. I hated them for seeing something was "wrong" with me, and I hated myself for not being "perfect."

In sixth grade Miss Galloway gave our class an assignment to complete over the Thanksgiving break. We had to write a short story about something we considered "important." When the story was done, we were to put it in a folder and write the title and our name on the "cover of the book." Miss Galloway also wanted us to create an illustrative cover design. All of us loved Marge Galloway. She was young, gentle and always listened to us encouragingly when we answered in class. I wanted to please her very much.

The title of my story was: "She Was Different." It was a four-page narrative about "Jane", a 10 year-old Quaker girl, and the injustices inflicted on her in school because she was different from everyone else. I made a cover of blue construction paper. In the center I pasted a two-inch, round picture of a smiling, blue-eyed "Jane" cut out from an ad in my mother's *Ladies Home Journal*. I made six index fingers out of salmon colored construction paper; each about four inches long, and pasted the six fingers in a circle around Jane's picture, all pointing at her. Each finger was twice as big as Jane and the six of them dwarfed her completely. In the story I was Jane's advocate, successfully defending her from all attackers. I explained to all of Jane's classmates why it was wrong to bully someone just for not having the same religion as everyone else. I adapted to sixth grade discourse the attitude and language my parents used when they had explained why it was important to be "nice to the Negroes." Jane liked and admired me. She was very grateful that I had rescued her from terrible situations. She couldn't find enough ways to thank me.

Miss Galloway showed my story to my parents because, as I was told, she thought it was "so interesting and well written." My parents never discussed the story with me, but my father mobilized immediately. He called a friend, a carpenter, and asked if he could build a six-foot wooden menorah as soon as possible. Traditionally, a menorah is a small ceremonial candleholder used in Jewish families to celebrate the eight days of Hanukah. The menorah holds nine candles, one for each night of the holiday and a ninth, which lights the others each night of the holiday. However, my father had other ideas about the use of a menorah. Three weeks after his call to the carpenter, a beautifully painted blue and white eight-branched wooden menorah, standing over six feet tall and topped with nine electric bulbs that could go on one at a time, appeared at our house. It became the centerpiece of a Hanukah party my parents held for my entire sixth grade class at the Caldwell Women's Club. They had rented the banquet room for the occasion. My father was the architect of the event, but my mother helped in the execution; she never disagreed openly with him if he felt strongly about something.

Located on Westville Ave about a mile from my home, the Caldwell Women's Club was (and still is) part of the General Federation of Women's Clubs. Devoted to community service, the organization meets monthly, sponsors cultural events and often rents out several of its rooms for community events. In the 1940s and 50s, the women who ran the club were all Christian stalwarts of the community. When I was in fifth and sixth grades, the Women's Club sponsored a "Cotillion"—semi-monthly ballroom dancing classes on Friday nights for grade school students of my age, boy and girls. The fee made it accessible, and most of my friends attended. For them it was primarily a social event, and I wanted to go too. My mother's response to my request was terse and abrupt: "You can't go to the Cotillion. Damn goyim." I was angry at her for the Yiddish slur she used to refer to the non-Jewish people I went to school with every day, but I did not say anything. I understood I could not go to Cotillion because I was Jewish. The subject never came up in the family again. When several of my friends asked me why I was not going to Cotillion, I told them I already had so many ballet lessons, I did not want more classes related to dancing. However, the Caldwell Women's Club was willing to accept my father's money to rent its banquet room for a Jewish event.

The Hanukah party took place on a Saturday evening and the whole class came, including Miss Galloway. My parents decorated the banquet room with blue and white crepe paper streamers that flowed out from the huge menorah in the center—the Jewish Christmas tree. On one side of the room, long tables covered with white tablecloths hosted mounds of sugar cookies, each cut in the shape of a six-pointed star-the Star of David. Each cookie had either blue or white frosting; the blue ones were topped with white sugar sparkles and the white cookies had blue sparkles. Later, the class would be introduced to more Hanukah treats: trays of potato latkes [pancakes], bowls of apple sauce and sour cream, and heaps of round pieces of chocolate, each wrapped in gold foil the size of a quarter. This was edible Hanukah *gelt* [money] used to play a game with dreidels.[4] At the end of one of the tables was a pile of small wooden *dreidels*, one for each guest. Two large presents beautifully wrapped in glittering blue and white Hanukah paper and tied with wide, shiny gold ribbon, sat next to the *driedels*. They were destined for the winners of the spinning game the guests would soon play. In the background, a victrola played Hanukah songs from my father's record collection.

The evening started well. Classmates flooded into the room, gobbled sugar cookies and bounced around to the music. They barely seemed to notice the carefully constructed symphony in blue and white, the colors of the flag of the recently created State of Israel. I thought they seemed quite pleased to be there as they chatted, picked up dreidels, and drank coke or ginger ale. Immersed in a sense of wellbeing, I glanced at my parents. They were smiling with pleasure; the plan was working. It occurred to me that it might be okay to be Jewish. All the kids seemed to like being here, I thought, even though the party was blue and white instead of red and green. My relaxed contentment was brief; out of the corner of my eye, I spotted Sean Murphy and Dick Killigan, the two most popular boys in the class, huddled together in a corner, looking at the menorah and laughing. They were covering their mouths trying to muffle what they were saying. Suddenly they could not contain their laughter and, embarrassed, ran out of the banquet hall, heading toward the men's room. I could not hear what they were saying, but it did not matter. It was bad; I knew it. For me, the party was over. My momentary sense of belonging, that temporary euphoria of being as worthy as everyone else in the class, plummeted. Sean and Dick were surely making fun of the menorah, of my being Jewish. The familiar wariness returned: Don't relax, watch very carefully what you say and do.

At one point we all sat on the floor around the menorah to eat latkes while my father explained the meaning of Hanukah. The class listened politely. I remained silent, hoping everything would end soon. Lynn, the judge's daughter, and Marilyn, the child of working class Scottish immigrants, asked questions and wanted to know more of the history. But I did not feel any better. What mattered to me was the mockery I had perceived by Sean and Dick. I felt worse than ever as the evening progressed because I had to pretend to my parents that I was having a wonderful time at the party they had gone to so much trouble and expense to give, to convince me that it was okay to be Jewish.

Before I went to kindergarten, my most treasured possession was an original 1938 edition of *"Babar et sa famille"* [Babar and His Family] published in Paris. It was a large book, 11 by 18 inches, in French, with wonderful illustrations of a family of elephants who all loved each other dearly. My father gave it to me for my fourth birthday and often read it to me in French. The language sounded pretty and although I did not know what the words meant, I understood my father relished the moments he read it to me. I did too. It was like being far away in a new country, just with him. This attachment to foreign languages, initially associated with paternal love and attention, would grow with the years and take many different directions.

My father also left me another legacy: a love of beauty, good taste and aesthetic excellence—his friends called him "Mr. Gracious Living." Not having money to implement the "high life" was not that important to him; what was crucial was to know what was "best" and to understand why.

When I was six years old, my father bought me a bottle of Chanel No. 5 perfume and explained that it was "the best." This gift not only signified a special bond between my father and me; it also cemented my special status in the family. I understood that little bottle of perfume placed me in a category separate from and superior to my mother and sister. In first grade, I became the chief repository of my father's unfulfilled hopes to move beyond the confines of the Jewish community. Each time he introduced me to a new touch of luxury or excellence, it was to help me take a step toward a bigger, wider world "out there." "Out there" initially meant the educated upper middle class gentile world. Later it became Europe.

At eight years old, I rode with my father overnight on a train to Boston in a parlor car (the most luxurious accommodations then available)—my mother's objections at the cost were silenced by his fiat: "it is good for her to know what is available in life." My mother's resentful expression did not bother me a bit; in fact, I rather enjoyed it. The family hierarchy was clear.

During the trip to Boston, my father and I ate in the dining car. In the late 1940s, eating in a dining car on a train was an elegant, decidedly pre-civil rights experience. The headwaiter, a tall Negro, as African Americans were referred to, dressed meticulously in a stiffly pressed black and white uniform with large gold buttons, showed us to our table. Two other waiters came to serve us. They were also Negroes, wearing the same uniform but without gold buttons. The tables had starched white tablecloths; each place setting consisted of a white linen napkin, white plates with a gold band and a bevy of forks, knives and spoons that my father said were sterling silver. Three different shaped glasses completed the setting: one for water, one for red wine and one for white wine, as my father explained. I glanced around the dining car. I took it all in. It was fun. But I had a question. "Daddy, why is everyone who works here a Negro?" Hesitating a moment before he answered, my father responded, "Because it is one of the best jobs Negroes can get now." The answer satisfied me, and we moved on to discuss more of the marvels of the dining car and our impending meal.

Some months later my father took me to the Metropolitan Opera in New York to hear Jussi Bjorling, at that time the world's greatest living tenor, sing Rodolfo in Puccini's *La Boheme*. It was at the old Met on 39th Street and Broadway; Lincoln Center had not yet been built. We sat in the orchestra and I wore my new shoes, black patent leather MaryJanes. My father bought me candy covered Jordan almonds in case I got hungry before the intermission. Suddenly the lights darkened; the thick, luxurious gold velvet curtain rose, and we were transported to Paris by the opening notes of Puccini's exquisitely sweet melodies. The grand world of beautiful people, glorious costumes and decorations, all blending with the music, captivated me immediately. Everyone was singing and looked happy. Then Jussi Bjorling stepped slightly forward and sang "*Che gelida manina*" [What a frozen little hand], "*se la lasci riscaldar.*" [Let me warm it for you]. I had no idea what Rodolfo was saying to Mimi, but it didn't matter. I sobbed from the sheer magnificence of the voice, the passion, the all-encompassing warm sensuality of the experience. I glanced at my father. He had tears trickling down his cheeks too.

I have never forgotten that moment and the evening that made me the opera buff I have been for over 60 years.

The legacy left to me by "Mr. Gracious Living" would turn out to be somewhat of a mixed blessing. Over the years, I have tried to balance (often precariously) my attraction to a sybaritic lifestyle with my devotion to political principles of social justice for the poor. Attempting to reconcile my attraction to a life of comfort, beauty and privilege with my concern for the exploitation of the poor on which such lives have often been based created a permanent tension in my life. My commitment to a political world in the United States that was contemptuous and dismissive of all things sybaritic heightened this tension.

My father died suddenly of a coronary thrombosis in May of

my freshman year in Caldwell High School, the same school from which he had graduated. He was 42. It was a thunderbolt: sudden and inconceivable. When my mother came home from the hotel in Cherry Hill, New Jersey, where she and my father had gone to spend Memorial Day weekend, and she told me "Daddy is dead," my first thought was: "How am I going to protect myself from her now? She'll never let me go." It took many years for me to allow myself both to realize this was not an ordinary — or even a normal — thought to have at that age, and to have feelings of compassion for my mother's situation. I was single mindedly bent on holding myself together emotionally and that meant ignoring the rest of the family's needs.

I handled my father's death by first being furious with him and then by blocking it out and numbing myself to all emotions that might confront me with the loss. I refused to go to his funeral because I could not bear the thought of the possible overflow of my feelings. I had to protect myself. With his death, I lost the only mooring I had ever known. I built instant, impenetrable armor that no one in my family thereafter breached. Robot-like, I garnered strength to return to school five days after my father's death (that was as soon as my mother would let me) in order to take final exams in early June. I studied even more than usual. I had to be successful at school, for that offered the only possible ticket out of Caldwell. When I got all As on my report card that June, I missed my father's warm smile of approval. No one else said anything to me.

After my father's death, my mother alternated between emotional collapse and unpredictable bouts of strength. She was not a warm or affectionate person (never kissed or hugged her daughters) but with the loss of her husband, my mother became brittle, harsh and defensively judgmental. She was unhappy, scared and lonely and I was a natural target for the venting of her frustrations: the oldest of three daughters, "Daddy's pet," and his big hope for entrée into mainstream America. My mother was too frightened to continue to support any of his ambitions for me. Constantly criticized and never affirmed, I lost most of my earlier confidence in my ability to do something "great." High school turned out to be a disaster. I was overpowered by the all-American ethic. Most of all, I wanted to be popular and especially to be liked by boys. I was crushed when, several weeks after my father's death, I was not elected to the cheerleading squad. I was convinced that something must be wrong with me: Was it because my legs were too heavy, because I still wore braces, or could it be because I was Jewish?

My mother did not work outside the house until my father died. At that time, I could not appreciate the strength and determination it took on her part to spend a year at Montclair State Teachers College (now Montclair University), only months after my father had died, to get a Masters Degree in Education and become a high school English teacher. My sole reaction to her new situation was to become even more resolutely determined to get out of Caldwell.

My mother was ambiguous about my aspirations to fly to new, unknown venues. (She had been confined to the house and forced to deal with a myriad of frustrated, unarticulated ambitions, so how could her children expect to succeed "out there"?). Without my father's admiration and encouragement to excel, each day was a potential battle to keep the end goal in sight. However, shortly before his death, my father gave me, probably unknowingly, a powerful tool to deal with the future. He gave me permission not to believe in God. "Daddy, what's an atheist?" "Someone who does not believe in God and has no religion," he responded. I was thrilled—a way to stop being Jewish! Maybe everything would change for me if I became an atheist. As my father and I discussed the pros and cons of believing in God (I never mentioned to him my plans to use atheism as a way to shed my Jewishness), I realized he did not believe in God, but was trying to present both sides of the argument to me. When I announced to my parents several days later that I was atheist, my father said, "Fine, that is your decision."

In my high school yearbook I wrote that my ambition was to be a bilingual secretary. Quite a step down from prima ballerina or my subsequent, short-lived desire to be a journalist. I had been socialized well throughout four years of high school and almost convinced that the main reason for going to college was to find the right husband. However, I had not totally given in to American high school socialization—the fact that I placed "bilingual" before "secretary" represented my consuming desire to travel. The sound of Babar's exotic French still lurked in the background.

I read the *The New York Sunday Times* want ads religiously all during high school. I did not know any other way to find out about opportunities for planning my future. The most exciting job under the "Female" column (all ads were gender segregated then) was Spanish-English secretary to an American corporate executive based in Latin America. Mexico, Argentina, Peru—locales far away from New Jersey, my family, being Jewish and the continual fear of unanticipated rejection. Freedom. Unpredictable experiences and dark, gentle, sensitive men. That sounded like the kind of future I wanted and one that I might be able to make work with the right kind of preparation.

I was the best student in Miss Abbot's Spanish class for the four years I took Spanish. She often remarked on "Roberta's linguistic ability." I loved the class. Miss Abbot was a tiny woman about 50 years old with horn-rimmed glasses, a permanently pleasant disposition and a ready smile. She had spent a summer in Spain years before and told us glorious tales about the Prado Museum, *tortilla de patatas* [Spanish omelet], flamenco dancing, the Alhambra, and friendly people who loved chatting in Spanish to American visitors. I did not know it then, but she had visited Spain in 1933 during the Spanish Republic, before the civil war and the Franco dictatorship. Miss Abbot made Spain sound intense, warm and exciting. On occasion she would get dewy-eyed relating bits of her trip to us. There must have been a dark, gentle, sensitive male tucked into those memories somewhere. French class was not nearly as much fun. Miss Liot, originally from Quebec, was in her thirties. She had short, straight black hair and bangs, a sharp pointy nose and thin lips pursed together into a straight line. Pinched and proper, Miss Liot was always telling us how we should sit, think, eat, speak and dress because that was how it was done in Paris. "The French have very good taste," she would invariably add. It was left to the rest of us to silently finish her thought: "and the Americans do not." I imagine she exempted her native Quebec from the sweeping denunciation, but maybe not. At any rate, France did not sound very welcoming.

One day during my junior year, Miss Abbot brought a man named Pedro to our Spanish class to play the guitar and talk about Spanish music. Pedro, who was about 30, had been born in Spain but now lived in New York. Miss Abbot did not tell us his family had fled the Franco dictatorship in 1939; I found that out years later. In preparation for Pedro's visit, Miss Abbot devoted several classes to discussing the "whole Spanish-speaking world." In addition to Spain, more than twenty other countries spoke Spanish throughout Latin America and the Caribbean, and we should know they existed and something about each one. But Miss Abbot's introduction to Latin America had a subtext: the continent to the south was interesting, even exotic, but backward and underdeveloped. Many people did not even know how to read; in short, it had no "culture." In 1950s America, Latin America was a geographical footnote. Hundreds of millions of people might speak Spanish throughout South America, but Spain was what counted. It was located in Western Europe, and Europe was the Western world's cultural citadel.

Pedro was a lovely man. Slim and graceful, he was of medium height with tan skin, olive green eyes and black hair with a slight wave. He was not "movie star" handsome, but emanated a gentle charm as he tried to engage us in his world. He spoke in Spanish, enunciating clearly, wanting to make sure we understood. I liked him immediately. As Pedro began strumming a *fandango*, I started to fantasize about romantic encounters with Latin men.

My first vision of Latin males came from pictures in *The New York Sunday Times* travel section and in my high school textbooks. I was attracted to these men because they were never blond, like all the popular boys in high school, and nothing about them resembled teenage boys in Caldwell. In my imagined world, Latin men not only lived far away, but they also belonged to an intellectually stimulating, elegant society that did not care about differences between Christians and Jews. My generic Latin male—a quintessentially "interesting man"—was the polar opposite of the fair, blue-eyed, ruddy lower middle-class boys of Irish and German descent that populated the classrooms of Caldwell High, several of whom were repositories of anti-Semitism imbibed from their parents.

The fascination with my platonic ideal of a Latin male—exotic, romantic, sensual, elegant, and most of all, madly in love with me—would last for years.

Although I had given up glorious ambitions by my junior year of high school, I still had the Jewish American drive "to achieve," so I applied to Harvard (then Radcliffe, for women). I was not accepted and instead went to the University of Michigan in Ann Arbor, mainly because it offered a full scholarship that my mother urged me to accept.

# CHAPTER 2

# NEW JERSEY TO HARVARD TO SPAIN

Like most college admission forms in the 1950s, Michigan asked all applicants to declare "Religion." I filled in the blank: Jewish. I wondered about the consequences of choosing an identity before I had even seen the university. I had an intimation when, on page 2, the form asked the applicant to describe "characteristics you would like in a roommate." I wrote that as long as the person was tolerant and honest, I did not care about anything else. I thought I was telling them that I did not want to room with a Jewish girl (sex segregation was a given) just because I was Jewish. They did not get my point. My roommate turned out to Lois Goldberg from Winnetka, Illinois, a wealthy suburb about twenty miles north of Chicago with a sizeable Jewish population.

The second issue on the application form that made me uneasy was raised by a question about "Greek Life." Was I interested in joining a sorority and did I want to "rush" in September? It sounded perilously like trying to get elected to the cheerleading squad at Caldwell High School. Another road to rejection. I would have liked to undergo the sorority vetting process and be chosen to belong, but I was too frightened of failing. Because rejection would hurt too much, I decided not to risk it.

When I got to Ann Arbor, I learned details about what was involved in the "live or die" selection process for members of sororities. The principal divide was between Christians and Jews. (There were so few non-white undergraduates at the university that no one was even aware of a racial divide. Blacks simply did not exist.) The second division was between rich, less rich and least rich. Poor girls never joined sororities; Greek life cost money. It was also very important what you looked like and how you dressed. Academic achievement was not one of the criteria. Over a dozen choices of a sorority were available for Christian girls, but just three for Jews: Alpha Epsilon Phi was "the best." Sigma Delta Tau for those "in the middle" and was considered comfortably above the third sorority (whose name I have forgotten), which was where Jewish leftovers went. Most girls who did not "rush" were either "nerds" or poor or both, although everyone I spoke to who did not "rush" said it was because she did not believe in the sorority system. I said that too, but I would have loved to have been invited to join Alpha Epsilon Phi. From the beginning of life in Ann Arbor, I felt excluded simply by the existence of a social life that was based on a sororal (and fraternal) hierarchy.

I lived in Alice Lloyd Hall, a huge dormitory with hundreds of rooms.

During the first semester, I shared a small basement room with Lois. We did not become friends. During the second semester, as the Dean of Students sought to empty the basement rooms, I was moved to the third floor. I shared a room with Bugs Smith, a tall athletic blonde from Northern Michigan. We were polite to each other, but never became close. Christians and Jews did not socialize either inside or outside the Greek system. Football and fraternities dominated daily life and molded the campus hero, the revered Michigan Man: a strong, beer-drinking athlete, who was decidedly not intellectual or sophisticated, and who was interested in women only as conquests, not comrades. In short, a total anathema to my idea of an appealing male.

The Jewish boys that I occasionally dated — usually just once — did not play football; they were studying to be doctors, dentists and lawyers. None of them seemed to like me; I am sure I was a somewhat unappreciative audience for their self-promoting monologues on how they planned to make money and triumph after graduation. None of them ever asked me what I wanted to do, and it did not occur to me to say anything. After a date, I would invariably return to the dorm feeling lonely and rudderless. What was wrong with me? Why didn't any of the boys call me back?

I did at least make a female friend: Doris, a tall, slim, attractive brunette, a Jewish girl who knew Lois from Winnetka, and who lived in the room next to me on the third floor. She was very popular with the budding doctors and lawyers. Warm, lively, kind and confident, she was devoid of all personal ambition — a real crowd pleaser. Doris was very comfortable being just who she was, an upper-middle class Jew from a wealthy suburb. She had been invited to join Sigma Delta Tau, but decided that if she could not get into Alpha Epsilon Phi, she would not join any sorority. Although not religious, Doris was quite clear about having come to Ann Arbor to search for a suitable Jewish husband. After two years, she left college to marry someone she met during her freshman year. I was a bridesmaid at her wedding in Chicago, and soon after we lost touch.

Doris was a nice person, and so were many of the other wealthy Jewish girls from the Middle West she introduced me to. But they were all satisfied with their niche in life and did not want to reach beyond what they were born into. I, too, wanted to find the "right man," but that was only the starting point! And I was not doing too well at anything either academic or social in Michigan. I did not get brilliant grades; I was not a leader in any way; and I was not popular with the boys. The main prop that high school had supported my constantly wavering sense of worth - being an academic star - was swept away amidst the competition offered by thousands of first year students. In spite of my friendship with Doris, I lived in a state of perpetual anguish, insecurity and semi-desperation. She must have perceived some of my unhappiness but we never discussed it. I was too vulnerable to try to articulate the causes of my misery. I was incapable of talking about the gloomy, sad twilight between acceptance and rejection in which I lived and constantly wondered: What should I do? Where should I turn?

I knew I had to get out of Ann Arbor. Some place urban, back East; that would be better. Maybe I would not be so lonely in a large city where I could learn and discover on my own, beyond the classroom. New York was out of the question; too close to Caldwell. Boston perhaps? Harvard had rejected me, but the prospect of being near "the best university in the world" appealed to me. My father had told me Boston was the intellectual capital of the United States and was home to the largest number of colleges and universities of any American city. New possibilities might unfold there. Okay, then; Boston, that's it. I applied to Boston University because it was easy to transfer there from the University of Michigan. By the end of April, I had arranged to start my sophomore year in September at BU and live at 175 Bay State Road, a small townhouse that housed just a dozen young women.

Joanie Berkowitz also lived on the third floor of Alice Lloyd Hall; she gave me an idea for an even earlier way out of the Caldwell/Ann Arbor axis. Joanie was a tall, cheerful blonde from Long Island, constantly flooded with invitations to go out on dates. She had big breasts, wore tight sweaters, and was an energetic problem solver. "Roberta, why don't you go to Europe this summer? I went to Italy last year and it was wonderful!" This was 1957 and study abroad programs were not yet a part of university curricula. How had Joanie managed to go to Europe? I saw a picture of her family's large, elegant home in Great Neck and assumed she had visited Italy with her family. But I was wrong. "I went on The Experiment in International Living and lived with an Italian family for a month. You can go too; it's easy. Come on, I'll show you how to apply."

From an early age—when my father died—I learned that if you wanted something you fought for it yourself and counted on no one else. Learning that lesson and having it continually reinforced was a lonely and painful experience, but it gave me a kind of strength before I understood that the American ideal of the "rugged individual" was a political creation and not the measure of a magic moral fortitude. I knew that if my unhappiness at Michigan were to change, I would have to do something to change it myself,

I had my own savings account containing $1000 my grandfather had left me when he died the year before I went to college and $236 saved from my babysitting money. Joanie said the whole trip cost less than $500, with everything included except spending money. Without consulting my mother, I applied to The Experiment in International Living to spend the summer of 1957 in Madrid with a Spanish family. There was no question but that I would try to go to Spain; I knew a bit of the language and Miss Abbot's narratives had sparked my desire to visit Spain more than any other country in Europe. I knew that Spain was a dictatorship under General Franco, but I didn't care. What would that have to do with me? I was an American exploring a new world.

Over spring break I informed my mother that I had been accepted to go on The Experiment. She snapped, "They kill Jews in Spain, but perhaps you didn't know that." Enraged, I screamed, "Mom, that was 500 years ago during the Inquisition!" To my surprise, one explosion took care of that issue. She did not pose further objections. I didn't understand then that she was both proud of my capacity to arrange a trip to Europe and resentful that I, not she, could realize a long-term goal of her own. When she was in her 70s she made several trips to Israel and England with her second husband, but we never shared travel experiences.

We both lived with a deep hollowness after my father's death, but since we could not speak about it, nasty, bitter exchanges filled the gap. I did not have a warm, nurturing parent and she had lost a beloved partner and, perhaps unconsciously, leaned on me, but I was too emotionally fragile to help her in any way. I wanted her to support me with love and warmth and not ask anything in return.

The Johan van Oldenbarneveldt docked in Rotterdam where we stayed the night before starting the long train ride to Madrid. My first day on European soil was memorable. We went to the top floor of a new building with a splendid view of the "old and new

Rotterdam." "Old" as I found out, meant the part of the city not rebuilt since the Germans bombed it during the War. That jolted me. Goodness! World War II and the Nazis had been right here! But that's okay, I assured myself. The world was fine now. "We" had won.

The group spent the night in a small, impeccably clean hotel, but I could not sleep from the excitement of all that was to come, beginning the next morning. After a huge breakfast of delicious variations of cheeses and breads—none of which I had tasted before—we went to the railroad station to locate the train where we would spend the next two days and nights en route to Madrid.

I liked being surrounded by people who did not speak English, even though I did not understand a word of the Dutch, German, and French I heard on the train as we traveled from the Netherlands to the Iberian Peninsula. The indecipherable words promised unforeseen adventures, new people, and different ways to think and act. Wonderful! I could not wait to discover more.

In the summer of 1957, there were not many tourists in Madrid and children would often stare at me, struck by the novel sight of someone covered with freckles and with red hair piled on top of her head. "¡*Mira! ¡Parece una jirafa!*" [Look! She looks like a giraffe!] They pointed fingers at me and burst out laughing, but I did not feel rejected and hurt because I was being singled out as different. Here I found it endearing. The gaze of the Spanish children was admiring, not scornful as in Caldwell. They welcomed this "different-looking" person and wanted to talk to me, find out where I came from, and what I was. After a while, whenever I saw children staring at me, I would wave and go chat with them as they started giggling.

Franco's *Guardia Civil* was all over Madrid—generally passive, but a perpetual warning not to step out of line. Due in part to my ignorance, I was never afraid of the "Civil Guard," the soldiers with the funny three-cornered patent leather hats whose image, I would later learn, Federico García Lorca had scathingly immortalized. But I did find the ubiquitous presence of long robed priests bizarre, even a bit comic. They strutted along the grand boulevards of all the Spanish cities I visited, confidently dedicated to upholding the moral edicts of the Franco regime. I was in a country run by a fascist government, but as a complete outsider, a young student tourist from a rich country, it did not occur to me to consider the possibility of personal danger.

I was relaxed, happy and at ease in this intense Mediterranean land in a way I was not in my own country. I had fun actually using the present and past subjunctive on a daily basis instead of just memorizing it for an exam. Years later I would realize that one of the reasons I had felt so welcome on my first trip to Spain was that differences between Christians and Jews were not part of the Spanish discourse. If you were a Spaniard, you were Catholic. That was it. At that time, no one ever spoke of "minorities;" all Spanish citizens were Spanish-born. All restaurants served only Spanish food. Except for foreign tourists, everyone in Spain was Spanish. (I did not know then about Franco's relentless suppression of Spain's regional differences and languages, particularly in Catalonia.) As a member of The Experiment, I fit into the only non-Spanish category, and it was a desirable one: foreigner. I was simply an American, just like the other eleven members of our group. Our hosts were Spanish; we were Americans. Those were the terms of the discourse. No one asked what my religion was, and I never spoke about it. For the first time in my life, I walked into rooms full of unknown people and did not immediately sort them into Jews or Christians to identify possible points of danger. I loved being in Spain, made rapid progress in learning the language, and connected easily with the expressive spontaneity of the typical Spaniard. I threw myself into exploring as much as I could—enjoying the new freedom of not having to view society through the prism of an externally imposed ethnic identity.

The big divide in Spain was political; Spaniards were either pro or anti-Franco. That was fine with me. Cognizant of being a representative of the world's foremost democracy (as our group leader had explained in the orientation session), I was politely anti-Franco, but fascism was not my primary concern. I was more interested in exploring what I liked and could learn about the country.

On the ship back to the United States, I decided I would major in Spanish. The trip took five days—lots of time to think about my next steps. I wanted to learn more about this engaging land in the throes of working itself out of the ravages, despair and profound scars of a devastating civil war—a country where I had felt so welcome and so at ease. It would, however, take me some years to figure out how to get back to Spain.

During my nautical musings on the trip back to the United States, I decided that moving to Boston would signify a new beginning and Ann Arbor would be permanently erased. With Boston as the backdrop, I would set about inserting myself into the "big world out there" my father had begun to describe for me and whose existence I had confirmed in Spain. I had not defined specific goals, but like a puppy searching for an appropriate tree, I was on a mission.

My Boston dorm, the small brownstone at 175 Bay State Road, was less overwhelming than the huge, cold Alice Lloyd Hall in Ann Arbor. My room on the second floor looked out on a cobble-stoned street where local people, as well as students, passed by. It was so much more welcoming than the seemingly endless empty sprawl of perfect green grass that had surrounded the Michigan dorm. I had two roommates who were pleasant enough, but neither shared the curiosity that drove me to explore the world, either geographically or intellectually.

Although Boston University had a football team and sororities and fraternities, sports and clubs were not the arbitrators of social life as in Ann Arbor. In fact, they were barely visible. BU did not have a campus clearly separated from the city. The university consisted of a series of buildings blended into Kenmore Square in the stately, historic Back Bay section of the city. The main building for the College of Arts and Sciences was (and still is) on Commonwealth Ave, the dorms were scattered along Commonwealth Ave, Bay State Road and Marlboro and Beacon Streets. I loved the rows of 19th century brownstones graciously scattered among the buildings that belonged to the university. Many of the three and four story brownstones were still private homes, and I never tired of gazing at them and fantasizing about their furnishings and inhabitants.

The whole city was accessible either on foot or on the "T" (subway). I spent hours wandering alone through the web of narrow streets and boulevards that formed Back Bay. I explored the majestic Boston Public Library in Copley Square, the elegant stores on Newbury Street, the big department stores downtown, and the theatre district and Chinatown on Washington, Boylston and Tremont Streets. I bought boots and underwear in Filene's Basement, walked across the Boston Common, up Charles Street and thoroughout Beacon Hill with its elegant Federal-style mansions, many with original 18th century purple glass window panels. I read histories of Boston and learned that Louisburg Square, which was developed in the 1830s, was the crowning glory of the Beacon Hill district. In 1890, Henry James had called Mount Vernon Street, which flanks the Square, "the most civilized street in America." This was where the original Boston Brahmins lived. I then went to the North End, Boston's first neighborhood, and for over a century the center of Boston's Italian community. I visited Paul Revere's house, and I sampled Italian food at all the restaurants I could afford on Hanover Street. A *flâneuse* from New Jersey, I was etching out space, molding myself into an urban citizen.

Late in the Fall I got a job working from 5:00 to 9:00 three evenings a week in the Jordan Marsh Department Store on Tremont Street. I wanted the extra money to go to concerts, operas and the theater. After my father died, my mother did not take us to New York to go to museums, concerts or anything else. In hindsight, I realize it was too complicated and expensive for her to undertake. Caldwell was only 15 miles away from Manhattan, but it might just as well have been a continent away. If we left Caldwell, it was to go to Newark and to shop during sales at Klein's Department Store. In Boston, I was free to go to the opera and anything else I wanted; I just needed to pay for it myself.

Each Monday, Tuesday and Thursday evening I took the "T" to downtown Boston. I rode the Green Line from Kenmore Square to Park Street to work in Jordan Marsh's Authorization Department on the 6$^{th}$ floor. In the pre-computer age, each time a customer wanted to use a charge account, salespeople had to call up to the authorization department to get approval. The work was repetitive and dreary, but I did not care. I daydreamed the time away by planning my next excursion. On weekends I went either to hear Arthur Fiedler conduct the Boston Pops or to the Boston Symphony Orchestra. Once I bought an orchestra seat to hear Zlinka Milanov sing *Tosca*. It cost twenty-two dollars—about what I earned for a week's work at Jordan Marsh. I loved going to Huntington Ave to visit Symphony Hall and the Museum of Fine Arts (MFA). I considered certain paintings in the museum personal friends—especially Renoir's dancing couple with a bouquet of violets and several of Monet's landscapes. At the end of my first year in Boston and my many visits to the MFA, I decided to minor in Art History.

After spending the summer in Spain and a year in Boston, I had a new sense of possibility. I had concrete evidence there were other worlds "out there," but I still needed to plot the route to get there—wherever "there" turned out to be. The only given was that I would have to manage the journey completely on my own.

I believed what the other girls (as we referred to each other) did—the right man was the ticket to everything. Finding that evasive male would be the permanent ticket out of Caldwell, but dating at Boston University did not lead to his discovery. However, my apparent failure to snare a future husband from either side of the Charles River (a Harvard mate was the goal of the Boston University coed) bothered me less in Boston than had similar unsatisfactory dating experiences in Michigan. During my first year in Boston, I discovered I possessed enormous reserves of energy, both mental and physical. In the late 1950s, BU still bore the stamp of a commuter school for new immigrants and members of the working class. It was not the major research university it is today. Academically, the university was not a challenge for me, and after the first semester I decided to merge three years into two and graduate a year early. Then perhaps I could find a way to live in Europe, although "bi-lingual secretary" and "airline stewardess" were still the only jobs in the female want ads that promised foreign travel.

I did well academically and my Spanish professors nominated me for membership in Phi Sigma Iota, the Romance Language Honorary Society, in the fall of my second year at Boston University (my last year of undergraduate work). I graduated in June of 1959. Señora Osorio, the only female professor I had ever known, asked me what I was going to do after graduating. Then she made some suggestions: *¿Por qué no sacas un doctorado en Harvard o a lo mejor prefieres pedir una beca Fulbright para estudiar en Latinoamérica?* [5] (Why don't you study for a doctorate at Harvard or would you prefer to apply for a Fulbright in Latin America?) Latin America could not compete with a permanent trip across the Charles River.

That is how I came to study at Harvard.

Maria Luisa Osorio was the key agent in engineering my transition to the other side of the Charles River. Luisa, as her friends called her, was the daughter of an educated middle class Cuban family and had come to study in the United States in the mid-1950s and stayed. She was intense, vital, outspoken and charming. Usually dressed in black and white, she had a bohemian flare that signaled potential excitement. Petite and agile, her face and expression recalled the German actress Maria Schell. Her husband Miguel was a Spanish artist and jewelry maker. They had met in Paris and both were ardent progressives. "Señora Osorio," as I called her until very recently, believed in my potential and introduced me to her friends at Harvard's Spanish department. In 1958, she had also introduced me to the name of a young man she admired in Cuba who was fighting to overthrow that country's dictatorship. His name was Fidel Castro.

Being accepted to Harvard was a momentous event. It marked the moment when I crossed the threshold into the wonderful world of "interesting people" that I had long been seeking. Now I was sure that my days would be filled with dynamic, handsome intellectuals, stimulating discussions, theatre, ballet, and French restaurants. But Harvard turned out to be hard work, and the challenge to succeed intellectually absorbed most of my time for my first year. I never saw a female professor at Harvard, but two male professors were instrumental in my life that year. I was immediately infatuated with one of my Spanish professors, Steven Gilman. (I had never met a gentle Protestant intellectual before.) After he said, somewhat casually as I remember, "Are you here to find a husband or are you going to take all this seriously?" I plunged into my work with a vengeance. I was determined to be a success (and win his approval) no matter what. Raimundo Lida was the other "important man" who took me seriously. He was a soft-spoken Argentine and a highly respected scholar and teacher in the world of Hispanic letters. From the first day I met him in Widener Library he assumed I was a serious scholar who was simply coming to him for aid and guidance. I was astounded. ME? An ex-cheerleader (I had eventually been elected to the silly squad) might be a real scholar?

During the first year, I worked long days and many nights in Widener Library and in the little room I rented at 369 Harvard Street. I was driven to study in part by intellectual curiosity, but principally because I was on a mission to succeed, which for me meant getting all As. I did everything asked of me in the graduate courses, too scared to question methods or content. Just get the As.

And I got them, in all 8 courses during the first year. So my Harvard professors, the gods I had endowed with the power to judge not only my intellectual capacities, but also my intrinsic worth, deemed me a success.

By the end of my second year in Cambridge the newness and glory of belonging to Harvard Square had worn off and I was discontented again. I had met some of the highly prized "interesting people" but I had not found the elusive "right man" yet. And what was more troubling, studying Spanish literature was beginning not to make much sense.

I saw I could do what it took to succeed at Harvard, but I did not know enough in 1960 to understand why I felt constrained and vaguely dissatisfied with my classes and with how I was being taught to analyze literature. I simply believed this is what it was like to be in graduate school in Romance Languages at Harvard. I lacked the intellectual confidence and political formation to question the methods used in the teaching of literature at Harvard.

Plagued by the insecurities that weighed down many Harvard graduate students (especially the young females), I could not parse the reigning approaches to literature—all of them, I subsequently understood, unspoken reactions against 1930s socialism. I was offered various methods of textual analysis, none of which related to my still undefined quest to make sense of the world. Unable on my own to cast off the sedimentations of McCarthyism that still cast a pall on the study of culture in the United States, I had no mentor or guide to help in sorting out the politics of literary scholarship in the United States in 1959-61. I remained unaware of the existence of people on the left in the US who were searching for a way to relate literature and politics that offered an alternative to socialist realism. Had I known about books such as Ian Watts' The *Rise of the Novel* [6] or texts by Marxist critics Christopher Caudwell, Georg Lukacs and the French sociologist Lucien Goldmann, I might have found the courage to think outside the hegemonic approaches favored by Harvard's Spanish Department.

During my two years in residence at Harvard, I was unable to use my chosen discipline in a way that would empower me to delve more profoundly, more satisfyingly, into major issues. I could not identify why, and I attributed it to something wrong with me. I was too frightened of failure, of displeasing authority figures, of going beyond what I was taught in classes. I did not even know that I was looking for a way to study literature that entwined culture with politics, economics and history.

I was briefly introduced to Henri Bergson's "stream of consciousness theory," Erich Auerbach's *Mimesis,* and René Wellek and Austin Warren's *Theory of Literature.* That was about it. I could not articulate then why Wellek and Warren's study, highly regarded in many quarters at Harvard, made me feel passive and confused. For these two widely respected pundits, good literary criticism, the New Criticism, meant a close formal study of the text, closed off from "extrinsic" influences. Wellek and Warren advocated an "intrinsic" study of literature separate from and superior to biographical, psychological, sociological and historical criticism— pure linguistic existence as independent of the surrounding world as possible. Agentless phrases or depersonalized pronouns such as "there is" or "one points out" gave the impression of "scientific" objectivity and left no room for authorial judgments and viewpoints. It depressed me and I could not explain why.

Less than two decades later, a vehement reaction against this kind of literary study would sweep over the humanities, but by that time, I had moved on to another life.

The fall semester of my second year at Harvard, John F. Kennedy was elected President. He was young, handsome, a Harvard graduate, a Native son. "Ah, someone we can finally identify with!" one of my professors said in class. "This hasn't happened in America since the election of Woodrow Wilson." It was then I learned that Woodrow Wilson had a Harvard PhD in political science and had been president of Princeton University.

I decided to look around for a group to join in order to "get more involved," as I phrased it then. I read the *Harvard Crimson*, the daily student paper, looking for a way to insert myself into the larger world beyond the study of literature. One day I saw an ad placed by a group called the John Birch Society: "Students, get involved! Be part of change in our country. Come to our meetings." When I asked a friend in the history department about the John Birch Society, he laughed, scornfully, and said they were narrow-minded conservatives. Chagrined and ashamed of my ignorance, I stopped looking for ways to become politically active. I did not know that at the same time that the John Birch Society was seeking student members, Todd Gitlin, an undergraduate at Harvard (then still an all-male college), was talking with friends about organizing what would merge with other incipient student movements across the country to become SDS, Students for a Democratic Society. However, I am not sure if a curious, but politically naïve, female graduate student would have been welcomed into their circle.[7]

Thus, when early in 1961, midway through my second year at Harvard, Steve Gilman (who had agreed to be my thesis advisor) suggested I spend the following year in Madrid to improve my Spanish and prepare for the doctoral exams, I leapt at the opportunity. Finally, a chance to return to Spain without having to relinquish my enjoyment at being able to say I was still a part of Harvard! Gilman would speak to "Miss Sweeney" about my going to teach at the *Instituto Internacional* [International Institute] in Madrid. Miss Sweeney was the Boston contact. The teaching would be minimal and all my expenses covered. Several weeks later, I had an appointment to meet Miss Sweeney.

A 1923 Radcliffe graduate, Mary Sweeney (along with her sisters) had for decades been the American-based driving force of the *Instituto*. When I met her, she was a tall, thin, grey-haired Bostonian in her sixties. Very erect, she wore sensible shoes with shoelaces, and clothes that would always seem to be grey, beige and navy even when they were not. Mary Sweeney epitomized my stereotype of the socially conscious East Coast Yankee I had read about in histories of the American suffrage movement and in Edith Wharton's novels. And here she was, sharing a bench with me in Harvard yard. As Miss Sweeney examined me and my potential suitability to teach in Madrid—I can't say it was a proper interview; it was an examination—I became acutely aware of using my hands too much as we talked. Hers never moved. She had kind, but somewhat piercing blue eyes, and as she spoke, her very straight back leaned slightly toward me with a quiet, firm authority that I had not encountered before in what I then considered an elderly woman. She was gracious, but distant and when she got up and left, I had no idea what she thought of me. Did she know I was Jewish? Was it all right to be Jewish? Would they give a fellowship in Madrid to a Jewish girl? As a Jew, it was not hard to feel like an outsider with tenuous status at Harvard in 1961, but I never shared these anxieties with anyone. I just hoped that they would fade away and not get in my way.

Apparently, I passed Miss Sweeney's scrutiny. Gilman told me I would be offered the teaching fellowship at the Madrid Institute for the 1961-62 academic year. I was to teach English classes to adult Spaniards several evenings a week and do research and prepare for my doctoral exams in Romance Languages and Literature during the day. I was thrilled! Finally, a chance to re-immerse myself in the culture where I had felt so welcomed a few years back. I knew a lot more about Spain now and could not wait to embark on the new adventure.

Several weeks after I arrived in Madrid and settled in at Manolita's house on Lope de Vega Street, I started to teach and to familiarize myself with the entity known as *"El Instituto,"* which was and still is, located at Miguel Angel 8 in what was then considered the northern part of the city. Madrid developed from south to north. What is now referred to as modern Madrid starts about a mile or so north of Lope de Vega Street, where I was living, close to the Prado Museum, and extends east and west of the grand boulevard everyone called *"la Castellana."* The elegant Barrio Salamanca, socially equivalent to the combination of luxurious residences and boutiques found on New York City's Upper East Side, lies to the east of the *Castellana*. To the west is Miguel Angel Street. The *Instituto* was at number 8, and at number 18 lived the family of the Spanish student I was to marry in a year.

Founded at the end of the 19th century by Boston-based American Protestant missionaries Alice Gordon and her husband William

Gulick, the original idea of the *Instituto* or "El Boston" as it was known, was to provide a socially and culturally progressive education for Spanish women and to disseminate emancipated ideas about the role of women. Adamant about their mission to modernize women's education in Spain, the Gulicks called on prominent Boston pedagogues James Russell Lowell and George Ticknor, and on many friends connected with Harvard. In 1901 the group formed a corporation and bought the building in Madrid, which still houses the *Instituto*. Smith and Mount Holyoke Colleges provided models for the early development of an educational vision and curriculum for Spanish women. This was due both to their reputation as innovative colleges for women's education and to the personal links between these institutions and the Spanish female educators who were instrumental in the formative years of the *Instituto*. In addition to educating "young ladies," a private, coed K-12 school was established in the *Instituto* during the first decades of the 20th century. It was the only school in Spain to provide a secular, coed and quietly progressive grade school education, principally for upper middle class *madrileños*. Familiarly known as the *Instituto-Escuela*, the school closed in 1936 due to the outbreak of the Civil War. It reopened in 1940 under the name of *Colegio Estudio*. Many of the Spaniards I came to know had attended the *Colegio Estudio*, including my future husband.

The educational functions of the Institute ceased during the Civil War. But the Franco government (that put an end to every undertaking hostile to Spanish fascism) was never able to confiscate its building. Miguel Angel 8 was the private property of American citizens and therefore deemed untouchable. During the war years, members of the corporation (chiefly Mary Sweeney, based in Boston) published *Notes and News* to inform the Institute's members of what was happening to prominent Spanish Republicans in exile around the world. Outstanding among these were: Américo Castro, Jorge Guillén, Federico García Lorca's brother Francisco, Salvador Madariaga and many others. During these chaotic years, the little newsletter maintained a vital communications network for anti-Franco intellectual exiles scattered around the globe (some at Harvard, Columbia and Princeton; others in Latin America or Europe) and otherwise often lost to one another.

Although its early 20th century feminist founding principle (progressive education for women) faded throughout the Franco years, the *Instituto* itself remained a beacon of cautious liberalism. It continues to be a focal point for varied intellectual activities as well as a center for American universities' study abroad programs. In 1986, mindful of its original purpose, the *Instituto* initiated a series of Colloquia on the status of women, often in collaboration with North American feminists.

During my first year in Spain, I learned three important things. First, it was acceptable, even desirable to be Jewish. Years of solitary living under a veil of mostly "polite," but quietly vicious anti-Semitism in Caldwell had left indelible scars. From childhood, I remained on the lookout, waiting to be hurt. But the educated Spaniards I met in 1961 made fun of the stereotypical WASP American with a grace and humor that allowed me to regard large segments of the American Anglo-Saxon population as hamburger-loving, insensitive, unsophisticated clods despite being the people in power in my country. Spaniards valued my vituperative tongue, facility for speaking foreign languages, and appreciation of good food. Wit and intensity became positive attributes instead of occasions for inappropriate social gaffes. The Spaniards I met thought of Jews in America as "French intellectuals" (then the highest compliment from a university-educated Spaniard).

My second lesson was the discovery of the meaning of real poverty for the first time. Watts had not yet burned and although my hometown was only forty-five minutes away from Harlem, like the majority of white Americans, I knew nothing about it. It hadn't even occurred to me to care. During the summer of 1957, as part of *The Experiment in International Living,* I explored the working-class districts of Madrid and traveled through poverty-stricken southern Spain (Granada, Malaga and Seville). Other Americans in our group blamed the victims rather than trying to understand the bigger picture. They made comments like: "Why are they so poor? Why don't they have a democracy like ours? I guess some people just like to be poor." I was troubled by these remarks, but did not contradict them because I was not ready for any kind of conflict, particularly the kind that can result from observations of social inequities.

When I returned to Spain in 1961 and saw the same humiliating poverty, I started to feel an anger that was to develop into deep rage. Without initially understanding it when I moved there, I was confronting an example of the devastating effect the civil war had had on the rural poor. In those days everyone who had a home and enough to eat had a live-in maid for there was an abundant supply of girls and women who had only two routes out of dire poverty: domestic service or prostitution. Victoria had been Manolita

Roesset's live-in maid for decades; I never knew exactly how long. Orphaned by the war, Victoria had never learned to read or write and had left the countryside to work as a domestic in exchange for food and a bed. Some years younger than Manolita, she was already stooped, wizened and wrinkled. A tiny woman, Victoria walked with a limp, spoke very little, and was missing several of her front teeth. Blank submission was the only expression I ever saw in her tiny, pale blue eyes.

As I would learn, Victoria worked six and a half days per week and slept on a straw mattress in a tiny, windowless cubbyhole off the kitchen where she cooked three meals a day for Manolita and her female boarders. As Victoria cleared the plates from the large, round, dark wooden table, I occasionally saw her pile all the leftovers onto one plate. It was several weeks before I realized this was what she ate for dinner. It reminded me of when I was a child and we used to feed our collie Sandy the leftovers from our plates. In fact, Manolita treated Victoria with the compassion one reserves for a maimed, loyal dog. She would lament if Victoria dropped a glass or served the soup a bit too soon or a bit too late: "Poor woman, if I were to throw her out, where would she go? At her age and in her condition no one would take her in." Only Manolita spoke directly to Victoria; somehow the rest of us knew we should not engage her in any way beyond a murmured *gracias* as she served the meals.

I have often regretted not disobeying the unstated rules of the house to find out more about Victoria's life.

My third insight came from the discovery that I was a woman whom men found attractive. American men had always made me feel dirty. I went through high school thinking that if I was "sexy" (as on occasion I was told I was), it meant I was in grave danger of becoming a "bad woman." Spaniards made me feel that anything I did was fine and desirable. It took me years to learn that to be placed on a pedestal and unquestionably adored is only another form of not-too-subtle male domination. I marvel at how long I was able to accept the sticky, stereotyped flattery meant to perpetuate the doll-like status of most Spanish women. It was so pleasant to hear nice words that I refused to examine their validity.

I welcomed the attention from certain Spanish males, namely the ones who were progressive intellectuals, elegant, energetic and electric. It was fun being a "sought after commodity," as I would phrase it years later. And part of the pleasure of being the object of this new kind of male desire was that nobody rejected me because I was Jewish. I didn't even have to think about that.

# CHAPTER 3

# MARRIAGE AND FASCISM

From the start, my marriage was chaotic, turbulent, and absurdly romantic. The Cuban Missile Crisis of October 1962 provided the international context for my first weeks of married life. Discussing politics was part of our daily fare, but for me, in Spain, both Cuba and the United States seemed far away. Therefore, I reacted to the Missile Crisis through a Spanish lens. Spain was not a major global player, and while the government was solidly in the pocket of the United States, Franco never broke relations with Cuba. After all, Fidel Castro was a *gallego*; his father had immigrated to Cuba from northern Spain, from Galicia. Although passionately anti-Communist in the 1960s, Spain maintained a certain admiration for Fidel. He was the Spanish-speaking David even though Goliath was underwriting Spain's economy. Everyone I knew in Madrid cheered the victory of the Cuban revolutionaries.

Gabriel and I married in Gibraltar because civil marriages were not permitted in Spain for Spanish citizens. I refused to get married under the aegis of the Catholic Church that helped enforce Franco's 1939 Civil Code, which dictated that "A man must protect his wife, and she must obey her husband." I considered the duty "to obey" the most egregious affront to my dignity. Other mandates were hardly less humiliating: a woman could not take a job or open a bank account without her husband's permission; adultery by a wife was always a crime whereas a husband could be unfaithful as long as the act was not done in his home or he did not live with his mistress. A Church guide for new brides stated: "When you are married, you must never confront your husband, never use your anger against his anger, or your stubbornness against his. When he gets angry, you will shut up; when he shouts, lower your head without reply; when he demands, you will cede."

In addition to this preposterous ideology, the Franco regime, like Hitler's Germany, emphasized a Spanish woman's duty to the state. It held that women served the state and the nation, as well as God and society, by rearing children and inculcating in them suitable values and attitudes. Women between the ages of 17 and 35 were required to take a six-month course on how to be "a proper

Spanish woman." This was called "Social Service" and was administered by the Women's Section of the Spanish Fascist Party. Among its admonitions was the warning: "never be a girl crammed with book learning; there is nothing more detestable than an intellectual woman."

All foreign women who married Spaniards in Spain were obligated to adopt Spanish nationality and obtain a national identity card by application to a myriad of Spanish authorities. I was not willing to submit myself to Franco's government. I would not get married on Spanish territory. Gabriel's parents, although not religious, were upset for "social reasons" that we didn't marry in the Church. As responsible parents, they wanted their son's life to be free of as many obstacles as possible. Gabriel and I both wanted to be married for that was what people like us did then. In 1962, simply living together was not an option in Spain.

Gabriel did not care how we got married, but as a Spanish citizen, his civil marriage to me was never recognized in Spain. Under Franco, only Catholic marriages were legal for Spaniards. In fact, when we traveled throughout Spain in those years, we were forced to rent two rooms in hotels. His passport (which he had to show to rent a room) said *soltero* (bachelor) and unmarried persons could not rent a room together. My United States passport did not reveal marital status. It was, however, fine with the innkeepers if we paid for two rooms and used just one.

In Gibraltar, two Andalusian, English-speaking taxicab drivers served as the required witnesses when Gabriel and I stepped into the British judge's chambers to be married in a civil ceremony on October 2, 1962. "*Lo hacemos para mucha gente, señores, no se preocupen*" [We act as witnesses for a lot of people, don't worry] the two young men assured us as Gabriel handed each of them a generous tip. Gibraltar was Great Britain's spot of sun in southern Spain, a fact that convinced the Spanish that England's empire had not yet shrunk quite enough. The general population was bilingual. The locals spoke English with a British accent and Spanish with a lilt typical of many parts of southern Spain. Gibraltar's main street had an ordered, deliberately tidy character totally absent in the rest of Spain.

A huge portrait of Queen Elizabeth hung on the wall of the judge's office; she smiled benignly as Gabriel and I exchanged simple gold wedding bands. The marriage ceremony took ten minutes and cost the equivalent of twenty-five dollars.

We then took a train to Cádiz, in southwestern Spain, to spend several days at the Hotel Atlántico, a grand, traditionally luxurious hotel that reminded me of the setting for an old romantic Alain Resnais film. Gabriel's father called the hotel several times a day to ask when we were coming back to Madrid, and to inform us that he was arranging a wedding dinner for about 30 friends and family at Llardy's, one of Madrid's most elegant restaurants. A Frenchman established it in 1839 on the Carrera de San Jerónimo, near the Puerta del Sol. I was never consulted on any of the plans for the celebration of my wedding.

As I would later realize, my father-in-law's dominant presence in my marriage dated from those phone calls. I would have no voice when he was around. The conversation took place between men, father and son. It was futile for me to try and interrupt, to inject my presence or opinions. No one paid attention to me; it was as if I did not exist. Later I would complain to Gabriel. He always agreed with me, and affirmed how important my opinions were to him. He just could not confront his father and would never recognize that this created a problem. Gradually I observed how my sister-in-law and other women I knew assumed the passive, secondary status in public while manipulating men in private. I understood that social mores forced them to act that way, I just did not know how to imitate them, even if I had wanted to. It takes years of training to become skilled in social manipulation of that order.

When we returned to Madrid, we moved into the Tortella's country home in Pozuelo de Alarcón, a small village 10 miles west of Madrid.[8] We were to live there for a year or so while Gabriel finished his studies. Gabriel's father gave him a monthly stipend to support us. It maintained us, if not luxuriously, quite adequately.

As I look back to understand the road to the political person I became, the first moment that stands out is an April 1962 student-run strike at the University of Madrid.

In the spring of 1962, Gabriel was finishing a degree roughly equivalent to an American Masters in Economic History at the School of Economics at the University of Madrid, located on San Bernardo Street in the heart of downtown. San Bernardo was dotted with the wonderful little bars characteristic of *castiza* [old, traditional] Madrid. Enticing aromas of *tortilla de patatas* [Spanish potato omelet], grilled sardines, marinated anchovies, spicy potatoes, olives, fried salt cod, and *serrano* ham floated in and out of open doorways. Large wheels of Manchego, Idiazabel, Cabrales and Roncal—the unique Spanish cheeses then still unknown outside the country—sat on worn marble counters and under the counter, olive pits competed for floor space with cigarette butts.

Gabriel and I had just met at the beginning of February, and we saw each other some part of every day. One afternoon in April, he told me that a group of students in his *Facultad* was planning a strike at lunch hour the following day to protest new government restrictions against student assemblies and demonstrations. The School of Economics was at that time the most radical in the University; it was here that the young socialists and communists flocked to try to figure out how to oppose fascism and build a New Spain.

Widespread student unrest throughout the Spanish universities in 1956 had been decisive in hastening Franco's rapprochement with non-Falangist sectors of society and heightened his need to broaden his base of support. So, in the early 1960s, as a thaw began in the totalitarianism of the earlier years and a certain (albeit unreliable) elasticity in government repression became apparent, sporadic eruptions of dissent took place. The University of Madrid was one of the first nationally important centers of public protest. The first major anti-government student protest had taken place there in 1956. Gabriel had, in fact, played a role in that uprising and spent a brief time in jail as a consequence.

The new, coming strike would attract national attention because of the *Facultad's* central location, which gave its strikers the ability to do something roughly similar to blocking traffic during rush hour in New York's Times Square. Also, leaders of outlawed unions and political parties gathered at the university to lend solidarity. Gabriel said we might not be able to see each other because going on strike meant students would lock themselves in the building and refuse to leave until the authorities conceded to their demands. Without hesitation, I said I wanted to be part of the strike too. He warned that if the students could manage to circumvent university administrators and stay inside the building, the police would come to San Bernardo Street. This would cause a huge snarl in traffic and result in a lot of commotion and media attention. But, Gabriel was sure the police would not barge into university buildings, beat up students or drag them off to jail. Franco's police adhered to the centuries-old, sacrosanct practice (common throughout most of Western Europe) of not entering either a university or a church. Universities were safe because their student bodies were almost entirely composed of sons and daughters of the bourgeoisie, even though some of these progeny were a bit too left-wing for the authorities. The church was secure because the hierarchy and bureaucracy of the Catholic Church worked hand in hand with the Falangist Party.

The picture described to me did not make immediate sense. I had never witnessed a student strike, let alone participated in one. Strikes were not part of life in Caldwell, although I knew that all of us had a right to freedom of speech and assembly. I had never seen students rallying for a cause. Yet here I was, an outsider, about to be the only non-Spanish participant in a student strike against repressive measures of a fascist government. I was conscious of the fact that, for the first time in my life, I would take direct action against a political vision I didn't believe in—fascism—in favor of another that I did—democracy. I wondered why mature persons who had nothing to do with the university—people (almost all men as it turned out) from trade unions and political parties, not student organizations— would participate in a student protest. (It would be a while before I understood the complex relationship among the then outlawed Communist and Socialist political parties and university activities.) And I wondered why Franco's all-powerful Guardia Civil would respect a centuries-old tradition of not entering the university to break up an illegal protest meeting.

Most of all, I did not comprehend why, if the police were not going to storm the university, it was so important for me to remember to bring my passport to the strike. Later someone explained that it could be serious to be jailed without a national identity card, particularly if your appearance did not immediately convey membership in the bourgeoisie. I did not, however, barrage the politically savvy Spanish students with questions born of my political naiveté. I would go to the strike and see what it was all about. It was an action against Franco. That was reason enough.

Mid-morning of the day of the strike I went to the university with Gabriel. It was a glorious spring day: brilliant sun, crisp clear air, and balmy breeze. Friends congregated in the halls and heatedly exchanged last minute opinions about how to proceed. I remember crowded hallways, general confusion and an atmosphere charged with tense expectations. People seemed more excited than afraid, but everyone made sure they had their identity cards with them in case they were arrested.

We had been inside the university building for about an hour when I realized the doors were locked, the police were outside, and a delegation of students had been sent to negotiate with university officials. I did not notice that there were no women in the student delegation, nor were any of the student leaders female. The lack of women in leadership positions seemed perfectly natural to me in 1962.

While the student leaders went to communicate our political demands, the rest of us congregated in groups or just milled around. Several hours passed. It was way past lunchtime; we were all getting hungry. I stood on a chair to look outside: the entrance to the university was blocked by dozens of grey uniformed police, each of whom carried a club and a gun. Then someone said, "But Roberta has an American passport, she can come and go!" (Being an American guaranteed considerable immunity from Franco's police.) I agreed to go buy some sandwiches, and a collection was taken up. It didn't occur to me to be frightened, such was my faith in the stars and stripes and the slim blue passport to anywhere. It is hard for me to believe that I calmly opened a side door, showed my passport to a young policeman and walked across the street to buy thirty cheese sandwiches. To this day, whenever I eat the wonderful Manchego cheese (one of Spain's lasting gifts to international cuisine) in the familiar Spanish oval shaped hard roll, I remember the thirty sandwiches that I bought in the bar across the street from the university during the strike that sunny spring afternoon.

"*Es americana, déjenla pasar,*" (She's American, let her pass) one of the policemen said to the others as I walked back into the building with a huge brown bag full of sandwiches. The *bocadillos de queso* were delicious, partly because I was hungry, but mainly because I enjoyed the experience of handing them out immensely. Toward the end of the afternoon, the rector (roughly equivalent to Dean of Faculty) appeared to address the students. An accommodation was reached and soon after we all dispersed. The police disappeared, traffic resumed, and the strike was over. The students had won some of their demands and deemed the event a political success. I was a bit sorry when the strike ended. I liked being part of a community of peers who were working together to achieve a common goal. Not only was it fun, it was also empowering. I wanted to continue.

The next day, instead of buying just the *International Herald Tribune,* I also bought the *ABC, Arriba* and *Ya,* the most widely read daily papers of the heavily censored Spanish press. With intense anticipation, I scoured the three Spanish newspapers for reports of the strike. The result was confrontation with a personal example of Francoist censorship. Later that day I shared my outrage at the distorted journalistic descriptions of the strike with some of my co-strikers: "Communist-infiltrators lead battling students in strike to close university building. Police immediately restore order...no concessions granted to unruly students." That was the final word on the public version of the strike. No response to the official reporting was permitted in the media.

It flashed through my mind to write a letter to the editors to point out the inaccuracies in their published report. I was an American, after all, and that is what we do. Fortunately, it only took me several minutes to realize that not only was it ridiculous to try to contradict a fascist-controlled press, it was also dangerous. It would reveal to government authorities not only my views, but also call attention to those of my soon-to-be Spanish relatives and that was never advisable.

From then on, I read the Spanish press daily and asked friends a lot of questions. These students were well informed about Spain and the rest of the world because they were convinced they were in a position to have an impact on national politics both then and in the future. They knew much more about politics and history than I or my Harvard colleagues did, even when they were getting degrees that nominally had nothing to do with politics and history. As dissidents in a fascist society, they automatically questioned authority and constantly evaluated all received information. Thus, they learned to see in fundamental ways how authority, power, the press, and government propaganda worked. My life in the United States had been geared to teach me not to see, not to question basic premises of the American way of life. Eventually I realized that in the United States, the mainstream population internalizes the values of corporate America as if this vision were the objective starting point for subsequent judgments, as if it were the natural way for everyone to view the world.

In spite of the repressive conditions under which Spaniards were living, my friends had a sense of entitlement to public acts of dissent that I found very appealing. It surprised me at first and subsequently enticed me. I was attracted by how confident these young Europeans—Spanish intellectuals who were mostly socialists or communists—were in their belief that it would be possible to form a society where the great ideals of liberty and equality would finally exist. At the time it seemed to me that the strength of their faith in the future would be enough to transform the world.

Life in Madrid in the 1960s was intense, intellectual, and culturally eclectic for those of us huddled together in opposition to *El Caudillo* and his cohorts. There were only two sides: Him and Us, right and wrong. "One day we will change Spain", my friends often said, and "*seremos dueños del país*" [we will be in charge]. They were right. A surprisingly large number of the people I knew in the 1960s became, and still are, major players in the reconfiguration of post-Franco Spain.

From that student strike I gained a sense of what philosophers, particularly Marx, mean by "agency." By deciding to take a position and actively participate, one can become part of a social force that can engender changes in societies, policies, and cultures. I also experienced the elation that comes from being part of a group of peers united by a sense of mission. Agency and mission are powerful elements to incorporate into one's life.

Paradoxically, the stifling passivity so characteristic of the intellectual wasteland Franco had created would become the stimulant that propelled me to political understanding and action, and perhaps most significantly, to feminism.

To complement the growing first hand knowledge of fascism that I ingested from daily doses of the Spanish press, my friends recommended books to encourage my "political development." They had to be personal copies that circulated because these books were not available in bookstores or libraries. I read Fichte, Plekhanov, some Hegel, a considerable amount of Karl Marx and Friedrich Engels, and I plunged into intense discussions of these works whenever I could. *The German Ideology*, Marx' and Engels' critique of Georg Hegel's idealism, first gave me the intellectual tools to analyze history and current politics in a way that made sense to me. The interrelatedness of events and ideas, the notion that human beings were their own agents and generated all ideas (including the idea of god) rather than being products of an all-powerful extra human force was exactly what I had always believed. I had not known, however, that this fundamental concept was also the foundation of Marxist dialectical materialism. Subsequently I began to understand how history could be explained as a reciprocal interaction between individual and social forces.

The essence of what I gleaned from those months of reading and conversing in 1962 was something like this: The use of the dialectic as a historical method is the strongest element in Marxist theory. In its broadest terms, it is a way of viewing each aspect of a historical moment—its art, its industry, its politics—as being part of the whole and of understanding that every dominant idea depends on and defines itself against whatever it suppresses or excludes. Dialectical thinking is a brake on the tendency to assume that things will continue to be the way they are, only more so, because it reminds us that every paradigm contains the seed of its own undoing. I came to understand that most cultural products work in several ways at once, that each element in a cultural system depends for its value on all the others, and that to alter one element is to alter every element. This was very different from any approach to history to which I had previously been exposed by my formal and informal education. Previously, no framework for a "big picture" analysis had been available to me. Rather, what I had been offered as models to emulate were binary analyses, right or left—subjects studied in fragmented, isolated ways. This was due in part, no doubt, to the nature of Hispanic studies in the United States in the early 1960s. With this limited vision, it was almost impossible to get a sense of a "whole". Thanks to the books to which I was exposed in Franco-controlled Spain, I felt an intellectual light bulb flash on. There was a superb touch of irony in this that I did not appreciate until some years later.

It was while living in fascist Spain, paradoxically, that I learned to overcome the knee-jerk American anti-communism that pervaded the United States throughout the 1950s, an attitude that kept most of middle class America in a patriotic fog and blind to the fact that we, too, were a society divided into classes. In those days, a few people were very rich; many were poor and most of us floated in the middle, lulled into complacency by material well being. Poverty was tucked away in rich, post-World War II 1960s America. It was not omnipresent and obvious as it was in poor post-World War II Spain.

Some weeks after the strike at the University of Madrid, there was a "buzz" among progressive students: Lauro Olmo, then a young radical playwright from Galicia in northern Spain, had gotten permission from the government controlled censors for one of his new plays to have a short run in a commercial theater. This was exciting news, as Olmo was an anti-Francoist—not a militant radical, but strongly opposed to the regime. Did this permission signify a positive trend? Would literary censorship lessen? Speculations were rampant in the cafes and bars students frequented.

As I entered the theater that evening in April 1962, I noticed that a lot of the people (not just my friends) who were milling around and finding their seats seemed to know each other. An atmosphere of camaraderie and controlled tension enveloped the audience even before the curtain went up. I had never read anything by Lauro Olmo and had no idea what to expect. No one had mentioned the theme of Olmo's new play—perhaps no one had read it, as the text had not been published. All I knew was that my friends enthusiastically attended the opening because it signified an act against the government.

Spanish theater had been in a dreary state during the two decades that followed the Civil War. With the exception of very occasional presentations of works by Alfonso Sastre and Antonio Buero Vallejo, first-rate contemporary drama had not been staged publicly in Spain since the days of the Republic. How poignantly tragic this was for a country that had inspired the great works of Federico Garcia Lorca and the authors of a high point of European culture, Spain's Golden Age of drama: Cervantes, Lope de Vega, Pedro Calderon de la Barca and others. In Spain, classical (as well as non-classical) theater has been part of popular culture since the Middle Ages, and in the 1960s one still met Spaniards without formal education who could recite from memory passages from Lope de Vega or Garcia Lorca.

Official theater, however, had been reduced to a largely trivial exercise. The plays of Alfonso Paso, Spain's most financially successful dramatist in the 1950s and 1960s, typified the sanctioned canon: light comedies of manners, devoid of ideological content. Paso was a prolific writer, and one or two of his plays were always in major theaters. I once went to see one of his popular comedies, *"Cosas de papa y mama"* [Things About Mom and Dad], a fatuous undertaking, ineffectual and insipid, a not very clever soap opera about little glitches in the lives and families of the people who were in power in Spain at that time. Once the curtain went up, the play made avatars of Francoism *simpático* and approachable, just like part of the family. Lines of class and privilege were temporarily blurred; everyone was equal and all were happy. This subtext was probably the principal reason for the play's popularity. Tickets to the theater were relatively inexpensive—so different from the United States, where going to a Broadway play cost 10 or 12 times as much as seeing a new film, but tickets to first-run theater in Madrid were slightly more than the price of a movie. This made Paso's plays accessible to a lot of people, even in Spain's lean years.

So it was a big event in Madrilenian oppositional circles when Lauro Olmo was given permission to present his new play in a commercial theater. *La Camisa* [The Shirt] tells the story of the family of Juan and Lola who had come to Madrid in the 1940s with the huge wave of people driven from the countryside by the destruction of the Civil War. Survival was the goal. The play takes place in Madrid in the early 1960s—the time when I saw it. Like thousands of the capital's poor, the family is plagued by chronic unemployment and one of the consequences is alcoholism. Olmo's characters, like other destitute Spanish workers, see emigration to Germany, France or Switzerland as the only way out. Their poverty is symbolized by not having a shirt to wear to look for a job. When one of the characters declares he wants to leave this *"perra vida"* [dog's life] and look for a better life in Germany, sections of the audience gasped, and I did not immediately understand why. Instinctively, however, I knew the gasp was politically inspired.

Only four or five months previously, in fall 1961, I had taken a long bus ride from Barcelona to Munich to visit a friend. The bus was German made and the two drivers and two hostesses were Germans in their late 20s or early 30s. It was my first direct contact with Germans; the Nazis had been defeated just fifteen years earlier. The gleaming new bus exuded an efficiency and technological confidence unknown in Francoist Spain. But it was the encounter with the tall, robust, ever-smiling blond Germans that is most clearly etched in my memory. Most of the passengers on the bus were impoverished Spaniards, many single men, some families, all going to work in Germany. I was the only American taking the thirty-hour ride to Munich.

At lunchtime the first day, the bus pulled over to something akin to the rest areas that dot American highways. However, there were no restaurants or rest rooms, but only a series of rundown picnic tables scattered randomly over a grass plot. We all carried food with us. I went to sit down with a Spanish family. (After all, I spoke fluent Spanish and practically no German.) Almost immediately, I spotted the four Germans who had gone off to a table by themselves staring at me. Then the young man who was evidently in charge of the bus walked over to me, and unequivocally made it clear that I was to come and sit with them. He was smiling grandly, evidently pleased to have the opportunity to rescue the blue-eyed freckled American with red hair from the swarthy folk surrounding her. He explained that I did not want to *"fressen"* with the Spaniards. I should come to *"essen"* with them. My Teutonic limitations did not prevent me from knowing that *"fressen"* was how animals ate, while *"essen"* was the verb applied to humans. I looked at the representatives of the nation defeated by the Allies and felt a tightening in my stomach and a little wave of nausea. I suppressed the nausea and succumbed to the "flattery" of being selected to join the club that would have rejected me since I had been born Jewish. I wanted to know what it would feel like, so I got up and followed the blond man to the German table.

As I try to understand why I did that, memories from my childhood in Caldwell jump into focus. In fifth grade, in homeroom where the class congregated first thing every morning, Bobby Esenbach sat behind me and Ben Groo sat next to him. Bobby was gawky and fair with a small pug nose and a swagger. I only remember two words he said to me. Every morning, right after we saluted the flag and said the daily prayer. ("Our father who art in heaven...") He hissed over my shoulder: "Jew girl! Jew girl!" A tightening in my throat and intimations of nausea rendered me incapable of responding. One day Ben, a placid, slightly overweight boy who wore frameless glasses and never antagonized anyone, got tired of listening to Bobby, turned to him and imitated the hiss: "Jew boy! Jew boy!" I knew Ben was trying to help me, but I remained silent. I just wanted it all to go away. Bobby eventually stopped his bullying and at the end of the year left the Caldwell school system. His parents had decided he would get a better education in the local Catholic grammar school.

The second snapshot is from my senior year in high school. I was a cheerleader and therefore putatively one of the "elite" females in the hierarchy that reigned in the middle-class suburbs of 1950s America. One Saturday morning right before a football game about six of us from the twelve-member cheerleading squad gathered at Andy Unruh's home. Andy lived in a nice house and had lots of older siblings who had been successful athletes in high school. Her parents clearly enjoyed their children's public recognition and liked having young people drift in and out of their house. On that Saturday morning Andy's mother was stretched out on the living room couch, sipping a beer and chatting with us. She had faded red hair and freckles and a large potbelly. I only remember one sentence she spoke: "Hitler should have killed all the Jews." I became slightly nauseous. I said nothing and tuned her out as Andy's mother continued with a long harangue against Jews. Andy knew I was Jewish as did all the other cheerleaders, but it was evident from the grimace on her face that Andy had not shared this knowledge with her mother. I left the house with Marilyn Walker, a best friend in those days, who said, "But Andy's mother didn't mean you." I smiled limply and said, "Yeah, I know." None of my friends ever spoke to me about that morning and I never mentioned it either, for over forty years.

These formative moments had left me a little afraid of the four Germans in charge of the bus. As requested, I moved to their table, but I didn't stay for lunch. My awareness that the Spaniards were watching me and understood why I had been invited to join the Germans gave me the courage to smile, get up from the table, and walk back to eat with the Spanish family. In getting up to join the German table, I reacted as a scarred member of an unpopular minority who, given the opportunity, leaps to accept membership in a "top" group just to see how it feels. The seduction of "belonging" is so strong, that even if it is false, entails offending others, and lasts only for a few moments, it is difficult to resist.

At the end of the day, when the bus stopped at a small hotel in Lyon, the driver asked me if I was going to sleep with my friends too. This time I was ready. I ignored him and negotiated my own sleeping arrangements with the French receptionist. The Vichy government was no longer in power, and I knew more French than the Germans.

It was the recollection of my bus trip to Munich with the Spanish emigrants that flashed through my mind in the theater that spring evening in 1962 as I heard the audience gasp during the production of *La Camisa*. Why were they shocked? I knew from firsthand experience that the situation Olmo was dramatizing was true. If I knew it was true, surely they did too.

That was exactly the point. Olmo was telling a big truth, and very publicly. Between 1959 and 1962, over half a million Spaniards emigrated for economic reasons. The play illustrated how unemployment, dire poverty and alcoholism (the consequences of two decades of Francoism) were driving Spaniards out of their own country in order to survive. This was frontal criticism of Franco's policies. The play received a standing ovation, and as we left the theater, Olmo's courage was the main subject of praise. (¡*Qué cojones tiene el tío!* [He really has balls!]). No one seriously discussed the quality of the play itself. That was disappointing. Political courage took precedence over critical literary acuity. The fact that a political truth about the Franco regime was being presented to the public in a theater in Madrid was an end in itself.

Later I would learn more about Olmo from José [Pepe] Ruibal, a friend of ours also from Galicia in northern Spain. (In 1963 Pepe married the woman who had introduced me to Gabriel, Consuelo Vázquez de Parga.) Pepe, like Olmo, was attempting to create new theater for Spain in the 1960s. He was more than ten years older than the rest of us and had lived in exile in Buenos Aires and Paris for over a decade. One afternoon over a few *copas de tinto* [glasses of red wine], Pepe talked about the short pieces of drama he was committed to writing. They were designed to be produced in cafes with little scenery or action, Pepe explained, smiling sardonically, so if the police arrived, the actors simply sat down and became customers of the café. This alerted me to the existence of underground theater in the sixties in Madrid, a genre of social protest that Olmo and Ruibal were instrumental in creating.

A couple of weeks later some of us got together to comment on an early draft of Pepe's new play, *El hombre y la mosca*, [The Man and the Fly], about a dialogue between a man and his double and how they are affected by the various faces of tyranny. I don't remember my reaction to the draft, but the finished product became one of Pepe's very successful works.

Dressed in Left-Bank black and speaking Spanish with a strong Galician accent, Pepe was not "refined" in the way our *madrileño* acquaintances were. He remained socially marginal to the upper-middle class world of Madrid dissidents that he, like I, had joined by marriage. However, Pepe's class origins, unlike mine, were immediately apparent to our sophisticated relatives and friends. His long, ill-kept hair and rumpled, careless demeanor bordered on an aggressive rejection of the well turned-out folks who surrounded him. I, on the other hand, enjoyed occasional trips to the beauty parlor and to my mother-in-law's seamstress Chelo to have clothes made for me.

I never saw Pepe after I left Spain in 1968 - he died in 1999 - but in the post-Franco years, he became a nationally and internationally renowned fixture of the New Spanish Theater. In recent decades I learned first-hand of Pepe's success from academic colleagues in the US, some of whom had interviewed him, published studies of his plays, and taught his underground café-teatro to American students of contemporary Spanish theater.

That night at *La Camisa* was the beginning of my actual grappling with—not just intellectually understanding—what it means to live subject to the often lethal power of a dominant, highly centralized government opposed to freedom of the press and any oppositional thought or action. My friends often mentioned that they used so much energy in combating the political system that little was left for the intellectual subtleties I took for granted. None of them had examined the literary qualities of *La Camisa*; all their energies had been used in celebrating the fact that it had been staged.

This, it seemed, was a form of unconscious self-censorship. Internalized self-censorship had become an intrinsic part of growing up under Francoism, even if one were consciously fighting against the political system. During the next year, I would trace more and more of the pall Franco's long shadow cast over Spain. I did not know that in the not too distant future, New Left activists in the United States would struggle with many of these same issues, especially the relation of esthetics to the objectives of political protest.

On November 8, 1962, about a month after our honeymoon in Cádiz, Franco's police apprehended Julian Grimau, a fifty-one-year-old Spaniard, on a streetcar near Cuatro Caminos, a lower middle-class district in northern Madrid. Grimau was officially charged with illegal entry into Spain. But that was not the whole story, as I learned bit by bit over the next months.

Julian Grimau, a staunch defender of the Republic, had joined the Communist Party when the war broke out in 1936. After the defeat of the Republic, he continued the campaign against Franco for the rest of his life. Living in southern France as a leader of the exiled Spanish Communist Party, Grimau made frequent clandestine trips to Spain to aid the opposition. After being jailed for "illegal entry" he was tortured almost beyond recognition. His family, from their base in France, and his political associates mobilized the international press. When Franco's security police realized Grimau was too badly injured by his torturers to be seen by foreign doctors or press, they threw him out of a second story window of the General Security Headquarters in the Puerta del Sol and alleged he had tried to commit suicide. The police assumed he would die, but he did not.

Grimau was medically "patched up" so that he could be tried in a military court for crimes allegedly committed during the Civil War as an anti-Franco combatant. No proof of any crime was offered during the trial. In 1939 the Franco government had instituted a retroactive law that allowed for those deemed responsible for political "crimes" previous to that date to be jailed at will. Everyone understood that Grimau's trial was about the "crime" of having been a leading Republican combatant.

The international press attended the trial, and the Grimau affair became an international cause célèbre. Demonstrations supporting him took place in Belgium, Italy, England and France, and letters of support came from, among others: the Queen Mother of Belgium, the Mayor of Florence, and Nikita Khrushchev. Contrasts between the reporting done by the Spanish press and the European press were astonishing, despite the fact that reporters from France's *Le Monde*, London's *Guardian* and other leading European newspapers were not allowed into Spain. The US based *International Herald*

*Tribune* barely mentioned Grimau or the trial.

Not surprisingly, Grimau was found guilty, and at dawn, on April 20, 1963, he was executed in Carabanchel Prison, in the center of Madrid. He was to be the last person put to death for Civil War crimes, but in April 1963 this was not obvious. The fascists were still firmly in control, and international opinion had made little difference.

The noisy "liberalization" campaign managed by Manuel Fraga Iribarne, which had allowed *La Camisa* to be commercially produced, was orchestrated in large part for external consumption, especially the United States. In 1959, Washington had saved the Franco regime from economic collapse by providing nearly a billion dollars in non-military aid, on top of military assistance that had begun in 1953 with the establishment of US military bases in Spain and offers of American military and technical training. Internally, Fraga Iribarne used the Grimau affair to demonstrate to the Spaniards that despite a certain lip service paid to "liberalization," Franco and his ministers still tightly held the reins of power. I understood that the Grimau trial and execution were one of the ways Franco kept the population terrorized, under control, always fearful, insecure, and often grateful the *caudillo* was "keeping the peace."

During the six months of Grimau's incarceration, I wrote my first piece of partisan political analysis. In the process, I underwent a transformative progression of political awareness, much like the careful, steady process of bringing a blurred camera into sharp focus. Not only did I gain insights into the mechanics and machinations of Spanish fascism; I also learned a lot about how my own government worked.

In those days *The New Republic* was a progressive magazine, and I had a subscription and received it regularly in Pozuelo de Alarcón. In 1962, Salvador Madariaga, a distinguished writer and historian who had been Spain's ambassador to the United States during the end of the Republic, wrote an "Appeal to Americans" in that journal. It urged Americans to recognize the evils of the Franco regime and to apply pressure for a change in Washington's policy of supporting the Spanish government.[9] Several weeks later, Louis J. Halle, a veteran State Department diplomat, published a reply explaining the advantages of maintaining the current US policy towards Franco, and the benefits Spaniards were receiving from their leader. Halle's letter coincided with Grimau's arrest.

The chance to view the effects of American foreign policy "from the other side" marked a crucial point in my political evolution. I saw firsthand how Eisenhower's and then Kennedy's support for the Spanish regime had become the linchpin of Franco's strength. Without US dollars, the Spanish government would be gravely weakened. This was the first time I was aware of the blatant discrepancy between what the State Department said about democracy and American ideals, and how it was capable of acting. It was an odd feeling, being on the receiving end of American foreign policy. I shared the anger and frustration of the anti-Francoist Spaniards, and I felt I had to do something. I decided to write an article for the American press on the Grimau trial. Some months later Paul Sweezy, editor of the *Monthly Review*, sent me a handwritten letter kindly explaining why he couldn't publish my article. I don't remember what nice words he used to say that it was too inflammatory. I was touched — and emboldened to continue to investigate and report.

These political events – the strike, the theatre and Grimau's trial – transformed my understanding of how societies and governments work. They profoundly affected my capacity not only to define myself as a political being, but also as a young American woman on the path to becoming a certain kind of feminist and socialist. Weaving through these events, as well as through those of the following years, are memories of women's voices, many forgotten until now. Decades ago I heard some of them; others remained unheeded for many years. The absence of female voices often accompanied me too, consciously and unconsciously, and had its part in the formation of the feminist I am today.

# CHAPTER 4

# MADRID AND ESCAPE

Gabriel and I never confronted any serious problems. He believed love would conquer all, and I was sure I could get my way. After I gradually realized what life married to a member of the Spanish upper middle class (albeit among the liberal faction) would be for me, I did not want to continue living in Spain; I wanted a career as a university professor in the United States. Gabriel's parents were horrified to think I would abduct the family jewel to the wilds of America. Gabriel tried to keep us all happy by never making his desires and plans clear to anyone.

Soon after we were married I urged Gabriel to apply for a Fulbright to study in America. (I had arranged for a year's leave from Harvard.) Because I was petrified of taking my PhD Generals and convinced that I did not have what it took to get a doctorate there, I welcomed the excuse marriage gave me for a year's respite. For six months, I was an exemplary wife. I made a fetish of cooking gourmet meals, did the dishes, entertained family and friends, and tried to forget how much I hated my father-in-law's constant intervention in my life. Handsome and charming, my father-in-law was, at the time, the owner of Tecnos, a small, but important publishing company. He was also a frustrated intellectual whose promising university career was ended by the Civil War — and a dictatorial Latin patriarch. He smilingly tyrannized his wife and children economically, psychologically and intellectually. I never had the courage to stand up to him — probably because I did not fully understand my situation. I did, however, spend long hours contemplating how pleasant my life would be if he were to disappear.

After six months of marriage I suddenly lost my appetite, became very thin, and was constantly depressed. I hated my life as a married woman in Madrid, had numerous fits of hysteria, and could think of nothing but returning to America. Apparently my instinct for survival was telling me that if I did not get back to the States soon and finish my degree, life would be over for me. Occasionally, I would reflect on what a 'wonderful life' I might have as the wife of a wealthy Madrid technocrat, the life everyone was pressing me to accept. Gabriel would have an interesting job; Gabriel would travel; Gabriel would have entry to decision-making positions. But what about me? All I could see in the future was a comfortable apartment, a maid or two, vacations on the Mediterranean, and boredom and isolation. I could not do it.

Gabriel finally received a Fulbright to study economic history at the University of Wisconsin. Madison was a long way from Cambridge and Harvard, but I did not care. I would commute; I would sprout wings; I would do anything to be free of Madrid and his family. Without his father and other family pressure I thought everything would be perfect.

We lived from 1963 to 1966 in Madison as graduate students. I passed my doctoral exams, finished my thesis, and published a scholarly article. I also carried responsibility for cooking, cleaning, shopping, and every administrative problem in our lives while working fifteen to twenty hours a week as a project assistant in the university's Spanish department. Despite being harassed, nervous, emaciated, and suffering severe headaches and insomnia, I thought I was happy. Gabriel's family was an ocean away.

Madison was a politically exciting spot. Like Berkeley and Columbia, the University of Wisconsin was a center of activity against the Vietnam War and in favor of civil rights. Several of our friends went to Mississippi to participate in the 1964 Freedom Summer during which three young civil rights workers were killed, two of them from New York. I met "Red Diaper Babies" for the first time—sons and daughters of American Communists and Socialists who were adapting family traditions of radical politics to the 1960s student movement.

In 1965, one of the early anti-Vietnam War teach-ins was held on the University of Wisconsin campus. I became friendly with a graduate student in the history department, Joan W. Scott, one of the organizers of the teach-in, who would go on to become a major figure in American academia. From John Coatsworth, a graduate student in Latin American history who would one day become the founding director of the David Rockefeller Center for Latin American Studies at Harvard University, I heard a first-hand account of the Cuban Revolution. He and his wife Pat met on an "illegal" trip to Cuba in the summer of 1963. I never forgot the glowing description they gave of the new revolution, and it crossed my mind that one day I would want to visit the Caribbean island that had been transformed by those larger-than-life-leaders, Fidel Castro and Che Guevara. However, in Madison, I did not immerse myself wholeheartedly in student politics, for I was obsessed with finishing my thesis. I also realized that Gabriel was ambivalent about taking part in US radical politics as a foreigner. Therefore, we socialized with student radicals, but I limited my participation to attending marches and other big public events.

Every once in a while I resented being "forced" to remain on the margins of political life in Madison chiefly because Gabriel was afraid that public participation might be dangerous for him, either in the United States or back in Spain. I was never sure if the danger was real, or if Gabriel simply did not want to make a commitment to living in the United States. It was a topic neither of us could discuss rationally, so I pushed my spurts of anger away and plunged even more determinedly into finishing my dissertation.

Because Gabriel had come to the States on a student's visa, he had to return to Spain for two years before he could apply for status as a "resident alien." The question of where we would live permanently was never settled between us. Gabriel simply would not face the issue. He did not realize that more was involved than could be solved by saying, "Darling, you are right. You absolutely must have your own career too." During our last year in Madison, I taught Spanish literature at a small, non-accredited college nearby. I resented the fact that I had to take that job and did not have the freedom to choose another place and city because Gabriel was still working on his degree, but I accepted it as my fate. However, my unacknowledged frustrations emerged in a thousand ways—screaming, fits of hysteria, and petty fights. These "inherently feminine" weapons are, in truth, tools any human being uses when she or he feels suffocated, trapped and helpless.

In September 1966, we went back to Spain. Gabriel had a fellowship to write his thesis, and I had a postdoctoral research grant from Harvard to investigate something I thought was not particularly important. I wanted to stay in the States, teach, and increase involvement in radical politics. Madison had become a hot bed of what would come to be known as "1960s radicalism." It was too early for the Women's Liberation Movement, but by the time we went back to Spain, I knew about Students for a Democratic Society, had attended "teach-ins" against the Vietnam War and made what would turn out to be life-long friends among Madison's student radicals.

I dreaded returning to Spain. By 1966, my love of Spain was overshadowed by the struggle to separate the country from the suffocating role of a Spanish family in my marriage. To keep some distance between the family network and our life, I persuaded Gabriel that we should live in Barcelona, not Madrid. I imagine his father was furious, but since neither he nor anyone else in the family ever brought up the issue in front of me, I just let Gabriel handle all of that. We rented a small apartment in Castelldefels, on the beach a few minutes drive from Barcelona. Gabriel went to an archive every day and I mostly stayed at home and tried to convince myself that I was converting my thesis into a publishable book. I walked on the beach in the mornings, felt lonely in the afternoons, and picked petty fights with Gabriel in the evenings.

This arrangement came to an end after three months. Gabriel said he needed to be in Madrid to do research in the archives of the Central Bank. The grant I had received from Harvard required research in the Madrid-based newspaper library, so I could not make a rational case to stay in Castelldefels where, in fact, I had not been particularly happy anyway.

In Madrid, we again lived in one of the properties my father-in-law owned. This time it was an apartment he had bought for his daughter and son-in-law at 9 Amado Nervo Street, in Madrid's Barrio del Niño Jesús. My sister-in-law Teri, her husband Carlos Bustelo and their two young children were its permanent inhabitants, but they were going to lend it to us since Carlos' job was taking them to Paris for almost a year. Being "housed" by the family I felt hemmed in once again, but there was nothing I could do about it. Gabriel said it was ridiculous to spend money for an apartment when we could live rent-free. What could I say that would make sense to anyone else but me? It was a lovely apartment and Carlos and Teri generously left us whatever we needed. When they returned from Paris, Gabriel and I rented an apartment several blocks away at Plaza del Niño Jesus, 5.

The Plaza del Niño Jesus is on the southeastern side of the Retiro Park, an elegantly designed park that was the 17$^{th}$ century private playground of the royal family. The district was a solidly bourgeois neighborhood with three and four story apartment buildings that were, at the time, about thirty or forty years old. They were mostly made of the yellowish/beige stucco so familiar throughout the Mediterranean. Our side of the Retiro, the eastern side, was not as elegant as the other side, the Jerónimos district. There the gracious Alfonso XII Street, which extended along the western side of the Retiro, boasted some of Madrid's finest residences and most sought after addresses.

Most of the inhabitants in number 5 Plaza del Niño Jesus owned their apartments and lived there for their entire lives. Similar residences on both sides flanked the plaza in front of the pleasant entrance to our building. On the ground floor, the street level, was a typical *madrileño* assembly of small businesses: a *panadería* where I purchased fresh bread each morning, a "bar" that served *café con churros* (delicious fried dough sticks, a Madrid specialty) as well as wine and liquor, a shop for fresh fruits and vegetables, and a few other small stores, each devoted to specific merchandise.

Several of our friends lived around the corner: Javier and Gabriela Pradera, Gabriela's brother Rafael Sánchez Ferlosio and his wife Carmen Martín Gaite. These neighbors were some of the dissidents couched in class entitlement who would, some years after Franco's death in 1975, be celebrated as leading political and cultural figures of the New Spain. None of us knew that in 1966, but I did realize that in *el barrio* and beyond, I was socializing with cutting edge novelists and dramatists, daring political rebels, independent movie producers and actors, and relatives of some of Republican Spain's most illustrious figures. Because of my marriage, I had readymade access to the cultural and intellectual core of an entire country, albeit all dissidents. An equivalent of this world would not have been available to me in the United States when I was in my early twenties. In my own country, I had no family or social connections and being a graduate student at Harvard only insured access to one's professors.

Among these men and women, and without entirely realizing it, I consolidated my own formation. I discovered new avenues to explore: different ways to think, talk, eat and dress. I became, or realized I was, an intellectual with an internationalist perspective and a coherent left-wing understanding of how the world worked. I also perfected a layer of good taste and wit. But most of all, I forged a deep, conscious commitment to feminism.

I had first met Javier Pradera in 1963 in my in-laws' apartment. My father-in-law had given Javier a job when he was virtually unemployable, having just gotten out of jail where he had been confined for anti-Francoist activities. Javier and Gabriel had both participated in the first major uprising against Franco, the university demonstrations of 1956, but Javier (unlike Gabriel) had a close relationship with the outlawed Communist Party, so his jail stint was harsher and longer than Gabriel's.

I always liked Gabriela. More a sympathizer with her husband's solidly left-wing politics than an activist herself, Gabriela's family network was remarkable, but not atypical during those early Post-Civil War times. Her father was Rafael Sánchez Mazas, a founding member of the Falange [the Spanish Fascist Party] as well as a member of Franco's government in 1939. Sánchez Mazas, who died in 1966, was also a well-known pro-fascist journalist and novelist, a proponent of the "Catholic novel." His son (and Gabriela's brother) was Rafael Sánchez Ferlosio, a staunch anti-Francoist and a leading avant-garde novelist. Sánchez Ferlosio was married to a woman who was not only a strong anti-fascist, but also a feminist: Carmen Martín Gaite, a prize-winning novelist.

Martín Gaite was the only female literary figure I knew relatively well during those years in Madrid. In 1958, she won one of Spain's most coveted literary prizes, the "Premio Nadal," for her novel, *Entre Visillos* [Behind the Curtains]. However, when I met her, it was clear that her husband, Rafael Sánchez Ferlosio, was considered the major new literary voice — his wife "also wrote novels." Ferlosio's *Jarama* caused a stir because of its formal innovations, and for some years after its 1956 publication, his star status remained unique among anti-Francoist intellectuals. However, Carmen, his (then) wife became in 1978 the first woman to receive the Spanish National Prize for Literature for her novel *El cuarto de atrás* [The Back Room], published in English in 1987. Within a few years, she was to become the doyenne of Spanish letters, feted the world over, her novels and essays translated into dozens of languages.

Carmen had published only one or two works when I met her. I had not yet read any of her novels, and I must confess what I most remember about our first meeting was her unconventional manner. Madrid was — and is — an elegant city where concern with physical appearance and apparel is tailored by a class system, so it was rare to encounter a woman in her thirties with a passport to membership in the Madrid upper middle class who dressed in bohemian garb. Carmen wore no make-up, flat sandals, had long straight hair and projected a resolutely intellectual demeanor. She was vintage Greenwich Village. Her deliberate lack of social pretension conveyed an oppositional strength that I found attractive and endearing.

One afternoon, while I was having coffee with Carmen, I blurted out my frustrations about feeling controlled by Gabriel's father. "Why am I the only member of the family who reacts so negatively to the control and infantilization of his wife and the other females around him? Gabriel says he agrees with me, but everything Gabriel does contradicts what he says. I feel like I am living in a velvet prison!"

Carmen looked straight at me with her intense, intelligent eyes and leaning a bit forward said, "*¿Sabes lo que son la Sección Femenina[10] y el Código Civil de Franco?*" [Do you know what the Feminine Branch of the Falangist Party and Franco's Civil Code are?]

Carmen introduced me to the fundamental institutions and texts that supported the Francoist brand of misogyny. She was the first Spanish female who spoke to me seriously about the status of women in Spain; a subject no one I met ever spoke about openly. We were not close friends, and I was moved that she took my emotional outburst seriously. I wondered where she, living in a society so overtly scornful of female achievement, had found the grit and confidence to produce first-rate literary works. Somehow Carmen, born into a conservative religious family in northern Spain, had developed a defiant, resolute clarity of vision and purpose that I did not possess—at least not yet. I needed support from people who surrounded me. But what I usually encountered were strutting, immature males and passive, submissive females. Many years later, in 1987, when I read Carmen's groundbreaking study of male/female relationships in postwar Spain, *Usos amorosos de la postguerra* [Courtship Customs in Postwar Spain], I realized how much more she had probably understood on that day about my frustration with my role as "Gabriel's wife."

Almost thirty years passed before I had contact again with Carmen Martín Gaite. In 1993 I was writing and co-editing a book on gender and Valle-Inclán[11]. Carmen Martín Gaite's perspective on the then somewhat unorthodox subject of gender in the literary works of Valle-Inclán would make her a highly valued addition to our list of contributors; I wrote to her and described our project. Her answer was hand typed on the onionskin paper we all used then for airmail letters. The pages are a bit yellow now, but the immediacy, frankness and warmth of the words have not faded. She was in the middle of a novel and didn't want to interrupt its progress, but—"*¡qué bien recibir noticias tuyas, que me han hecho recordar aquellos tiempos tan ricos!*" [How good it is to hear from you...your letter has made me recall those splendid days.] By "those splendid days" I imagine Carmen meant both the boundless optimism and the intense camaraderie shared by all of us who were united in the opposition movements. I was touched that she remembered me and momentarily nostalgic for the 1960s and Spain. A few years ago I clipped Carmen's front-page obituary from *El País* and tucked it into one of her novels that she had inscribed for me.

My mother-in-law, Maria Teresa Casares de Tortella, was a

member of the Spanish Association of University Women. In 1960s Spain, this organization consisted of a relatively small number of Spanish women who had had access to the university, most of them before the Civil War. In Madrid, members tended to be progressive, and they often socialized together. They held their monthly meetings in the *Instituto Internacional* and many women in the Association had educated their children at the *Colegio Estudio*.

Several months after Gabriel and I returned to Madrid, Doña Soledad Ortega, the president of the Spanish Association of University Women and a friend of my mother-in-law's, asked me to speak on some aspect of the American university. She had heard that Maria Teresa's daughter-in-law was from Harvard and writing her dissertation with Steve Gilman.[12] Without hesitation, and somewhat to my own surprise, I said I would talk on the role of women in the university. I knew nothing about the subject—but I would by the time I gave the speech. The Association's annual lecture series would be held in the lecture hall of the *Instituto*, where I had taught English to adults when I came to Madrid as a graduate student on a fellowship from Harvard in 1961.

Doña Soledad Ortega, an elegant, educated woman in her late forties, was a driving force in the small but important group of the Spanish bourgeoisie who kept intellectual debate alive in Madrid in the 1960s. As the daughter of the internationally renowned Spanish philosopher, parliamentarian, professor and social critic, José Ortega y Gasset (1883-1955), Doña Soledad belonged to one of Republican Spain's most prominent families. Ortega was also remembered as a man who publicly declared, in Spain, that he was an atheist. At any point in Spain's history, from its incipient moments as Western Europe's first nation state in 1492 until 1975 when Franco died, these were fighting words—especially when proclaimed in a public forum. *The Revista de Occidente* [Magazine of the West], the cultural journal Doña Soledad's father had founded in 1923, remained in the family and served as a center, even if necessarily a polite one, of opposition to the Franco regime.

Ortega y Gasset had not been a proponent of women's equality, intellectually or personally. However, the intellectual and social prominence of the Ortega family counted for a great deal. The importance of the father created a certain public space for the daughter. For Doña Soledad, familial social status took precedence over gender, as it had for Indira Gandhi and other daughters of prominent men in Third World countries where the vast majority of women were treated like second class citizens, or worse.

As I watched Doña Soledad move in and out of public and private spheres so confidently and competently during those months in 1966 and 1967, the ability of social class to erase a "gender handicap" that limited women's access to the public sphere first became apparent to me. I had never considered this before because it was not an option for me. Class privilege could, to a certain degree, erase gender prejudice. The number of educated women in Spain's oppositional elite was so tiny and their situation contrasted so dramatically with the lives of the large majority of women in Spain, that these few women were quietly sheltered under the male wing, as it were. For Doña Soledad, living under a repressive fascist regime that had no pretentions to being a "classless" or democratic society, her social status simply eclipsed her gender handicap in many, though never all, venues.

I had never met an American feminist, but had read Betty Friedan's *The Feminine Mystique* and reread it to prepare for the speech I would deliver in April 1967 at Madrid's *Instituto Internacional*. Although I recognized my mother's plight in Friedan's descriptions of married life in the 1950s, and I certainly shared some of the malaise Betty Friedan identified in her book, I did not know anyone else who did and Friedan's analysis did not satisfy me. She talked about "the illness with no name," that awful psychological oppression—the enormous frustration, anger, bitterness that lay just below the surface for countless women who had been socialized into believing that "true women" accepted secondary status in society. All of that certainly resonated with me, but the solution she suggested was incomplete and did not go to the root of the problem. Her answer to combating male supremacist practices was to fight for certain reforms that amounted to getting men out of the way so as to make room for women; that is, freeing women from the institutionalized discrimination that maintained male dominance. Crucial reforms, but Betty Friedan was talking about improving the lot of women like herself, and I knew that middle class women were only a part of the female population.

I had seen what working class poverty did to too many women in Spain to forget about them. Abolishing discrimination against women might open the way for a female head of state, a corporation president, and female generals, but a factory girl would remain a factory girl; a maid would remain a maid. It seemed to me that unless a women's movement made changing the status of women like Juana and Vicenta, the domestic workers I knew, as important as achieving more opportunities for my upper middle class Spanish sister-in-law (or for me in the United States), the fundamental causes of women's oppression would not be eliminated. But I knew, even then, that the arena where I would be most effective in promulgating progressive change for women would be in academia, among middle class women. My roots were there and the stimulus to revolt had sprung from this world.

As I searched for more data for my lecture, I found that there were practically no books that dealt with women in the university — a subject generally assumed to have little intrinsic, let alone market value. I wrote to Dean Kirby-Miller at Radcliffe, who responded immediately, sending me Jessie Bernard's *Academic Women*, several other leads and a note saying not too much had been published on the subject. Over forty years have passed since the Dean of Radcliffe airmailed me these materials, a gesture that I believe I rather took for granted at the time. Radcliffe administrators always helped the women at Harvard. Having been an academic dean myself in the ensuing years and having worked closely with many other (mostly male) university administrators, I realize the uniqueness of Dean Kirby-Miller's support, and, in hindsight, remain touched by her generosity.

My research clearly showed that women didn't get a fair shake in any market place, at the university or elsewhere. The evidence was unequivocal. The deck was stacked against females who wandered into the public domain, for the men who dealt the cards made the rules. Power was not suitable for women; the exercise of power simply was not ladylike. As I wrote the speech, I became angrier and angrier at the injustice of it all. Halfway through the speech I read Simone de Beauvoir's *The Second Sex*. I had tried to read it before, but somehow never managed more than twenty pages. It made me too uncomfortable. But Beauvoir's courageous text now sustained me as I accepted the consequences of understanding that my condition as a woman was a social problem and not just a matter of my "silly, personal neuroses." Years later I would thank its author by naming my daughter Ana Simone.

The ire born in me during the course of writing that speech was not a surge of fury. Rather, it was a steady, methodical, and deliberate passion that generated an intense, permanent white-hot heat whose embers still glow within me.

I gave the speech, and toward the end I speculated about the future for women in American universities. I was also very much aware that I was speaking to a Spanish public. "A society that does not have the confidence to permit its intellectuals to work freely is almost, by definition, incapable of creating first-rate universities," I said. I also put my distinguished audience of about 200 (a mix of academics, well-heeled ladies, some prominent husbands, college students, and various priests) on warning: "In addition to a civil rights movement that has been gaining momentum for five or six years in the US, since February 1965 when the government began to bomb Vietnam, an anti-war movement has been developing throughout my country. Although it is difficult to say at this moment what lasting effect the antiwar movement will have, history has shown that often one progressive movement engenders others; perhaps we are on the verge of witnessing a new women's movement too." I didn't know at the time that I was talking about the impossibility to separate — the infrangibility of — the civil rights struggle, the national outrage at the Vietnam War, and the beginnings of the second wave of feminism in the United States.

The closing paragraphs of my speech urged the formation of a new definition of femininity in which the roles of wife and mother are made compatible with their maximal intellectual and professional development. I advocated government-sponsored aid for women, usually wives and mothers, to allow them to go back to school to finish interrupted or postponed educations; the establishment of government and/or work place sponsored day care centers, and provision of birth control education at the national level, free and accessible to all.

The last item rocked the boat in Madrid. I knew it would, but I could not refrain from saying it. I thought I had been quite temperate by not mentioning the word 'abortion.' Perhaps the slightly blander phrase "birth control" would pass. It did not. The robed priests in the audience — there, after all, as custodians of national morality — leapt up to disagree. Nominally, I was speaking about women in the United States, but national borders did not count when it came to control over human reproduction. We all knew that. I looked directly at the outraged priests and summoned up a properly polite smile. My demeanor was conciliatory and diplomatic. The priests mistakenly thought I was contrite, so they folded their skirts and sat down, pudgy arms resting on rounded paunches. The 'patria' would remain pure.

It took a certain amount of courage to make that speech, I now realize. But the opportunity to be courageous and take a political risk publicly in front of an audience that "mattered" erased any thought of potential negative consequences. My American passport and Gabriel's social status would take care of everything, I assumed. And I was right.

As I would learn almost twenty years later, among the students in the audience that day was Soledad Varela Ortega, Doña Soledad's daughter, known to her friends as Paloma. In 1985, I ran into Paloma in the history department at Tel Aviv University in Israel. I hadn't remembered meeting Paloma, now a Madrid-based professor of linguistics, in 1967, but she had come to hear my speech. She recalled that lecture as a wake-up call. It was the first time she had heard a feminist speak publicly.

In 1978, during the creative ferment of the first post-Franco years, Doña Soledad and her family established the Ortega y Gasset Foundation, an independent center for research in the social sciences and humanities, policy formulation and a sponsor for seminars, and some post-secondary instruction. Two years later Doña Soledad took over as Director of the *Revista de Occidente*, the literary/cultural magazine her father had founded almost sixty years before. The prestigious journal had always remained in the family, but until 1980 it had always been under the control of a male relative. The Foundation has become one of the major independent research and policy centers in Spain with branches in Toledo, Spain, and Buenos Aires.

In 1985, I returned to Madrid for my first extended stay in newly democratic Spain. Paloma had arranged for me to give a summer course for American students studying in Spain on "Women in Latin America" at the Foundation's Toledo Center. It was personally and politically rewarding to be able to measure the inroads academic feminism had made in Spain since I gave my speech in 1966. By the mid 1980s, women's studies had become a staple in Spanish institutions of higher education.

***

The Spanish sense of the family unit is intense and overrides all other concerns. It bridges generations, transcends politics, and is ever-present in conversations. It is at the heart of everything.

Gabriel's parents expected us to come to lunch every Sunday at their home. In the Spanish style, this was an elaborate affair that started sometime after two o'clock and lasted two or three hours. At Miguel Angel 18, two maids were in charge of the four-course meal served at the long rectangular dining table that on Sundays often hosted a dozen relatives and friends.

Juana and Vicenta, the Tortella's maids, were very different from Victoria, Manolita Roesset's domestic servant at Lope de Vega 31. When I met Juana and Vicenta, they were in their late teens, perhaps early twenties—three or four years younger than I. They shared a bedroom in the back of the kitchen. Their room had a tiny window and was sparsely but decently furnished. Next to the bedroom was a tiny bathroom reserved for the maids and for anyone else who might be doing temporary manual work in the apartment. Juana was strikingly pretty: slight and slim with gentle brown eyes and chestnut hair that fell to her shoulders in an uncomplicated manner. With her delicate features and graceful manner, she could have been on a Spanish travel poster advertising Iberian beauties. More pleasant than intelligent, Juana served the meals, answered the door and the phone, while Vicenta did the cooking and heavy cleaning. Vicenta had the stocky build of a peasant girl and a twinkle in her eye. Their rules of employment were nominally the same as Victoria's: Sunday afternoons off and certain food reserved for them. However at Miguel Angel 18 the maids ate what the family did, not just leftovers, and also had alternate Thursday afternoons off. On Sundays, after being served coffee in the living room at the end of lunch (usually around four o'clock) Gabriel's mother urged us to finish up because *"las chicas tienen que irse"* [the girls have to leave]. They were due back in time to prepare and serve a light dinner around 10:00 p.m.

After several months, I caught on to the code of conduct for "The Family" with respect to domestic servants. All family members were to be polite, even considerate to the maids. One also showed compassion if they needed to see a doctor. Part of the tacit accord between *"los señores"* and the maids was that the former group never spoke to the latter about anything other than the work they were doing in the household. Maintaining the proper distance was crucial for sustaining inter-class relations, particularly among those housed together under one's own roof.

With what I later recognized as a naïve, if well-meaning, all-American disregard for established social patterns, I decided to try to get to know Juana and Vicenta. Perhaps, I could teach them English or open up new avenues for them in some way. So, every now and then, and usually dressed in blue jeans, I would wander into the kitchen to "chat." I cringe now as I recall my suggestions of ways to improve their situation, and my attempts to let them know that I sympathized with their plight. They mostly just listened, occasionally offering to make me coffee or tea, which I was delighted to accept. I can't imagine what they thought of me other than wondering why the wife of *Señorito* Gabriel (oldest and favored son of a wealthy family) would dress the way I did when the family could obviously afford to have me decked out in a more appropriate manner.

Months later I learned my forays into the kitchen had led to a touching incident. At certain intervals Gabriel's mother had to sign government-issued papers for the maids so that their National Identity Card would be "in order." No citizen could be without this assurance of his/her approved presence in Spanish society. The card always asked "Occupation," and the answer defined your slot in the Spanish economic and social hierarchy. *"Doméstica"* [maid] was the lowest type of occupation available for women given that prostitution was not recognized as a category.

The time came for Juana to renew her card: "*¿Señora, tiene usted que poner doméstica este año?*" [Señora, do you have to put maid as my profession this year?] This was the first time it had occurred to Juana to question her status, my mother-in-law later told me. Juana knew that in 1960s Spain, once labeled a maid on your national identity card, it was virtually impossible to find other work. That stigmatum on her identity card would also prevent Juana from marrying even slightly above her present station, despite her good looks.

"*Bueno, pero Juana, eso es lo que eres,*" [But Juana, this is what you are], my mother-in-law gently replied. She was a nice woman.

*Pero señora, quizá no lo seré siempre,* [But perhaps I won't always be a maid], Juana answered.

"*Bueno, bueno. Ya veremos,*" [Well, we'll see], said my mother-in-law.

Her "we'll see" was a soft exit strategy from a difficult conversation. Juana had to have an updated identity card, and even though I argued that we find another category for Juana, it was out of the question. No one risked offending the government bureaucracy to help a maid, not even decent liberals. My visits to the kitchen gradually diminished as I realized the futility of my efforts to remake Franco's Spain bit by bit.

I did not like being expected to eat at my in-laws' house every Sunday. Even though the surroundings were elegant, the food good and the company often interesting, I resented being "summoned" to fulfill an obligatory role as the wife of the family scion.

The lives of women (even foreign women) in Spain were prescribed and confined—the particular manifestations varied, of course, according to the economic and social status of the individual female. A man had a legal right to "discipline" his wife by beating her. Signs of affection were also restricted. Holding hands in public was prohibited. In my case, it was not overt masculine brutality that crushed my dignity and independence. Rather, it was the many ways women were infantilized that infuriated and inhibited me. Sometimes the condescension was merely a gesture of dismissal for an opinion expressed by a woman or an unspoken attitude of scorn, barely perceptible to anyone except its recipient. Interrupting and silencing women in public seemed perfectly natural to most everyone.

The inability to take women seriously, to regard female adults as rational beings, was deeply ingrained in Spanish society at all levels. One had to wear armor at all times in order to conduct daily life with a minimum of dignity. And the likelihood of a female triumph was about as good as had been Don Quijote's chances of vanquishing the windmill monsters. I knew the polite, "well groomed" dismissal of women was a refined version and an indirect, unselfconscious corollary of those laws that advocated physical violence against women, but I could not separate the "dancer from the dance." I did not know how to construct a social discourse on the subject that would win me allies. One of my strongest memories of those years is of being constantly irritated and never being able to explain exactly why. Often I had temper tantrums and I could not identify the cause. As a result, I knew some people found me "oddly" unpleasant. It did not please me, but there was nothing I could do about it.

Even though Carmen Martín Gaite had explained to me the basis for Spain's legislated misogyny, I was unable at that point to make sufficient connections between society and self to parse the roots of my anger. I did not understand how my discontent was anchored to the protest against the Francoist social construct of womanhood. It took me a long time to sort all that out.

Sunday lunch often included members of the Bustelo family — Gabriel's sister Teri was married to Carlos Bustelo. He had several siblings who occasionally joined us at table. I instinctively liked Carlos' sister, Carlota Bustelo Kindelán, whom everyone called Milota to distinguish her from her mother Carlota Garcia de Real de Bustelo. After Franco's death, Milota would become one of Spain's leading feminists, but in 1962 no Spaniard referred to herself as a feminist. To be called a *"feminista"* was an unmitigated insult that vitiated everything a Spanish woman was expected to aspire to be.

After Franco's death in 1975, nuanced differences played out in the public sphere and gradually replaced the homogenous unity of "Them and Us." The wealthy Bustelo clan would evolve into a powerful banking and financial family in the new Spain, but in the 1960s, when I knew them, there was only one significant political distinction in Spain: in favor of Franco or against him. Other than the outlawed Communist Party, differences among anti-Francoists were not a subject of public discourse. In the wake of Franco's death and during the three crucial years of transition to democracy (1975-78), a spate of new political energies fractured the bubble that had unified the "anti-franquistas" and scattered them to unexplored points on a constantly evolving political map.

Milota Bustelo and one of her brothers, Francisco, became major figures in the *Partido Socialista de España* that won a landslide election in 1982 under Prime Minister Felipe González. Carlos Bustelo, my sister-in-law Teri's husband, was Secretary of Commerce in 1979-80 for the center-right party, Adolfo Suárez' Union of the Democratic Center. But in the mid 1960s, we were all just a large extended family of anti-Francoists and had no way of foreseeing the political fracturing that lay ahead for us.

My talk on the role of women in the American university had made my feminist views public, particularly among members of the Tortella/Bustelo families. No one in the family ever disagreed with me face to face. That was not part of their culture. Gabriel said he agreed with everything I said, and it seemed that my views on feminism were smilingly tolerated in the family. No one discussed the subject openly or ever asked me a question. To this day, I have no idea what they really thought. However, my public presentation caused a rupture in my own development. I grew more confident and resolute about pursuing my growing interest in feminism—both in the incipient feminist movement in the United States and, perhaps more urgently, in how the issue of sexual inequality was infringing on my own life.

In the 1980s, Carolyn Heilbrun would write "Power is the ability to take one's place in whatever discourse is essential to action and the right to have one's part matter."[13] This is true she went on, in the Pentagon, in marriage, in friendship, and in politics. I could not articulate in 1967 that part of what angered me was my lack of access to power in public and private spheres. One (if one were female) did not speak of power; it was considered pushy and crass for an educated woman to say she wanted power.

When, years later, I saw Carlos and Teri in 1989 at a reception in Madrid they told me about Milota's groundbreaking role in the

Spanish Women's Movement. She had been elected to the Spanish Parliament in 1977 as a Socialist Party delegate from Madrid. Then, when Felipe González and the Socialists won the national elections in 1982, Milota became the driving force in the Socialist Party for initiating feminist actions on a national level. This resulted in legalization of the sale of contraceptives and the establishment of Family Planning Centers across Spain. She was the first General Director of the Women's Rights Institute set up by the government within the Ministry of Social Affairs. Since 1988, Milota has been active internationally as a member of the United Nations Committee for the Elimination of Violence Against Women.

Later, when I learned more about Milota's role in working to eliminate domestic violence in Spain, I wryly recalled that when Milota and I knew each other, it was legal for our husbands to beat us.[14]

Sometime in the early spring of 1968, sitting in my living room in Madrid, I read an article by Marlene Dixon about the creation of a women's caucus in an organization recently formed in Chicago called the New University Conference. I don't remember if it appeared in *The Nation*, or maybe *The New Republic*. Dixon, a professor of sociology at the University of Chicago, spelled out the aims of the caucus — to achieve social, economic, and psychological equality for women — and related feminism to radical politics. Finally, I had found my soulmate! Elated, I wrote to Marlene. She answered immediately and said to visit her as soon as I got back to the States.

I had grown increasingly exasperated by my life in Madrid, trapped in an invisible cocoon that both smothered me and prevented me from talking about the politely constructed prison that confined middle class women in Spain. It was even worse being a married woman: in this case the inferior status both endured and supported the country's social system. I always felt like I was drowning, gasping for air. Wasn't America better than this? Or was I constructing a false reality on the other side of the Atlantic? Where was the way out? I had to find a lifeboat to somewhere.

Among the few times I had felt emboldened during my years in Spain were moments when I had tried to ameliorate the situation of domestic servants: e.g., helping Juana, showing solidarity with Spain's impoverished workers by having the courage not to eat lunch with the Germans, and participating in the student strike against a fascist government by handing out *bocadillos* at the university. I also enjoyed writing the article on Julian Grimau, except for my annoyance at Gabriel when he hung over my shoulder to make sure I "got it right." But most of all, I felt strong and happy when I gave the speech on the current situation of academic women in the United States. That was all mine. Standing in front of a large audience in a major venue in Madrid and calling for a struggle for women's rights made me feel good—and powerful.

The speech had been my major comfort. Formulating my thoughts on the situation of women and communicating them to the public, trying to convince people to change ossified modes of thought, had been an exhilarating experience. I wanted to do more of that. Marriage was suffocating me. I had to get out of Madrid. The women's movement was the lifeboat; the way out.

I always wanted to be a "player," but on my own terms, without compromising my personal and political beliefs and principles. Marlene Dixon's article gave me hope that perhaps there was a new path I could forge for myself. A potential visit with Marlene gave me an incentive to return to the States earlier than Gabriel planned to. We both had jobs teaching at the University of Pittsburgh for the fall. His two-year stay in Spain was not up until September, but I invented, and half-believed at the time, a need to return to the States in June to finish research on a book. The truth was I wanted to talk to Marlene. My relationship with my husband was tense, poised to collapse—and I could not stand it any longer.

# CHAPTER 5

# WOMEN'S LIBERATION AND THE NEW UNIVERSITY CONFERENCE

I finally met Marlene Dixon in July 1968 at her home in Hyde Park, Chicago. Although we had only exchanged letters, she welcomed me as an old friend. Marlene's apartment was in the basement of a large building that straddled a border between a prosperous, largely intellectual community informally linked to the University of Chicago and a low-income area, largely populated by African Americans. The small apartment was furnished in vintage graduate student "movement" style, filled with books, political posters and second hand furniture. The rather dark kitchen was painted the garish light green often seen in institutional cafeterias.

Marlene was a large, imposing woman with short blond hair, a welcoming smile and boundless energy. All of her was strong: her voice, her thoughts, her determination. (Her kin were white working class, from southern California.) Definitely an alpha woman, I thought. I liked her. When I told her about my Madrid speech on the role of women - I didn't have a version in English and academics did not read Spanish in those days, unless they were Hispanists - she roared with laughter over my encounter with the priests. Marlene loved to talk, and once she grabbed hold of an idea, she was unstoppable.

I still have the notes I took that day. Reaching for a glass of red wine, she said that the institution of marriage "perpetuates the oppression of women and has also been the spark to ignite women's rebellion throughout history." For emphasis, she punched the table. Her glass of wine quivered ominously.

Marlene gulped down the wine, got a glass of water, slammed it on the table dangerously near my purse, and started denouncing the links between racism and male supremacy. Her passion increased as she spewed forth: "Male supremacy is an ideology that affirms the biological and social inferiority of women in order to justify massive institutionalized oppression. And don't forget that the root of the ideology of male superiority is female inferiority, and white racism is a system of white male superiority."[15] I decided I needed a glass of wine, but in deference to Marlene's passion, I only filled it up halfway. I opened my mouth to ask a question, but it was impossible to interrupt the torrent of words. "Look," she said, leaning closer to me, "white male supremacy is part of the idea, the ideology, of imperialism... first the Europeans then the Americans looted Africa, Asia and Latin America of raw materials like gold and silver. They used slaves from Africa and cheap labor from Asia to build the wealthiest countries, empires, in fact, the world has ever known. Then to justify such brutal exploitation, they invented the doctrine of white racial superiority and the supremacy of European and American 'civilizations' over the 'heathens' in the rest of the world. And you know what? The doctrine of white supremacy includes the supremacy of white women as well as of white men."

I finished my wine. Marlene went to the bathroom.

No one had ever talked to me like that—justifying, acknowledging, even embracing, my constant rage at the second class citizenship of women and my frustrations with my marriage, and suggesting a way to channel my anger into social action. An image of Carmen Martín Gaite flashed through my mind. There she was, as I had last seen her some months ago, in Madrid, isolated from other like-minded women, waging a solitary feminist struggle, using her writing to resist suffocation in a fascist society. I wished she could have been here. Although these two feminists were geographically and personally worlds apart, they probably shared many long-term goals. But unlike Carmen's, Marlene's was not a solitary struggle. Surrounded by a growing community of feminists, Marlene was working day and night to help lead a movement for major social change in a liberal democracy, in the richest country in the world.

When she came back to the kitchen table, Marlene started telling me about the New University Conference and its women's caucus, both created only four months earlier. She leaned back on the wobbly wooden chair, which I was sure would collapse momentarily. The New University Conference was created in the wake of the dissolution of Students for a Democratic Society, the major student organization of the New Left.

Although a considerable number of young radicals in 1968 chose to abandon the university to carry on the struggle outside academia, many wanted to balance both a radical approach to the institutions in which they were located (by radical teaching, curriculum reform, democratic struggles for control) with activism outside their work—community struggles against imperialism, racism, sexual inequality and capitalist economic organization. NUC was a magnet for hundreds, then thousands, of like-minded radicals in the academy.

Great! This appealed to me. So far, so good. The organization had a double mission: theorizing "a new, American form of socialism" and—now Marlene was pure radical academic—replacing "an educational and social system that is an instrument of class, sexual, and racial oppression with one that belongs to the people."[16] The intent was to build on the New University Conference as the higher education section of a yet-to-be-created socialist party.

As I was to learn, NUC was never united on a definition of "American" socialism. It was not a Marxist-Leninist organization and didn't resemble the Marxist utopias I had learned about in Spain. Some members were anti-communist, others were "radicals" without a precise definition, some were anarchists and a few were diehard Marxists. The majority were content to agree on what we were against: capitalism, sexism, power of large corporations, the Viet-Nam War, racism, poverty in America and, importantly, any form of structural hierarchy, "imposition from above" that resembled the Old Left of the 1930s. To me, the goal of NUC's "socialism" meant striving to create a non-capitalist, non-sexist democracy. The Soviet Union was not a model.

The politics—the analysis and strategy—of achieving these long-term goals were never worked out, but I could live with that for a while, as long as women were in the forefront. Marlene made us more coffee and continued talking, zeroing in on the creation of the Women's caucus. I was captivated.

Suddenly she interrupted herself: "Wait, you have to meet someone else." She called her friend, psychologist Naomi Weisstein who lived nearby with her husband, historian Jesse Lemisch. Naomi, petite with long dark auburn hair, contrasted physically with Marlene. But they shared a political vision, and both had grand smiles that conveyed buoyant optimism and confidence. Marlene and Naomi were not just intelligent, they knew things I didn't, about America, politics and possibilities for a women's movement and radical social change.

We had dinner in Marlene's kitchen. With a large bowl of steamed fresh artichokes in the middle of the table, we continued talking, tossing artichoke petals into an empty bowl on the table and drinking red wine. Jesse was there with us, but he never interrupted. Having just returned from two years in Spain, I was not used to being with a man who not only was absorbed in what women were saying, but also never interrupted them! He listened and watched, the first male feminist I had ever met.

Marlene, Naomi and Jesse had been at the founding convention of the New University Conference in Chicago in March 1968. Over artichokes and wine, they told me about major NUC participants, founding principles and the context in which Marlene and Naomi were working to shape its women's caucus. A burning issue in the women's movement was whether feminists should work separately or join with men in New Left organizations to further the women's liberation movement. Debates about the role of the women's movement in shaping the objectives of male-run New Left organizations had already erupted in 1967, when Heather Booth and Jo Freeman and other Chicago-based women had left SDS to organize the independent Women's Radical Action Project.[17] At the same time, Freeman started the first women's liberation newsletter, *"Voices of the Women's Liberation Movement."*

That was the context for Naomi's organizing a women's workshop at the NUC convention. A small group attended, largely activists from Chicago who were already involved in women's liberation. Position papers were presented, for and against creating a woman's caucus within the larger organization. The vote for it prevailed, the consensus being that women needed to develop a sense of unity and consciousness that would foster their full and equal participation in the radical movement. NUC would become the first New Left organization to adopt a feminist agenda from its inception.

The tension between "the movement" and "the women's movement" would reach a boiling point the following year, after Richard Nixon had been elected President, at the January 1969 SDS counter-inaugural. Women were silenced and thrown out for demanding female parity with the men at all levels of the organization. When Marilyn Salzman Webb, a prominent leader of SDS, got up to discuss the role of women there, she was hooted and booed off the stage as individual men shouted "Fuck her!" "Take her into an alley and fuck her!"

This event accelerated the debate about the ability of feminists to work within male-run radical organizations. Roxanne Dunbar[18] issued a challenge: "Why should the organ for revolution be a masculine organ within which women's liberation is a function (caucus)?"[19] Kathy McAfee and Myrna Wood wrote, "The problem at the present time is simply: should a women's liberation movement be a caucus within SDS, or should it be more than that? The radical women liberationists say the latter."[20] In "Toward a Female Liberation Movement," an article widely circulated in 1968 and 1969,

Beverly Jones and Judith Brown critiqued the role women tried to play in SDS and called for an independent female liberation movement. They also took aim at the subtle and not-so-subtle sexism of radical male activists.[21]

I was never a feminist separatist, and I enthusiastically supported the opportunity to work for both women's liberation and socialism. The caucus defined itself as a "national organization of women with socialist politics who do our political work in the area of education." We were educators and would concentrate our political activism in our workplace. For me, "socialist feminist" meant that sexism, racism, capitalism and imperialism could, in different contexts, be of equal importance. I was committed to an autonomous women's movement, but I also wanted to make sure women's liberation was included in the core of the New Left.

I left Chicago several days later with a sense that there was a place in my country where I could fit. These people were like me: young academics passionate about changing the world and improving it for women, but not just for women. The idea of belonging to a community of shared ideals and goals that stretched from California to New York freed me from the solitude of my personal situation. I had not been able to bear the confinement of my life in Madrid, but there I had been part of a clearly defined, solidly entrenched segment of Spanish society. After being in Chicago for just a few days, I began thinking about new friends and stimulating situations offering unforeseen opportunities. I loved the Spanish word *compañeros* and what it evoked.

However, for the moment, I was still married to Gabriel and about to start a career as a Hispanist at the University of Pittsburgh. I immediately wrote to the national office of the NUC in Chicago and told them I wanted to join. I pledged 2.5% of my annual salary, something the organization asked, but did not require, of its members.[22]

I rented a large, old brick home at 4218 Centre Ave in the Oakland section of the city, where the university was located. The house sat on a hill overlooking the main building of the College of Arts and Sciences. I furnished it in a haphazard, temporary way, borrowing some pieces from colleagues and buying essentials like a bed and a television. Lurking in the background, but still unarticulated, was the knowledge that Gabriel and I would not live there very long.

Gabriel and I sent each other airletters every day, mine were blue and his were beige, bordered with the red and yellow of the

Spanish flag. We spoke on the phone about once a week (long distance calls were expensive in 1968). His letters were somewhat mechanical and distant, but I just filed that bit of knowledge away. Denial had set in. I busied myself meeting new colleagues in the Department of Hispanic Languages and Literature and I got in contact with Jim Holland, a psychology professor who was interested in NUC. Jim introduced me to other progressives on the faculty and I started to familiarize myself with Pittsburgh after working mornings in the library.

I knew something was wrong as soon as Gabriel stepped off the plane. *"Hola rica."* [Hello darling.] He smiled as he embraced me and gave me a peck on the cheek.

We went about the expected rituals: I showed him the house; he said he loved it. I cooked him dinner: *"Cocinas tan bien, cielo."* [You cook so well sweetheart]. Then we made love. It was mechanical and ritualistic, but this was nothing new, at least for me. I uttered the appropriate groans and moans in order to assure Gabriel of his capacity to satisfy me sexually—something that never occurred. It was important to him that I appreciated him as a lover, so I told him that I did.

Over breakfast the next morning, the truth spilled out. He told me he had fallen in love with another woman that summer. Josefina, he said, was *"muy comprensiva y sabe que será muy difícil para ti."* She was very understanding and knows how difficult this will be for me. He stared at me, proud of himself that he had the courage to tell me the truth and afraid of my reaction. I was hurt and furious.

*"Lo sospechaba,"* [I suspected it] I responded in a monotone.

He responded that he felt justified because it was impossible to live with my *"impaciencia y tus arrebatos contra mi familia y Espana"* [my impatience, and temper tantrums about his family and Spain]. Gabriel and I spoke Spanish, but his English was excellent.

*"Que gilipollas y cobarde tu eres "* I hissed at him. [What an asshole and a coward you are.]

When angry, Gabriel became more intense and tried to ignore my anger by not answering me. He never yelled. I, however, did scream. I became really good at it in Spanish.

We spent the rest of the day going through a familiar litany of accusations and insults that we had played out many times before, but without the existence of Josefina, Gabriel's safety blanket. Over the past several years I had threatened to leave several times; he would panic and beg me not to. We made up and peace reigned for a while. He was more afraid of being alone than of losing me. I think I knew that then, but I also was scared of starting life "all over again" alone, even though I said I wasn't.

The day ended as many others had, with a temporary peace. Gabriel promised to write to Josefina to end the affair, and he and I decided to give our marriage another chance. He did write to his Spanish lover. I know because some weeks later I went to his office at the university while he was teaching and found letters from her. In the last one, she was miserable and heartbroken. I thought good, at least he was honest about that.

The fall semester was about to begin. I diligently set about preparing my classes, seeing, for the first time, a way to combine my commitment to the humanities and European culture with my progressive politics. I was (and still am) a radical with classical tastes. I enjoyed reevaluating the past and making it alive and relevant to students who were protesting against the inequalities of 1968 America. I was teaching *Don Quijote* in translation to 50 students, and, in Spanish, an introductory survey of modern Spanish literature, and a graduate seminar on Valle-Inclán.[23] The students and I explored the nature of the humanism and idealism that defined the complex relationship between Don Quijote and Sancho Panza, as well as Cervantes' profound understanding of his country—at the time, a global imperial power ruled by King Philip II. My students discovered Cervantes' subtle defense of women, condemnation of religious intolerance and respect for the individual, even though he, the gentleman from La Mancha, was driven "mad" by a voracious, unjust society that refused to meet his ideals.

We also read the extraordinary poems and plays of Federico Garcia Lorca, assassinated by Franco's fascists in 1936. In 1968 Hispanists were not supposed to mention the open secret of Garcia Lorca's homosexuality. But when we read Lorca's magnificent, fierce "Ode to Walt Whitman," some in the class teased out similarities between living as a Spanish or American gay man in 1930 and in 1968. It was very moving. And this was before the Stonewall revolution of 1969!

Early in the semester, as I was getting acquainted with my classes, Bob Ross, who was in charge of the New University Conference national office in Chicago, asked me if I could form a chapter in Pittsburgh. This was an expansion of the organizing Marlene had unofficially asked me to undertake for the women's caucus, more opportunity to build something new. I knew I could do it.

I plunged into a whirlwind of political activity. The issues of women's liberation were still new to most people in Pittsburgh, and I felt an urgency to get the word out to as many women as I could reach. Organizing a chapter of NUC was not much trouble at all, given the campus's readiness for some organization that would help faculty and graduate students work for social justice and academic reform. Jim Holland, who had been at the university for years, assembled a list of potential sympathizers, so only a couple of months after I had arrived in Pittsburgh, we were able to convene an active NUC chapter of several dozen members. It offered instant community, and we had fun getting to know each other and helping the group grow. I loved being at the hub of all this new activity. Most of us were humanists and social scientists, but there were a few scientists and some folks from education and social work. We were a presence on campus, involved in anti-Vietnam War and anti-corporate demonstrations as well as issues of educational reform, launching struggles around the curriculum to expose how universities reinforced the supremacy of the white male.

One of our first activities as a chapter was to protest the Gulf Oil Company's recent and initial foray into Ecuador. In the late 1960s, many US based petroleum companies were in the first stages of extracting crude oil from Latin America. Gulf promised riches for the Ecuadorian people in exchange for access to their oil. In October, we organized a joint demonstration between the University of Pittsburgh and Carnegie Mellon University, located just down the road from us. Jim Holland and other NUC faculty warned several hundred demonstrators that Gulf would never allow any Ecuadorian government to stay in power if it advocated using the country's natural resource to benefit more than a privileged few Ecuadorians. I listened, recalling Spanish friends explaining how in 1953 the US Central Intelligence Agency overthrew Mohammad Mossadegh in Iran because he wanted to nationalize his country's oil resources and use them to improve people's lives. In Madrid I had also learned that on the heels of the coup in Iran a year later, the democratically elected Jacobo Arbenz of Guatemala was overthrown in a CIA-supported right-wing coup because he tried to nationalize some of United Fruit's plantations to implement a small program of badly needed agrarian reform in Guatemala. In Iran, under the newly installed pro-American government of General Fazlollah Zahedi (a World War II Nazi collaborator), new arrangements gave 25-year leases on 40% of Iran's oil to three US firms, one of which was Gulf Oil. The CIA's leader for this coup was Kermit Roosevelt, who became a vice-president of Gulf Oil in 1960. Guatemala followed the same pattern: General Walter Bedell Smith, director of the CIA when the Guatemala coup was planned, joined the board of directors of the United Fruit Company (now Chiquita) soon after Arbenz was forced out.

At the demonstration in Pittsburgh, I also came to understand how the International Monetary Fund (IMF) and the World Bank trapped countries like Ecuador in permanent debt dependency under the guise of lending them money to develop—a key insight in my political development.

While Jim Holland and I got the Pittsburgh chapter off the ground, I organized a small caucus of New University Conference women. Many of the women interested in the caucus turned out to be the same faculty, graduate students, and faculty spouses I was working with to start Women's Liberation in Pittsburgh. This group began in the university and soon extended into the community.

Throughout the fall of 1968 and all of 1969, the women's liberation movement took off by leaps and bounds around the country. In Pittsburgh we began as three or four female faculty working with undergraduate and graduate students, some staff, and faculty wives whom women from the wider community then joined. The zeal with which we set about consciousness-raising, speaking to as many women as possible, in the university and beyond, to alert them about the oppression and second-class status of women in America did not leave time for the discovery of potential political differences among us.

However, from the beginning, I was torn between organizing a chapter of NUC, speaking to NUC women separately about joining the NUC Women's Caucus as Marlene Dixon had suggested, and getting other women (not just those interested in joining NUC) together for "consciousness-raising" and "rap groups" as part of the women's liberation movement. The pull from different groups, at times overlapping, often separate, created a demanding, often tense situation for me, as for hundreds of other women across the country, who were similarly active both in radical politics and in the women's movement. What about women who were not interested in NUC but were passionate about feminism—how were we to relate to them?[24] We all struggled against racism, but why weren't black women interested in "our" movement? How much should men be involved in women's liberation and in what ways? The pressure was particularly acute at smaller centers of radical activity like Pittsburgh, where, unlike New York, Boston and Chicago, the options to join a group were limited.

In spite of my personal doubts about whom to organize for what, this first year of the women's liberation movement in Pittsburgh was a growing and unifying experience for all of us. Women were collecting and sharing new materials by and about the women's movement that were beginning to circulate. In 1968, Naomi Weisstein, co-founder of the Chicago Women's Liberation Union, whom I'd met in Marlene's kitchen, challenged Bruno Bettleheim and Erik Erikson, giants in her field of psychology. In "Kinde, Kirche, Kuche: Psychology Constructs the Female, or the Fantasy Life of the Male Psychologist," Weisstein took on Bettleheim's assertion that "as much as women want to be good scientists or engineers, they want first and foremost to be womanly companions of men and to be mothers." She challenged Erikson's insistence that "much of a young woman's identity is already defined in her kind of attractiveness and in the selectivity of her search for the man (or men) by whom she wishes to be sought." We all read Marlene Dixon's article in *Ramparts,* which called marriage "the chief vehicle for the perpetuation of the oppression of women; it is through the role of wife that the subjugation of women is maintained. In a very real way the role of wife has been the genesis of women's rebellion throughout history." Someone in our group learned that Kate Millet was writing her Columbia dissertation on a new kind of literary criticism, a feminist analysis of male writers and critics; we could not wait to read what would become *Sexual Politics,* a major publishing event for women activists. I devoured every new publication that the women's liberation movement produced—at that time it was still possible to read "everything."

In Pittsburgh, our activist agenda was the same as that of hundreds of other women's groups sprouting up on campuses and elsewhere throughout the country. In 1969, some issues emerged as central to a broad national movement: the right to create and disseminate new knowledge about women (what would soon be known as women's studies), accessible daycare, equal pay, and reproductive rights. At the time thousands of women were dying from botched abortions, for abortion would remain illegal in this country until 1973. Even though the birth control pill had been available for several years, the words "unwanted pregnancy" still made everyone shudder. Although not many of us were mothers yet, we knew enough to fight for university-based daycare[25].

Also during this time, national conventions of professional organizations and of NUC became magnets of radical activity. The NUC role in national scholarly organizations was one of its major contributions to higher education, and the growth of feminist activity was an intricate part of this undertaking. My participation was in the Modern Language Association (MLA) which starting in 1968, was where I learned some of the difficulties and contradictions of trying to be a socialist feminist while working within the administrative framework of an established bureaucracy, albeit a scholarly one. My MLA experience was also riddled by inherent difficulties in trying to participate as a socialist feminist in a "power structure" while identifying with those feminists opposed to this very structure.

The Modern Language Association, begun in 1883, is an august scholarly association of English and Foreign Language professors, scholars and graduate students with approximately 30,000 members. Its annual convention attracts several thousand members. In December 1968, with my marriage nearing the breaking point (again), but in one of our moments of reconciliation, Gabriel and I decided to go to the convention in New York together. He would see friends while I attended NUC/ MLA meetings and participated in convention events. During those four days in New York, tension between what had become two increasingly contradictory facets of my post-Madrid life reached a new intensity: How could I reconcile Hispanism and Gabriel on the one hand, and the US radical movement and feminist organizing on the other? I was anxious, stressed, torn between these two worlds. At moments I felt vaguely schizophrenic as I moved back and forth between the two groups. There were two Robertas, a version in Spanish and another in English, and I had trouble melding them into one functioning unit. I was torn between attending meetings of the NUC Modern Language Caucus (MLC) and joining Gabriel on visits with mutual friends. Most of them were Spaniards and Latin Americans who lived in New York or were there to attend the convention. I liked Nicolás Sánchez Albornoz, Clara Lida, Iris Zavala, and Antonio Sánchez Barbudo.[26] But the world of Hispanic luminaries was barely aware of the existence of a women's movement and uninterested in its goals. I never discussed the women's liberation movement with Hispanic colleagues.

NUC had a stunning and lasting effect on the MLA during the convention. Preparation had begun that fall, with an invitation to attend workshops and meetings sponsored by a newly formed "Radical Caucus," that was published in the *New York Review of Books*. By the time of the meeting in December, the MLA Executive Council had agreed that literature and information tables could be set up by the Caucus in both convention hotels, the Americana and the Hilton. On opening day, we were all milling about in the lobby of the Americana as Louis Kampf, Florence Howe and Paul Lauter and several others put up posters nearby and directions for finding our table, which had been consigned to a very remote location.

One of the announcements bore William Blake's words, "The tigers of wrath are wiser than the horses of instruction." When a hotel employee saw the posters, he alerted the hotel management that some "crazy radicals" were at work. Hotel officials immediately tried to remove the placards, but Louis, along with two graduate students, blocked their way. Using a walkie-talkie (there were no cell phones in those days), one of the officials called the New York City police. This was 1968 and rebellious students—or young people who looked suspicious—were the scourge of the American establishment. The management of the five-star Americana Hotel was no exception.

Two of New York's Finest arrived and ordered Louis away from the posters so they could tear them down. He refused to move. I was standing in the lobby, transfixed. It was clear that if Louis did not move, the police were going to remove him. [27] And they did. "They put me along with the two graduate students in the police van they had come in, and took us to jail," Louis recalled. "They put us in a cell with about ten other people, mostly drunks. The police treated us decently... the other people in the cell were shocked to see us, in our suits and ties and all."

Outrage at the police treatment of a tenured humanist contributed to Louis Kampf's subsequent election to the leadership of the organization. (*Goodness, next they'll arrest us!*) Using confrontational politics to force the academic establishment to listen to our ideas had paid off.

Although hard-won university positions were potentially at stake for many young protesters at the MLA, our protest did not feel dangerous to me. It was perfectly legal to demonstrate for or against almost anything in the United States, and it was frustrating that the powers in charge did not respect our request to disseminate our ideas as broadly as possible. Just six months after leaving Franco's Spain, I experienced the frustration of the American New Left at not being "heard." We had to "up the ante" to make our case. If Louis hadn't been hauled off to jail, it is doubtful that most of the membership of the MLA would have noticed the Radical Caucus. They certainly would not have elected a well-known radical to lead the MLA.

Watching Louis and the two graduate students being ushered into the police van reminded me of the student strike I took part in at Madrid University in spring 1962, but the Spanish strike for minimal student participation in university governance was illegal, as was any type of demonstration that opposed government policy. Spaniards did not have freedom of the press or assembly; in fact, any non-officially sanctioned gathering of more than five Spaniards was understood to be a challenge to the General's rule. When Louis refused to remove a poster from the wall of the Americana Hotel, no one thought he would be arrested. In Madrid, we all knew that in response to the smallest infraction of public order, the Guardia Civil would swoop in to beat and jail us to restore "order." The MLA convention involved only faculty and graduate students. The university strike in Madrid had hidden but significant help from the clandestine Spanish Communist Party and they provided that action with an added political dimension.

Although I could not have articulated this when I was in Spain, I liked the protests in Madrid in part because we directly confronted major players at the center of power and were threatened with physical danger, which made our participation more meaningful — or so we thought then. It is empowering to feel courageous. Most of all, I liked the shadowy and distant presence of an established political party whose generations of supporters overlapped, a party that knew how to defeat fascism and combat capitalism. To my knowledge, few of the people I knew in Madrid were actual members of the Communist Party, but its presence validated us even when our protests failed. While no victories were in sight in the short term, older voices and accounts of former victories reassured us that ours was just one step in a longer trip.

The driving force of the New Left was a determination to be one's own agent of change and to reject the perceived authoritarian structure of America's 'Old Left' of the 1930s. I realize now that we paid a price for that. Lack of contact with experienced folks on the Left meant that it was difficult to keep longer goals in sight. This was one of the causes for irreparable acts of violence born of frustration at failing to achieve immediate victories, like ending the Viet Nam War that hastened the demise of the New Left.

In New York I was part of a cultural movement, not a political revolt. (Paul Lauter and Louis Kampf later referred to our actions as "The Little Bourgeois Cultural Revolution of the MLA 1968."[28]) However, this was *my* struggle, *my* country. My nationalism surprised me. Lurking just under the glamorous surface of fighting fascism in Madrid was the knowledge that I had been an outsider, an appendage. Here I could be a "player." I was on my own turf now, and this was where I would stay and cast my luck. Although I was being pushed to examine the relationship between my marriage and personal life and my increasing political commitments, something inside me actually calmed down.

The Radical Caucus released an enormous amount of political and intellectual energy, giving rise, for example, to a seminar on "Student Rebellions and the Teaching of Literature" organized by Paul Lauter and Louis Kampf with panels such as "Language and Politics," "Class Bias and the Teaching of Literature," "Foreign Languages and the Third World." For women, the achievements were striking. During the convention we had organized a workshop open to all women in MLA. Dozens, then hundreds flocked to our meetings and agreed to send a delegation to the business meeting to argue for a commission to investigate the situation of women within the profession, with the aim of assuring equitable standards. The request was approved. The report would concentrate on criteria for admission to graduate schools, awarding of grants and fellowships, sex as a prejudicial factor in hiring, promotion and tenure, and salary schedules.

Florence Howe chaired the five-person "Commission on the Status of Women in the Profession." I was one of the four other members. We were to report back to the MLA the following year. Although this Commission was a major victory, we also needed a "mass" organization to involve as many female members of MLA as possible. Thus the original women's workshop became the MLA Women's Caucus, a vital, exciting group that overflowed with new ideas and that produced, among other things, the MLA Job Information List. This List, published for members several times a year, was a compilation of university employment opportunities. Soon emulated by other professional organizations, this posting helped ensure equal access to university jobs, important for female job seekers who were excluded from the "old boys' networks" that controlled the most prestigious academic jobs. Not revolutionary changes, but dents in the armor.

Soon after the MLA convention, Bob Ross asked me to host a meeting of the New University Conference Interim Committee, about 50 people, including the national leadership and representatives from other chapters that spring. I enjoyed staging this meeting. I found I was good at this sort of undertaking; it seemed to come naturally to me.

The meeting stretched over a long weekend, with sessions in my old brick house on Centre Avenue, and in the nearby College of Liberal Arts. The weekend was intense and stimulating—one event spilling into another, and all involving impassioned conversation, new ideas, new friendships and occasional flare-ups of temper and disagreement. Gabriel was not really interested in NUC, but he was well brought up and charming, so he circulated easily among the American Leftists. We had a pleasant dinner with Louis Kampf and Ellen Cantarow—Louis was born in Vienna and steeped in European culture, so I knew he and Gabriel would get along. Gabriel and I carried off the farce of a happily married couple and I rather enjoyed the play-acting, since I was the director of the whole production.

Parts of the Pittsburgh meeting were open to the public. I hosted a reception at home, where dozens of people mingled, exchanging wine and words. When I read my FBI file decades later, I discovered I had apparently served wine and cheese to an FBI informant: "[name of informant deleted] further advised that prior to the meeting of the NUC Interim Committee, a social affair was held at the home of Roberta Salper on February 28, 1969... approximately 35-40 individuals were present at this meeting at 4218 Centre Ave."[29]

That FBI surveillance of my house would turn out to be more than an isolated occurrence.

At the end of April, after the last day of the semester, and barely two months after the NUC meeting in our house, Gabriel announced he was moving out. He wanted a divorce.

"*Estupéndo*" [Great] I snarled. "*Yo también!*" [Me too]. He went to stay with friends, and there I was, alone in that big house, more miserable than I cared to show.

Without fully realizing it, the commitment I had made to the New University Conference helped me forge a way out of my marriage. Gabriel and my former life in Spain receded in importance as my dedication to the NUC and the women's liberation movement increased. I was gradually pushing the study of modern Spanish literature to the back burner; my professional and personal lives had been intricately linked with each other and with Gabriel, his family and his country. I had to find a way to start building a new life alone.

I had no familial or social safety net. I did not "belong" anywhere. I took care to have no contact with anyone from my New Jersey high school, and I had not made long-term friendships as an undergraduate. At Harvard, I had two close friends, but both had since married Europeans and were living abroad. My widowed mother had remarried and moved with her second husband, a math teacher, to a small town in Pennsylvania. What I saw of their life was defined by an unarticulated, but deeply felt fear of anti-Semitism. My mother's husband had been born in Russia and persecuted for being a Jew. This Jewish cloud of insecurity defined their lives, but was expressed in monetary terms: there was never enough money for anything other than absolute necessities. She saved everything (paper bags, tinfoil, buttons, ribbons, wrappings) and spent very little. A meal out was the 5:00 early special at the local diner. My mother had a floor to ceiling white plastic cabinet in her bedroom filled with canned food and other survival staples, just in case the Pennsylvania equivalent of the Russian Cossacks stormed into their neighborhood. I couldn't bear to look at that cabinet. It became the incarnation of everything I wanted to purge from my life.

I had married into the cosmopolitan European upper middle class and enjoyed the adventure, including all the accouterments that financial security afforded. I left the marriage with no money of my own. My only marketable commodity was my brain and the capacity to earn a salary in academia. I had very few female peers in the university, but in comparison with the vast majority of American women at the time, I was in a relatively privileged position.

Gabriel and I had very civil post-separation discussions. It had not occurred to me to ask for alimony. I did not think it was fair, and I wanted to be totally free and independent. It also did not occur to me to take wedding gifts of considerable value, like china, Belgian crystal or sterling silver. I chose to keep three items: a leather-bound edition of *Don Quijote*, the complete works of Pío Baroja, and two volumes of reproductions of Goya's etchings. When the divorce was final, Gabriel and I split the cost of the lawyer, and the marriage was over.

The New Left and the women's movement provided support and a ready community as I navigated my exit from a seven year-long marriage. New friends and constant activities helped. With absolute conviction, I embraced NUC's goal of helping to create a new kind of American socialism, and tried to forget how lonely and scared I was, especially at night. It took a while to get used to sleeping alone.

In June 1969 the first annual convention of the New University Conference was held in Iowa City. Several weeks before I was to leave for that, Jerry Schneewind, a distinguished philosopher at the University of Pittsburgh and a progressive educator, was appointed Dean of the College of Arts and Sciences. Although I was still an untenured faculty member, he asked if I would accept an appointment as Assistant Dean for the following fall. I knew nothing about the job, but I saw it as an opportunity to pursue feminist activities. I would have some power as an administrator and perhaps could help implement a part of NUC's progressive agenda. The timing was perfect: the women's movement had come of age in America during 1969, and proposals to establish women's studies courses were beginning to gain credence. I went to the meeting at the University of Iowa eager to ask questions about how I could fit together women's liberation with New Left politics and my need to earn a living in the academic world.

None of us could foresee the groundswell of feminist activity that would take place in Iowa that June, where the relationship of the women's caucus to NUC and the role women should play in the organization became a burning issue. Although the women's caucus had existed for a year, it was slow to gain traction. Our activities at the convention were the first successful attempt to pull the women's caucus together.

We were 60 strong at the initial meeting and we came with a variety of needs and priorities. Excited to be part of the now large caucus, I couldn't contain myself from interrupting frequently with what I judged to be earth-shattering observations. It was soon pointed out to me that this was "male behavior" and I should raise my hand and wait. I was duly chastened. Male chauvinism had maimed us all.

We met as a caucus frequently, whenever we felt the need. It was so empowering! I didn't sleep much — whenever I had an idea, I would rush to share it with someone in the caucus. One night after midnight, I was in my room getting ready for bed when Lillian Robinson banged on my door. "Roberta, come to Liz's [Diggs] room right now; we have to discuss tomorrow's meeting!" Lillian, one of the brightest critical theorists among us,[30] needed help with a proposal she was formulating. I don't remember the content of the proposal, but we gladly stayed up half the night working on it.

The issue of women's liberation was not confined to public meetings between groups of men and women or just among women. Personal relationships felt the strain also; couples huddled in corners, intensely trying to sort things out: *Is our relationship exploitative? Why am I a sexist? But I do help with the housework!*

We launched a defensive attack on male chauvinism, which

was at least temporarily successful, and certainly an initial consciousness raising experience for many of the men. Contentious encounters throughout the convention between men and women over the issue of women's access to power culminated in an all night heated discussion by the fourteen members of the Executive Committee. The ever-growing presence of articulate women in the women's caucus would carry the day and we would finally win the "right" to equal representation. Before we left Iowa, 50-50 male-female representation on the National Committee, which was made up of Executive Committee members plus chapter delegates, was written into the NUC constitution.[31]

This struggle was personal as well as political. Paul Lauter recalls that he and Florence Howe, longtime partners, disagreed about gender parity on the Executive Committee. After that contentious all night meeting of the Committee, he said, "We didn't speak to each other for days and for a while I was afraid we would split up over this issue. It took me a while to come around to the idea of gender parity."[32] Paul subsequently became a champion of gender equality.

The thorny process of creating trust for each other in the women's caucus involved intense political debates on the women's liberation movement, on what our personal position was and what position NUC should adopt. We were divided between those emphasizing economic or cultural oppression. One group felt that economic oppression and class oppression were more crucial and thus working class women were the key to the revolution. Another group saw cultural oppression of middle class women as valid and potentially revolutionary and felt that sectorial organizing of all women was the key. Each caricatured the other's emphasis to mean that one thought only working class women important and the other only bourgeois women.[33]

A parallel difference existed over separatism, a commitment solely to the independent women's movement, vs. NUC. For some, building a socialist revolution depended on working with men; the women's movement was not explicitly revolutionary or radical. They supported women's liberation as they supported black liberation and felt the only way to work for it was in a mixed socialist movement. Others saw women in the larger, mixed movement as anti-women, unable to recognize their oppression as valid. They believed that women could only be truly revolutionary in an independent women's movement, where women's oppression was understood as their own.[34] Beyond the obvious task of dealing with male chauvinism, some of us felt it was critical to develop an analysis of women's oppression; others believed that we had to develop a program around women's issues on which to begin fighting; still others thought that unless we had a structure for ongoing work and communication we would fall apart. In addition, strong voices advocated leaving NUC for the independent women's movement. These debates would continue for the life of NUC and beyond and are still part of the women's movement in the 21st century.

The women's caucus newsletter, begun in Iowa, is an ongoing record of all this ferment, important as one of the first movement publications to record early debates between socialist feminists and radical feminists. It was produced by Bread and Roses, an internal collective[35] coordinated by a full time NUC staff person, and its first issue explained that the publication "grew out of our frustration with completed arguments. We found that when we tried to write for the NUC newsletter we forced our ideas into a finishedness we didn't mean them to have. It seemed too formal for tentative thoughts or ideas in process."[36] Between the fall of 1970 and the end of 1971, ten issues were published; I wrote part of issue #8, which focused on the politics of women's studies. [37]

NUC men were probably the first in the New Left to engage nationally in a real discussion of the meaning and ramifications of sexism. Chicago-based biologist Len Radinsky, one of the founders of Science for the People, wrote an article about what he felt was "a refusal of many men at the convention to confront their own sexism."[38] Psychologist Bart Myers from the Brooklyn College urged "commitment to anti-sexist practice... as... the way for men in NUC to combat male chauvinism and aid in the winning of women's liberation." Reprints of the Iowa convention caused a modest stir in movement circles for it was the first time that a male-dominated movement organization recognized the importance of fighting male supremacy along with racism, imperialism and economic oppression. Despite the efforts of many men, the women's caucus was never successfully integrated into NUC and although women from the caucus continued to be active throughout the women's movement, to this day, the organization would only last another 3 years. Why?

By 1972 the women's movement was so strong and varied nationally and locally, that NUC became redundant for many women. In addition, the national office ran out of money, perhaps because we took on too heavy an agenda without sufficient funding to carry out many of the projects. In hindsight I realize what a monumental undertaking it was to attempt to "start anew" and remake basic premises of society and the way men and women relate to each other. We were courageous, but so were many Americans in those years.

One personal consequence of that convention was that NUC was invited by the University of Havana to send a 15-person delegation to visit Cuba and learn about their revolution and I was asked to be a member of that delegation. For four weeks, I would see Havana, travel throughout Cuba and see socialism in action!

Figure 1. Roberta with mother Louise and father Murray. Boston, MA. August 23, 1939. Credit: Cedric G. Chase Photographic Laboratories.

Figure 2. Roberta with paternal grandfather, Joe Salper. Caldwell, NJ. September 1939. Family archive.

Figure 3. Roberta with mother. Caldwell, NJ. 1943-44. Family archive.

Figure 4. Roberta in front of the Menorah my father had built for Chanukah. Mother is to the left. Caldwell, NJ. Date unknown. Family archive.

Figure 5. Caldwell High School Cheerleaders. Left to right: Andy Unruh, Marilyn Walker, Roberta Salper, Carol Weisel. 1956. Family archive.

Figure 6. Roberta at Caldwell High School Senior Prom. May 1956. Credit unknown.

Figure 7. Roberta, fourth from left, surrounded by adult English students at International Institute, Madrid. Fall, 1960. Credit unknown.

Figure 8. Roberta with Spanish husband, Gabriel Tortella. Madrid 1965. Family archives.

Figure 9. Roberta with Gabriela Pradera at Alianza Editorial book party. Madrid, 1967. Credit: Jesus, Calle Oviedo, 10, Madrid 20.

Figure 10. Roberta and colleagues from first women's studies class at University of Pittsburgh. Pittsburgh Press, March 1, 1970.

# CHAPTER 6

# CUBA, 1969: A 'NEW MAN'

From the time I separated from my husband at the end of April, life-changing opportunities had opened up: Assistant Dean of the College of Arts and Sciences at the University of Pittsburgh and joining a delegation to Cuba. If I were to describe these two events as some "magic reward" for renouncing marriage and deciding to be independent, it would sound like a bad feminist soap opera. But that is exactly how I felt. I had taken a big leap, and I did not realize then how good my timing was. The years 1968 and 1969 marked a splendid period in the history of major American universities. The world was ours to conquer, or at least we thought so. My first year as an academic administrator came at a time when the economy was flourishing, academic jobs were available, and social activists, even female ones, got access to a little bit of space in the public sphere.

Even though it was technically legal for United States citizens to go to Cuba, the US blockade prohibited "trading with the enemy." This meant that no money could be exchanged, making it virtually impossible to travel to the island in a manner the US government would consider acceptable. US passports were stamped "Not valid for Cuba or Albania," so the cooperative Mexican officials did not stamp our passports. We suspected, correctly as it turned out, that the FBI knew, or would find out, that we were traveling to Cuba without State Department authorization. Once on the plane, several members of the delegation mentioned that a small overhead camera had taken our photos as we left the airport en route to the *Cubana Aviación* plane. The sense of danger, of having done something illegal, heightened our expectations as the small plane smoothly came to a landing at the Havana airport several hours later.

Disembarking, I carefully climbed down the steps, trying not to trip on the fancy sandals I had mistakenly chosen to wear to the tropics. I plunged into a sensual whirl: the sun was brilliant, intense, all-enveloping; the cloudless sky astonishingly, almost piercingly blue, and everything smelled wonderful—thick, sweet, warm, seductive. I looked up at the sumptuous Cuban landscape, palm trees, dripping coconuts, big red, fuchsia and violet flowers; a huge poster of Che Guevara in bold colors welcomed us to the New World: ¡*Patria o muerte*! At the foot of the stairs, Nestor, our *responsable*, the person in charge, waited with a tray of frozen daiquiris. Sunshine, rum and socialism.

We guzzled as many daiquiris as the Cubans offered, and with giddy abandon, climbed into the little bus—later we would all call it la *guaguita*—that took us to the Havana Libre, né Hilton. Fifteen wannabe socialists from the Colossus of the North full of enthusiasm, solidarity—and rum (The politically correct NUC delegation, was composed of eight women and seven men[39]).

In the lobby of what had once been one of Cuba's most luxurious hotels, Nestor told us we would have double rooms, and asked us to pair off, girls with girls and boys with boys. Uh, oh. That touched a nerve. I was doing the translating for the group, and I did not spare poor Nestor an exact translation of what he had said. Nestor was an attractive 30 year old Cuban, about 5'9" with a compact build, quick wit, expansive sense of humor and a twinkle in his eye. He worked in the Ministry of Foreign Affairs and had probably been chosen to escort the likes of us because of his evident affability.

"No," I explained to him, expressing the will of the people (us), "that is not how we would like the arrangements to be." I explained the needs of the NUC delegation. Before we left for Cuba, the group had met for two days in the large Chicago apartment of Mel and Marcia Rothenberg to clarify our political goals. At the instigation of one of the female members, we voted to change roommates every three or four days, to avoid the formation of cliques, factions or splinter groups. To illustrate our lack of sexism, the changing of roommates would be sexually integrated, rather than women with women and men with men. Sleeping accommodations in most US colleges were still rigorously single sex; women had curfews and the university was assumed to provide conditions to "protect women" (principally our virginity), so what we proposed to do in Cuba, we therefore deduced, had revolutionary implications. Subsequently, however, I found out that the suggestion had a rather dubious revolutionary provenance; the woman who suggested it wanted to find a way to avoid the nightly company of someone who wished to be her roommate throughout the trip.

I never liked the anti-imperialist roommate idea, mainly because I had only brought one sleeping garment, a flimsy little semi-transparent item. But I was too embarrassed to object.

"¿*Qué*?" Nestor blurted, an incredulous look on his face, as I summoned up my best Spanish to convey the political position of my *compañeros*. It took him a moment or two to regain control of his facial expressions. I knew Cuba was not Spain, but it was still a Latin society. The gender discourse of the late 1960s was very different in Cuba than in the United States, even among "fellow" revolutionaries. Our *responsable* thought we were crazy, but I was loyal to the group and continued to try to explain why we wanted to proceed this way. It was difficult for Nestor to understand why we considered certain sleeping arrangements more revolutionary than others. For him, revolution was a question of taking state power. However, Nestor's Marxist training apparently had provided him with sufficient intellectual tools to judge that this little bump was not a primary contradiction. He laughed, made a couple of expressive gestures with his hands that I would learn were typically Cuban, and said, "*Está bien. Hagan lo que quieran.*" [Okay. Do what you like.]

I was put in charge of giving Nestor a list each morning of what rooms we would be in that evening. He had to know where his charges were. What a wonderful time he must have had relating all of this to his *compañeros* at the Ministry of Foreign Affairs.

The New University Conference delegation was the first university-based group from the United States invited to Cuba. We were a bit of a novelty and got considerable official attention and publicity.[40] Our little *guaguita* carted us around Havana to meet with the Dean and departmental heads of the Faculty of Humanities at the University of Havana, national officials of the Committees for the Defense of the Revolution, and Vilma Espín, president of the Federation of Cuban Women and Fidel Castro's sister-in-law. We visited a session of the People's Court, day-care centers, hospitals, clinics where abortions were free on demand, cut rice at an experimental agricultural station run by the university, and swam at the famed Varadero beach, the pre-revolutionary playground of the rich and famous. Including the mafia. We also saw Cuban films that were prohibited from entering the United States, avant-garde theatre, and dance performances. We talked with artists, poets, novelists, playwrights, critics, journalists, and directors of the new cultural bureaucracy. Some of us gave interviews for the press and a few gave lectures at the university. Then our little bus took us on a nine-day trip through the countryside, from one end of the island to the other. Che Guevara had made the creation of the "New Man" a priority of the socialist revolution. As I was to learn, the construction of the new woman was more problematic.

Javier Pradera, a friend in Madrid, had been to Cuba during the summer of 1967 traveling with other members of the clandestine Spanish Communist Party. He had sent me a list of key literary figures to contact, with José (Pepe) Rodríquez Feo at the top because, as he wrote, "*Pepe conoce a todo el mundo y te conecta con quien quieras.*" [Pepe knows everyone, and he'll link you up with anyone you want to meet.] Rodríguez Feo's family once owned one of Cuba's largest sugar mills. In 1944 he and José Lezama Lima,[41] the grand patriarch of Cuban letters, had co-founded (with Rodríguez Feo's money) *Orígenes*, an influential literary magazine. It lasted until 1956.

When I met him, Pepe was working for the National Union for Writers and Artists and responsible for selecting and translating foreign literature for Cubans. He lived in a small, modest apartment, around the corner from his good friend, Virgilio Piñera, one of the country's finest dramatists. I realized these three men were homosexuals (the word "gay" was not yet in use), but I never mentioned it to anyone, such was the force of homophobia in Cuba[42].

Pepe was in his fifties and extremely cordial in the way cultured middle-aged Latin American men who have been brought up with all the accouterments of wealth and privilege can be. He looked very Spanish; his ancestors had evidently not frolicked with natives. One of the first things Pepe said to me was how much he enjoyed not having lots of money any more; it was so much easier he said to live with only the essentials. I wondered if that could possibly be true.

Pepe arranged for me to spend time with Lezama Lima. When I met Lezama he was 57 and still living in an apartment in the center of Havana where he had resided since he was fifteen. The high-ceilinged, small living room was over stuffed with heavy Spanish furniture; the graying stucco walls adorned with elaborately framed pictures of himself as a young lieutenant and his mother in her wedding gown. A small, round marble-topped table displayed a leather-bound and gold-lettered copy of Flaubert's *Correspondance,* and next to the *Correspondance* was a slim violet vase containing one pink wax rose. An ancient Spanish maid who had emigrated from Galicia as a child—hunch-backed, pale, and subservient—hobbled in and out of the room. Lezama, a corpulent walrus-like presence, was settled into a huge green velvet armchair. Surrounded by reminders of the past, he emerged from the layers of his memories to answer my questions. "What do I think of Fidel Castro? He has done one magnificent thing: He has done away with Cuba's corrupt, worthless past. The future? I am not sure what he will do with our future. Did I ever think of leaving Cuba? Of course not. I was born here; I have lived my life here, and I will die here."

On another occasion, Pepe invited me to meet the poet Heberto Padilla and his wife, Belkis Cuza Male, also a writer. Padilla, born in 1932, was closely associated with Cuban revolutionary movements before 1959, and after the revolutionaries' triumph, he occupied important posts in the new government. By the summer of 1969, however, his book of poems, *Fuera del Juego* [Outside of the Game] had become the object of worldwide controversy. The book, published in Cuba the previous year, had won the National Writers' Union prize given by a committee of Cuban and internationally known personalities. After the book was selected for the prize, but before it was actually published, the Cuban Culture Council[43] objected to its "counter-revolutionary content." Heated public debate between Padilla and Lisandro Otero, head of the Culture Council, filled the pages of the Cuban press. The book was finally published with a prologue explaining the government's position, summed up as: "We believe our Revolution is stronger than any criticism, and we are demonstrating our confidence by publishing this book."

Some of the poems express some skepticism about the revolution. For instance, the following lines: *"The poet /Kick him out! /He has no business here. /He doesn't play the game. /He never gets excited/ or speaks out clearly. /He never even sees the miracles..."* Yes, Padilla was critical; his stance toward the Revolution was one of critical distance, not unconditional acceptance. But why, I thought, make such a big fuss?

Heberto Padilla was a paunchy man with frameless glasses and a sullen expression. It was evident he was intelligent—and unhappy. This was July 1969, less than a year after the outburst of controversy over his book. We chatted about American and European literature, and I enjoyed his penetrating, sensitive insights. He clearly loved literature. Although he was much more interested in what he was saying than in my comments, his arrogance could not hide an articulate, cultured mind. With eyes that clouded over and an increasingly surly attitude, he said, "You think everything's wonderful here?" They are like big children, playing with their new toys." His wife rested her hand on his arm and he quieted down.

Padilla had fought to establish the economic and social principles of the Cuban revolution, but had come to realize that he could not live with its philosophy. I knew that the upheaval of the past ten years in Cuba had produced a cultural revolution. But I wondered why there had been a need to redefine the concept of artistic liberty in Cuba. Was the motive only a desire to emulate the censorship practiced by the Soviet Union?

That afternoon in Pepe's apartment I had my first personal encounter with an intellectual's disillusionment with a socialist revolution. My initial reaction was impatience with Padilla. I did not like him; I thought that he should learn to be a bit more flexible. After all, wasn't he just one self-centered person caught up in the world's most exciting social transformation? But I kept recalling how Heberto's outburst had provoked flashes of anxieties—perhaps fear—in the eyes of the others in Pepe's apartment as they glanced furtively at me. They were thinking "There is a stranger in our midst. Can we trust her?" This was an eerie feeling.

In a similar situation, would I react like Padilla? He was almost ten years older than I, but we belonged to the same generation and shared a similar intellectual formation. This had made it easy to talk about international culture with him, but he had caused me to wonder about the deeper implications of the changes worked by socialism.[44]

Several days after I met with Padilla, Nestor said, "Why are you bothering *con esa gente?* [With those people] I'll arrange for you to meet *compañeros* who are writing literature for the New Cuba." He suggested I meet Miguel Barnet and Nancy Morejón; both also on Javier's list.

Miguel's Euro/Latin phenotype was familiar to me from my years in Madrid: medium height and build, brown eyes and hair, fair skin, everything about him conveying intensity. He had a pleasant round face with an expression that seemed to look for reasons to smile (which he frequently found). Born in 1940, Barnet was one of the most popular and widely read poets and novelists on the island. In ensuing years he would become contemporary Cuba's best-known novelist and literary personality. Miguel talked about the trilogy of "anthropological novels" (his term) he was in the process of writing: "It's sort of like Oscar Lewis' work but much better. The structure of my novels is more original; they are anthropological studies, historical testaments, and fiction all at once. The first volume deals with colonial Cuba, the second with the republican period, and the third will focus on revolutionary Cuba." We established an immediate rapport as we chatted about Cimarrón,[45] his first "testimonial novel," which I had read. I was at ease with Miguel in a way I usually am not with a man I have just met, so it occurred to me he might be gay, an impression I later confirmed.

Miguel asked my impressions of Cuba. I was surprised at the spontaneity of my response. I told him how I liked the overt sensuality and celebratory aspects of life there and the different racial discourse than in the United States. "I've never been in a society where all different colors of people interact easily. I know racism must still exist—you can't erase all that in just ten years—but the dynamic was so different from the one in my country." I didn't feel on the defensive, that I had to let everyone who identifies as "black" know that I am not a racist. It was such a relief. Also, the gender discourse was unlike what I was used to—I didn't find the same dislike or fear of the female body that is so much a part of the puritanical Christian tradition. I liked the love of pleasure and of the senses, so evident in many aspects of life in Cuba, absent in American culture, or Spanish culture, for that matter.

Miguel had lived in the United States as a child and knew Spain. He smiled in agreement. "It is a relief to be in a country where religion is not part of the fabric of daily life. I really hate religions, all of them," I said. My thoughts spilled out freely, some articulated for the first time, even to myself.

"Listen, I know that even though there is improvement in the area of gender, women are not equal here, but the ingredients of the cocktail of inequality are different than in the United States or Spain... there is something to be said for a government in a Latin society that officially proclaims equality of the sexes and provides free abortion on demand, even if women still do all the housework and childrearing and don't have much power on the national level." And then, as I wound down, I concluded by saying: "I guess I like connecting to the energy, the *choteo*[46]... there is something electric all around. This country is a really attractive mixture of Europe and Africa."

Miguel responded by insisting I meet Nancy Morejón right away. The next afternoon the three of us gathered at the hotel for mojitos. Nancy moved with the fluid grace many Cubans have; all their limbs interact so smoothly that an awkward movement seems impossible. As she and Miguel, arms linked, found my table, Nancy leaned over to plant a kiss on my cheek. Her eyes were dark brown, so intense they almost flashed; everything about her was vital and attractive. Nancy Morejón was Afro-Cuban, what in the United States we would call black or African American. Cuba has a grand variety of skin colors from very fair to dark black, and hair quality ranges from straw straight to tight "afro" curls. In the Cuban social construct, dark-skinned Cubans with tight curly hair are

"Afro-Cubans." All others are simply "Cubans."

Born in 1944, the daughter of a harbor worker and a seamstress, Nancy was the first Afro-Cuban woman to receive a B.A. from the University of Havana. That was in 1966. She studied French literature and also knew English. By 1969 Nancy had published three books of poetry. Since then she has written dozens of books, (both prose and poetry) and become the most internationally successful and widely translated Cuban woman writer of the post-revolutionary period.

Nancy was interested in learning why I thought Cuba was "a really attractive mixture of Europe and Africa." (Miguel had evidently recounted our previous conversation.) I knew it was a serious, complex question, and I thought about it for some time.

Weeks earlier, before I met Miguel and Nancy, when I stepped off the plane at José Martí airport, one of the first thoughts I had was: this is what was missing in Spain! Africa mixed with Europe; a counter to Spain's Jesuitical rigidity and imperial palimpsests. Everyone all mixed up, all different colors, but all Cubans. As the three of us discussed the subject, I became aware of the possibility of a new racial discourse—neither black or white, not grounded in a color, but an idea, a national idea of Cubanness; "*Cubanía*" Nancy would dub it some years later. Although the idea that "race" is a notion invented in the 19th century to justify enslavement of groups judged biologically inferior is widely discussed and nuanced now, it was new to me at the time. Both Nancy and Miguel were passionate about exploring Cuba's "africanity" and the concept of transculturation. By the end of the afternoon, I began to believe it might be possible gradually to create a new understanding of race in Cuba.

This was my first trip to the Caribbean. I had read what Jose Martí had written about Cuba being more than white, more than mulatto, more than black—something beyond these categories, something different—something better, bigger, and out of the box. Martí's observation had made sense, but I hadn't thought about it again until, as I told Nancy and Miguel, I set foot in Cuba. Could it be applicable in any way to creating a non-racialized women's movement in the United States? NUC and its women's caucus were committed to building socialism in an organization that was virtually all white. Cuba was building socialism in a multiracial society. The US was also a multiracial country, but we still had a long way to go towards redefining what "multiracial" might mean in our own country, and in the women's movement.

After Nancy and Miguel left, I had another mojito and tried to sort out my thoughts. They were just a couple of years younger than Heberto Padilla, and Miguel and Heberto shared a middle-class background of European ancestry. How does one reconcile a cosmopolitan vision with the narrower interests of the Cuban Revolution? This revolution had complicated origins. What made one person cast his or her lot with its new experiment, another unable to conform, and still others totally to reject it? It was more than just having been rich or poor before 1959. Not all poor people supported Fidel Castro, and not all wealthy Cubans rejected him, although the scales were obviously tilted that way. Other intangibles came into play — for example, that part of each of us that makes one take a risk and another run away, or creates the capacity to understand the "other" and the will to affirm him or her. I also knew that how one deals with power and control on all levels is one of the intangibles that goes into forming "revolutionaries" and "counter revolutionaries."

What would it be like, I asked myself, to be an intellectual living here? Could I ever fit in, be personally happy, professionally creative, and make a contribution? It was hard to imagine, but the adventure it entailed made it fleetingly tempting.

Some days later, our group set out in our *guaguita* to see the rest of Cuba. The Cuban bus had very little in common with the air-conditioned Greyhound buses all over the United States. Left over from pre-revolutionary days, *la guaguita* resembled a rickety old yellow school bus whose only concession to creature comfort was worn leather seats. But by that time we were all used to it, and even had a grudging affection for the ancient vehicle that was held together by Cuban ingenuity. The ten-year US embargo on spare parts had spawned a generation of spontaneous, clever Cuban mechanics able to fix just about anything with minimal materials. Occasionally our bus driver would hear *la guagita* groan and burp a bit, so he'd stop, hop out, jiggle a few wires in the motor, pat the faded yellow hood of the bus, and say "¡*Vámonos, mi gente!*" And off we would go.

A couple of days into the trip I began to have terrible stomach problems. I told Nestor and he said, "No problem, we will find a doctor right away." He instructed the driver to turn left after 2 kilometers. Where would we find a doctor in this isolated rural place? Fifteen minutes later, we stopped in front of a low, one story white stucco building, and the lone construction on a road narrower than the one we had just turned off of. Over the entrance, painted in green, was the word *Clínica*.

The doctor was a young man in his late twenties and extraordinarily handsome. He looked like the movie star Andy Garcia (also Cuban). *Compañero* Miguel smiled warmly and asked how he could help me. There was no way I could discuss my diarrhea with such an attractive man. It was out of the question. Especially since all I could think of was how pleasurable it might be to spend the night making love with such a superb exemplar of revolutionary manhood.

In the back of the room a woman was leaning over the counter arranging some papers with her back to us. "May I speak to the nurse?" I inquired in wobbly Spanish, trying to maintain what I considered a modicum of dignity. This was the solution; a woman. Diarrhea was not a complicated disease; a nurse could handle it. "*Compañera*," the soft velvet brown eyes and beautifully chiseled lips said to me, "*compañera Ileana es médica, jefa de nuestra clínica.*" Comrade Ileana was a doctor, head of the clinic. My physical misery was now compounded by a fragile emotional state. I glanced around for a bathroom as I tried to forget what an unrevolutionary, unfeminist *faux pas* I had just committed.

In 1969, in the United States, a female doctor was a rarity— two or three women graduated from medical school occasionally among thousands of men. Not until the 1980s did women routinely became part of the American medical establishment. Health care, following the Soviet model (the Soviets believed women are more compassionate than men and would make good doctors), was one of the success stories of the first decade of the Cuban Revolution. About half of graduating classes of doctors were female. *Compañera* Ileana, the recently appointed head of a rural clinic in the new Cuban health system, was about my age. She was small and compact, poised and self-assured, with long wavy black hair and tawny skin—physically she fulfilled the requirements for what the Cubans called a "cute mulatta," but the young doctor carried herself with such dignity and confidence it was impossible to think of her primarily in terms of her physical attributes.

The beautiful *Compañero* Miguel mercifully made himself busy with something in the adjoining room as *Compañera* Ileana saw to my needs. She was very professional and exuded competence as she examined me. I swallowed a pink liquid, chewed on several white pills and got some sort of injection. Then *Compañero* Miguel reappeared, and both physicians smiled and wished me luck. The one *faux pas* I did not make was to ask for the bill. I knew all medical care and medicines were free for everyone in Cuba, foreign visitors included. However, I had no idea of what it felt like to be a participant, albeit briefly, in its system. My first encounter with socialized medicine made me consider how the knowledge that you would always have access to free medical care, from birth to death would affect your attitude toward life. Again, our group's hegemonic equation flashed through my mind: Cuba, good; United States, bad. Obviously, in those days, I took comfort in the apparent certainty offered by binary judgments. I was not looking for nuanced political discussions about how to bring about reform. I was part of a youthful community that was seeking validation for expressing its anger with the Vietnam War and other unjust policies and practices of the United States.

Several days later we arrived in Santiago de Cuba in Oriente Province, the "cradle of the Revolution." In the surrounding mountainous country known as Sierra Maestra, the revolution had been nurtured into its final stage. By this time, I was recovered from my illness, in tip-top shape, and ready for new adventures—revolutionary as well as culinary. For three nights, we stayed in student dormitories at the university in Santiago de Cuba.

One day we went to visit the now legendary Moncada[47] and the headquarters of the Second Front located in Sierra Cristal, the northern, smaller mountain range of Oriente where Raul Castro had established his command post and base of operations. Prior to the revolution, the region of Sierra Cristal was largely cut off from the rest of country and was one of the pockets in Cuba where agriculture was carried on primarily by peasant farmers rather than wage laborers on huge sugar estates. The main cash crop in Sierra Cristal was coffee, and the land was owned by local *terratenientes* [landowners]. The peasant families worked the land, built their own homes out of local products, grew the food they ate and lived in isolation. They were frequently in debt to the owners, either because the coffee crop did not yield enough to meet obligations to owners or, if their subsistence farming did not provide sufficient food to keep the family alive (generally due to bad weather), because they had to borrow money to eat. It was among these peasants in the Oriente province that Fidel Castro consolidated the movement that would triumph on January 1, 1959, the day he and his column of revolutionaries triumphantly entered Santiago de Cuba. The next day Che Guevara and Camilio Cienfuegos arrived in Havana, and on February 16, Fidel Castro became premier.

Plácido was our local guide. Slight and reticent, he was a local Party member[48] who had lived all of his 25 years in the mountains of Oriente province. His many little facial scars were probably the effects of a poorly treated childhood disease. A gentle man, Plácido was immensely proud of the revolution and eager to host us in any way he could. At one point I showed him something in *Juventud Rebelde*[49] I did not understand. As he leaned over to look at what I had pointed out, he seemed a bit hesitant, almost frightened. I thought, oh my goodness, what have I done, maybe he does not know how to read. But Plácido pulled himself together, read the paragraph and smiled with relief as he explained the meaning of two uniquely Cuban words. With the special antennae developed by individuals who have spent their formative years humbled and learning to survive among people who control their right to life, Plácido had immediately perceived that I had noted his momentary discomfort with the written word, and he said: "*Yo aprendí a leer cuando tenía 18 años, en 1962 durante la campaña de alfabetización,*" [I learned how to read when I was 18, in 1962, during the literacy campaign].

Seven years before, he went to class with his parents, each then 42, and his two older brothers. His face lit up as he recounted the process of making sense of all those *garabatos* [scribbles] that had been a constant reminder of his ignorance and inferiority. His joy was unmitigated and reminiscent of the excitement of childhood discovery, as he described the expression on his mother's face the day she read her first sentence.

He asked if I would like to meet his parents, who were still growing coffee near Mayarí Arriba in the Sierra Cristal. We set out the next day, with several other members of the group. We boarded a public bus in Santiago for Mayarí Arriba. From there, we had to walk several miles up a mountain to reach his home. The heat was ghastly, but we good revolutionaries had assured Plácido that we could easily handle the mountain. We were "hardy *americanos.*" After half an hour, I felt like I was expiring from the effort and the relentless sun. I was the fairest in the group, but determined not to be the first to complain. I thought: "I bet no other freckled redhead has made it up this mountain alive." Thankfully, a wrecker headed up the road to meet a construction crew stopped and gave us a lift the rest of the way.

The smell of freshly roasted coffee was overpowering as we entered the compound of small, simple houses where Plácido and his extended family lived. It was one of the most intoxicatingly delicious odors I have ever encountered. Piles of fresh coffee beans were in various stages of drying and roasting on a huge cement veranda in back of the house.

Ramón, Placido's father, came out to greet us and show us around. A small man, wrinkled by the elements, he looked much older than his 50 years. Mirta, his mother, stayed in the background. She also looked older than her years and had a weary expression in her eyes. I thought she must be lonely, staying home all day and living in subservience to her husband and male children. An isolated rural life must be particularly hard on women. The only time she spoke was to present her collection of 6 books *"que me dió la revolución"* [that the revolution gave me]. Ramón then signaled to his wife to make coffee.

Mirta took some roasted beans off the outside pile and pounded them into grounds with a wooden mortar and pestle. With great care and attention to the process, she then heated water over the fire, put the ground coffee in a cloth filter and poured hot water over it. The smell was inebriating. Mirta put several teaspoons of sugar into each tiny white cup and filled all of them with the thick black nectar. Her pride in sharing coffee with admirers of the Cuban Revolution was apparent. The intensity of the taste of the tiny cup of coffee matched the intensity of the moment as we all toasted the Revolution. Amidst the plush landscape of a remote corner of Cuba, I felt like I was in a rarified zone, somehow connected to a unique political process by that dark nectar of the gods. I can still summon up the taste and the smell.

I understood that there were hundreds of thousands of Cubans like Plácido's family whose lives were radically improved by the revolution. They now had the right to food, health care and education. The revolution had given them dignity, and they would defend it with their lives. It did not appear that Plácido's mother was troubled by her subservient position in the family. She was content to have enough to eat and to be literate.

*"A male student at the University of Havana told me very seriously that combating machismo is one of the greatest social efforts of the revolution and that he wanted to discuss the question with me as someone from the US who was involved in women's liberation. He then leaned lightly closer and said, 'You have marvelously beautiful eyes,' looking intently into mine in the best Latin manner of red-blood passion and tropical nights."*[50]

Elizabeth Diggs, who wrote those lines was, along with Lillian Robinson and myself, the most vocal about our feminism, even though the entire 15-member delegation expressed strong support for the women's liberation movement and New University Conference's commitment to socialist feminism. It was our comradely obligation to share our revolutionary commitments about gender with the architects of the hemisphere's first successful socialist revolution. Even though we wanted more from the women's liberation movement than personal freedoms for ourselves, it did not take very long to come face to face with major differences in the meaning of socialist feminism for us in a developed capitalist country and for Cuban women, who were primarily interested in joining men to free Cuba from underdevelopment and imperialist aggression. Ten years after Fidel Castro's triumph, a Cuban woman did not work, study and carry a gun to free herself from an oppressive personal situation. Cuban women did not organize among themselves to fight for an issue or to oppose male-controlled institutions, as American feminists did. Unlike us, she was not fighting to achieve legal and economic equality with men and bring about major structural changes in a government. Rather, she sought to acquire the skills she needed to help consolidate a revolution. Cuban men and women condemned Cuban sexism and machismo, but it was little more than lip service.[51]

Shortly after arriving in Havana, our group had toured the construction site for a foundry to see evidence of the changed role of women in the Cuban economy. One of the revolution's achievements had been to incorporate women into what had traditionally been "men's work." In this case, the revolutionary definition of "men's work" involved physical, not political or intellectual, capacity. I thought of "Rosie the Riveter" — the American symbol of thousands of women doing "men's work" in factories during World War II while men were off fighting. Rosie the Riveter celebrated the ideal of the physically strong workingwoman. Sadly, however, once the war was over, Rosie had to make way for a male veteran and return to home and hearth. She was forced into the role of the 1950's passive homemaker. Discontent with this confining ideal was a powerful stimulant in the creation of Second Wave feminism.

In 1959, the incorporation into the labor force of hundreds of thousands of Cuban women who had been maids, peasants and prostitutes — the most backward elements in society — worked a permanent structural change for men as well as women. The organizational unit for workers, female and male, at any given workplace was the brigade[52], and often the Federation of Cuban Women played a major role in setting up certain brigades. In my speeches on women's liberation in the United States in 1969, I always devoted several paragraphs to "the primary importance of the needs of working class women and particularly poor black women who were doubly trapped by race and poverty."

As I entered the foundry, it struck me how different it was to call attention to a social problem from within a protected university enclave and to see in process a national, government-sponsored campaign focused on improving the lot of the most habitually deprived women. A brigade of women and men were all doing the same work side by side—an example of the feminism we had all read about and, of course, enthusiastically supported.

I had conflicted feelings about what I saw. The attention given to "rehabilitating" this population of women was impressive, but what if all the former maids and prostitutes didn't want to become factory workers? Maybe they preferred another profession. My understanding was that they didn't have much choice. Personally, I found the prospect of having anything to do with a factory quite unappealing, but then again, as I frequently reminded myself, the Cubans didn't make this revolution for women like me. Surely if I were a Cuban, the revolution would have found an appropriate position for me as a leader in the university or of a new intellectual undertaking. At the time, the fact that many socialist intellectuals like me had fled Cuba soon after the revolution did not cross my mind.

Our guide introduced us to Mariana, a construction worker in her late twenties or early thirties. She was operating a forklift and clearly occupied a respected role in the largely male workers' brigade that was building the new plant. Mariana looked up from her work, flashed an engaging smile and halted her work to talk to us. I translated her description of how physically difficult her work was and her explanation that before the revolution, women were not trusted to do this kind of "man's work." Mariana was clearly proud to have been selected by the leaders of her work brigade to talk to a group of *norteamericanos* about the revolution and her part in it.

She extolled the government that had created an opportunity for her to be part of the workers' force that "controlled the means of production," as she phrased it. Workers' brigades, we learned, also organized on-site instruction in revolutionary thought and Marxism for each of its units. Mariana had evidently learned some Marxist theory and was proud to use the terms in her discussion with us. No one questioned the scripted explanation; for us Mariana was an authentic voice from "inside" the young revolution. And we were happy to listen to her.

Mariana was about five feet tall, with a curvaceous, honey-colored body that she moved with sensual pleasure. When she walked, her round, pleasingly muscular buttocks swayed from side to side seductively, like part of a rumba. Like her co-workers (male and female) Mariana had been issued work clothes by the brigade: work pants and a shirt. Although her olive and beige clothes were identical to those of the other workers, Mariana had apparently tailored the mass-issue clothing a bit: her work pants were well fitting and very tight, as was the shirt that barely closed across her ample, well-formed breasts. A large belt was pulled tightly around her waist, emphasizing her voluptuous form. The men in our group tried not to react obviously to her overt sexuality.

It was clear Mariana enjoyed being admired for her physical attributes. She smiled broadly and her lively black eyes made contact with each of us. Her hair was rolled around large metallic curlers that covered her whole head. We later learned she was going out with her boyfriend after work and wanted her hair to be in good shape. When Mariana took off the heavy work gloves, her nails were carefully manicured and painted red. At the time, the women's liberation movement considered rejection of certain traditional female accouterments such as make-up, colored nail polish and bras oppositional actions for confronting the consumer society imposed on us by the capitalist power structure.

Mariana was dynamic, charming and clever—the perfect spokeswoman for the new Cuba. When I asked one of the group's favorite questions "Mariana, *¿qué hiciste antes de la revolución?*," [What did you do before the revolution?] she hesitated. Then she smiled coyly, a twinkle in eye: *"Diles que era… doméstica."* [Tell them that I was a maid.]

Nestor had told me that until the end of 1958, Mariana had been a prostitute in Havana's flourishing sex industry. Aptly dubbed "a floating brothel," Cuba was the site of a sexually insatiable tourist industry that boomed under Batista's dictatorship and poured millions of dollars into his economy. The most notorious "Red Light District" was Havana's Barrio de Colón—twenty city blocks devoted to prostitution. In addition to catering to a lucrative tourist trade, Cuban brothels were a necessary institution in the pre-1959 patriarchal society that valued machismo, sexually experienced men, and virginal women—of a certain class. At the onset of puberty, Cuban fathers took their sons to neighborhood brothels to be initiated into the mysteries of sex. This was also the practice in Spain when I lived there, Gabriel once explained to me.

On the eve of the revolution, over 100,000 Cuban women were working as prostitutes, meaning that out of a total female population of roughly 3,300,000 in 1958, one in 30 was a prostitute. Often she was the sole wage earner for an extended family. Female prostitution drew on the urban and rural poor, where one of every 15 or 20 women worked as prostitutes. One of the first tasks of the revolution had been to "rehabilitate" these women. The brothels were closed and schools were set up to teach the former prostitutes skills that the revolutionary economy needed. They became farm and factory workers and staff for communal laundries and dining rooms, as well as the plethora of state-run childcare centers the government started establishing as early as 1959. These young women were taught to read and write and instructed in the content and goals of the revolution.

Instinctively I was sympathetic with young females, who, in order to survive, had to degrade themselves physically and emotionally by fulfilling male fantasies.

A few days later, we visited the revolution's major organization for women, the Cuban Federation for Women, founded in 1960 to bring together all the revolutionary women's organizations — workers, peasants, students, homemakers, professionals and others. Almost 75% of the female population belonged to the Federation. Any woman 14 years or older was free to join. The president, Vilma Espín, was married to Raul Castro, Fidel Castro's brother. Espín was one of the three most important women in Cuba. The other two were Haydee Santamaría, the director of the Casa de las Américas (one of two major state-run cultural institutions created by the revolution) and wife of Communist Party leader Armando Hart, and Celia Sánchez, Fidel Castro's administrative assistant. She was known affectionately as the person who "looks after" Fidel. All three women were veterans of the revolution and had fought alongside men in the Sierra Maestra. Espín had been born into an economically privileged family and in the early 1950s had studied chemical engineering at the Massachusetts Institute of Technology.

"*Bienvenidas compañeras,*" Espín smiled warmly as we filed into the simple, sparsely furnished meeting room at Federation headquarters and sat around a large square table. *Compañera* Vilma was in her forties, pleasant looking with a calm, confident composure. She wore round glasses, no make-up and her chestnut colored hair was carefully collected and fastened with a barrette at the back of her head. We had done our homework, so we knew that Cuban women carry guns, serve in the militia and are trained to fight. We also knew that in Cuba women are officially — legally and economically — equal to men. The overt vestiges of the influence of the Catholic Church had been eliminated, and contraceptives and abortions were free and available on demand. Knowing that in revolutionary Cuba women had been given what we considered these "basic human rights," we wanted to hone in on the more personal aspects of what it was like to be a woman in Cuba. As properly educated revolutionaries, we were well aware that Lenin had pointed out that equality before the law is not necessarily equality in fact.

"¿Compañera, doesn't the revolution consider marriage a bourgeois and oppressive institution?" One of our feminist 'trash monogamy'[53] zealots asked. I winced. But *Compañera* Vilma didn't miss a beat and her official translator's rendition was flawless: "The Federation has never talked about the elimination of marriage. From the beginning, the Federation has been a mass organization to incorporate women into the revolution, not a feminist organization."

A subtle *frisson* of disappointment hit us all. "What a bummer," I thought, "all we are going to get is the Party line." Non-plussed, *Compañera* Vilma continued: "Before the revolution, the vast majority of Cuban women were too poor to afford a wedding and many, many were forced into prostitution. Only the very wealthy could have a proper wedding; it was the envy of poor women. Now the government has "marriage palaces" in large cities free and open to anyone. Free honeymoons for a week in special honeymoon resorts are a reward for outstanding workers when they marry."[54]

This was a socialist economy, the model for Cuban gender equality based on the Soviet system that, for example, encouraged women to become doctors but closed other professions to them. The primary goal of establishing new rights for women was to further the goals of the revolution, as it was in the Soviet Union. However, we were interested in how the revolution defined sexual mores and sex roles. How did men and women treat each other now? Was the revolution formulating an "ideology on sex?" Did the Federation favor men participating in child-rearing and household tasks? This time *Compañera* Vilma's answer was brief and succinct. She was probably losing patience with us: "The Federation has no ideology on sex. If you ask ten different people, you'll get ten different answers."

I had no sense of Vilma Espín as a person. I felt I would have learned just about as much if she had given us several sheets of printed matter to read. Espín's pleasant, but carefully structured, composure insured that no spontaneity ever intruded in her remarks or answers to our questions. It was irritating to be "spoken at" in such a prepared and wooden manner. Because she was an educated female leader, I think I expected a different kind of interaction. I was disappointed not to have been given even a tiny glance at Vilma, the woman. As laid out by Fidel Castro's sister-in-law, we knew official Cuban feminism was not a model for us.

Undaunted by the stiff presentation, some of us set out to do our own field research. We chatted with as many Cuban women as we could—government guides, university students and factory workers. Mercifully, we restrained ourselves from asking peasant women like Mirta, Placido's mother, to discuss their sexual ideology. We found that (not unlike Spain at the time) Cuba still placed a premium on chastity for women "one might marry". "Free love" was frowned upon, especially by the older generation. But unlike the Spanish university women that I had known in 1966-1968, who strongly advocated "remaining pure" until after marriage, most Cuban university women openly mocked the idea of female virginity. In Spain, the Catholic Church had a monopoly on dictating sexual mores. Therefore, pre-marital sex was a sin. In Cuba, the Catholic Church no longer had the power to regulate female sexuality. Thus, sex was not much of a sin before marriage or after with contraceptives.

But entrenched social patterns fade slowly. The idea of prizing female chastity (traditionally applicable, of course, only to a certain class of women) took years to wither away, and in 1969 it was still part of a fading social code. In response to my query, Adela, a nineteen year old university student exclaimed, "*mi amor, ¡el único problema para nosotras no es SI hacemos amor con un novio, sino DONDE!*" [Honey, the only problem for us isn't IF we make love with a boyfriend, but WHERE to find a place to do it!] Adela told us about two young lovers who were brought to trial in People's Court for using an uncle's apartment for lunch-hour trysts. There were no cheap hotels to check into, and young people lived with their families or in strictly sexually segregated dormitories. The *donde* was a big problem.[55]

We did not delve into potential defects of the new Cuban society. We glossed over points of disagreement. If anyone brought up contentious issues (such as access to political power for women who were not married to male leaders, or freedom of the press), the rest of us objected that we were in Cuba to learn, not to criticize. None of the delegation's ardent feminists—myself included—

openly criticized anything Vilma Espín had said. None of us believed the Soviet model for female equality could ever be useful for our movement, but, we all agreed, the Cuban Revolution wasn't made for us. It was natural that financially secure, highly educated white American women had different feminist goals than the majority of Cuban women. It was better to compare the Cuban female population with its like—the millions of poor Latin American women struggling under the double yoke of capitalist and macho exploitation. They were worse off than any Cuban woman who at least had sufficient food and clothing and access to free education, housing, medical and childcare.

I was well aware that the constraints of censorship and freedom of expression in Cuba defined the lives of both women and men. I had lived under censorship and lack of freedom of the press in Spain, but that existed in a different context. I was totally against everything Franco and the fascist government stood for and was committed to the struggle to rid Spain of fascism. I admired what the Cuban revolution had accomplished to make food, education, medicine and housing accessible to all Cubans. They were creating a rational society with equality for women and a new culture for everyone. The revolution had turned the former colonial society upside down and was committed to a kind of socialism I respected. Yet I knew I could never conform to the Cuban revolution's regimented way of thinking, which I found infantilizing. The knowledge that one could not protest openly against government decisions or have access to whatever one wanted to read would have been intolerable. I was not, however, ready to voice my doubts. Cuba deserved a chance to develop freely on its own, and I wanted the United States to stop meddling in its affairs. What harm could this little tropical island with its great big leader do to us?

Like youth in revolt across the globe at that time, we intensely admired—indeed were fixated on—the commanding images of Fidel and Che. Against all odds, the Cuban student leader and the Argentine doctor, the little Davids of the battle, had nurtured a tiny movement into a successful revolution. Maybe we in the United States could vanquish our Goliath too. Revolution—albeit undefined for our group—was in the air. And it was empowering to be taken seriously by high officials of the Cuban government.

I returned to Pittsburgh in late August, ready to start work as assistant dean. I had to figure out how to deal with Gabriel, who was now living several blocks from my house with his new Mexican girlfriend. In Cuba, I had been able to block out the hurt and sudden aloneness that accompanied the dissolution of my marriage. The constant company of our group and the stimulation of travel and new adventures were a helpful distraction. I knew the loneliness would surface when I returned to my home and I was afraid of it—afraid it would immobilize me.

I did what was most immediately comforting to me, plunging headlong into being the university's token female administrator and the local leader of the women's liberation movement. I was constantly busy and often the center of attention and admiration, both of which helped assuage a certain loss of focus and capacity for reflection that accompanied getting a divorce. At the same time, I was attracted to the emerging field of Caribbean Studies. It was so different from the world of modern Spanish literature that was dominated by conservative, tradition-bound male Hispanists. The study of the Caribbean was more progressive. Caribbean Studies, like the soon to emerge field of Women's Studies, was interdisciplinary; scholars from many fields were getting involved and activists were welcome, even respected. I kept thinking about the conversation I had had with Nancy Morejón and Miguel Barnet about *cubanía* and creating new concepts, Caribbean Studies and Cuba were free of Gabriel and my former life in Spain. Involvement with Cuba was my own undertaking. No emotional baggage was attached to it.

I kept pondering what it would be like to live in Cuba. I liked being among Cubans. Temperamentally I felt very much at home among these clever, spontaneous, fun-loving and sensually uninhibited people. I had enjoyed several memorable nights of making love with Cuban men and found them to be gentle, generous lovers. Part of their lovemaking was to make sure that a woman enjoyed maximum pleasure. That was lovely. I found that the Cuban men I knew really liked women physically, even though after they got up and took a shower, conventional male supremacy was immediately restored. They started giving orders and patronizing. But that was fine. I just said goodbye and went back to the hotel.

I regarded Cuba as a country full of *gente viva*, lively, quick witted folks who appreciated my sharp tongue and sense of humor. To be fair, I also liked many of the Cuban exiles I met in the United States who shared these same characteristics. But in Cuba I also felt exhilarated by being in a society whose long-term goals were in sync with mine. What would it be like not to be constantly in the opposition? More than that, what would it be like to live in a society based on the premise that you would always be expected to support not only the government's long-term goals, but also all its short-term strategies? I thought about that a lot.

Even though I knew the principal aim of the Cuban Revolution was to establish social justice and redistribute wealth more equitably, I was also aware that a dynamic intellectual life is central to the successful development of any country. The Cuban government maintained this, but the Cubans defined "freedom of the press" differently than we did. Heberto Padilla was a case in point. That was their right, but I did not want to live without access to anything I wanted to read even though I knew that "freedom of the press" is a multi-layered, at times contradictory concept in the United States, where a powerful minority controls access to the tools that mould the opinions of the majority of citizens. Minority opinion is tolerated in the United States, but minorities are not given access to the means to influence broad segments of the population. Part of our definition of freedom of the press entails "protecting" US citizens by constructing barriers—some subtle, some not so subtle—to wide circulation in the mass media of forceful opinions that are said to be harmful to the national interest—of principal concern are arguments for non-market economies and a religion-free society. However, the American system is a system in which I know how to operate. I was versed in the ways to enjoy the benefits and protest the shortcomings of our public media.

Yet I believed then, as I do now, that the Cubans had the right to build their own society. They deserved the freedom to go their own way, without the market economy if they wished. The attitude of my government seemed like senseless imperial strutting to me. I decided I would try to help Cuba, from here in the United States.

I made an effort to communicate what I had learned from my Cuban experience to American audiences. I participated (as the dissenting voice) in a public symposium on the Cuban Revolution that was sponsored by the Political Science Department of the University of Pittsburgh. Carmelo Mesa-Lago, the organizer of the symposium and a Cuban exile, explained that he could not publish my speech in the anthology he was compiling from the symposium because it was "out of tune politically" with the rest of the articles. I was too supportive of Cuba. Why didn't I send it to the *Monthly Review*? Carmelo was a nice man; we just viewed the world differently. As it turned out, his suggestion was a good one. My article on "*Literature and Revolution in Cuba*" would be published in October 1970 in the socialist monthly and subsequently circulated rather widely.

I also arranged to give a graduate seminar in the spring semester on "Literature and Revolution in Cuba" for which, the truth be said, I was not particularly well prepared. Most of what I knew about the subject was already published in the article. I had managed to send back dozens of Cuban books via Canada, but my credentials in the then emerging field of Cuban and Caribbean Studies were wobbly. The course was sponsored by the College of Arts and Science Deans' office (not my home base which was the Department of Hispanic Languages and Literatures). I was very junior to propose creating and offering a new graduate course, but because I was assistant dean, the department chair, Rudi Cardona, an affable, progressive Costa Rican, allowed students to receive department credit for it. I offered the course one evening a week in the Dean's conference room and occasionally at my home. Eight students, all delighted to share my zealous enthusiasm for the Cuban Revolution, participated.

From the outset, I was pulled in various directions: New Left activism, the women's movement, and advocacy for better treatment of the Cuban Revolution by the US government. I was intermittently aware that engaging in this constant, demanding round of activities shielded me from examining the debris of a collapsed marriage. My daily life was full of new friends and a new kind of personal power as administrator and movement leader. I started dating a newly hired assistant professor of political science. He was bright, nice enough, and attended meetings of the New University Conference on campus. The relationship, which lasted six or seven months, was one of convenience, not deep commitment. I had no desire to undertake the self-examination and intense reflection some people do after the collapse of a long-term relationship. It was easier and temporarily more satisfying just to bury the wounds and construct a different life.

As the academic year unfolded, I found it hard to sustain my focus on Cuba. I was being pulled in too many directions, so I put Cuba on the back burner, in hibernation for what would be several years. Nevertheless, every now and then I found myself thinking about Cuba, Spain and, by extension, about the lives of Latinos living in the United States. I knew that the East coast was home to a large community of Puerto Ricans and that tens of thousands of Chicanos lived in the western states. It would be some years before I became involved in the politics of Puerto Rico and Chile, but I would soon have the opportunity to meet Chicanos and learn about their movement.

# CHAPTER 7
# PITTSBURGH'S FEMINIST DEAN

Before stepping up to the "deanship," I had a "trial run" at being a public advocate when I was invited to give a talk on the women's liberation movement at nearby Allegheny Community College. Pittsburgh was just ending its years as a big time steel town. In the city of Carnegie, Frick and Mellon, generations of coal and steel workers were being displaced — and impoverished. The students at Allegheny were probably the first in their families to set foot in a college. I remember them as all white. Many were in their late teens and early twenties and female, but about a third were male. There was a sprinkling of people in their thirties, more than would have come to this kind of talk at the University of Pittsburgh.

During the question and answer period, a man in his early thirties, perhaps late twenties, asked the first question: "You say there should be more women leaders in politics and business, but how can you women be leaders if you get menstrual cramps once a month? Look at all the times you'd miss work."

The room was utterly silent; everyone was looking at me. I smiled slightly but I felt the old numbness that had stopped me from fighting anti-Semitism in grade school and from rejecting the German bus driver's invitation to lunch on my trip to Munich. I was mortified, standing on the stage, trying to look sweet and unthreatening after having given a strident feminist speech.

Then a short man with a round, smiling face, slightly balding, with frameless glasses, stood up and introduced himself as Professor with an Italian-sounding-last-name. He said, "For heaven's sake, a woman can take a pill for a pain, just like we do!" The audience was relieved and many smiled or laughed in agreement. Two young women in the front row clapped their approval and looked me straight in the eye, communicating support and empathy. I quickly moved on to the next question. The numbness had disappeared and I was able to do a credible job with the rest of the questions. Although I had spoken in colleagues' classes about the women's movement throughout that academic year, this was the first time since my 1967 talk in Madrid that I had laid out my ideas on women's liberation to a large, unfamiliar audience. It had not occurred to me to prepare myself for an inability to react to only a moderately hostile question.

When the event concluded, a woman in the audience came up to me. She was small, thin and taut; I judged her to be in her late thirties. A mound of short blondish hair framed a lively, intense face. Her eyes were brown and looked straight at you. She radiated energy.

"My name is Joanne Gardner. Your talk was great, but next time don't let them silence you. It used to happen to me and I'll tell you how I conquered it. Anytime you don't know how to respond, or get frightened and suddenly can't talk back, force yourself to say something, anything, even if it is wrong, not at all what you wanted to say. The key point is not to remain silent. The first four or five times you will not be happy with what you say, but by the tenth or eleventh attempt, you will stop being afraid and be able to think quickly on your feet."

Her words have stayed with me and I have often shared them with other women.

Joanne Gardner lived nearby and was in the process of launching a feminist press called KNOW, Inc. Did I want to come to her house on St. James St., not far from the University of Pittsburgh, and see her basement operation? Her husband was still working on the finishing touches of the household conversion.

She and other members of Pittsburgh's National Organization for Women (NOW)[56] chapter were creating a national clearinghouse for feminist news and views. They planned to publish pamphlets, bibliographies, and papers written by movement and academic feminists. Joanne was spearheading the first feminist media enterprise. Women outside of Pittsburgh learned about KNOW, Inc. in 1970 when the little press published the first nationally distributed collections of syllabi for new women's studies courses.

Joanne was on a mission and constantly in motion. I liked her, and during the two years I lived in Pittsburgh, we collaborated on several feminist projects. She introduced me to Wilma Scott Heide, from Johnstown, near Pittsburgh. Wilma was head of the Pittsburgh chapter of NOW and in 1971 she was elected national president of NOW. Wilma asked me to speak at their fall meeting in Pittsburgh, and I agreed. The evening in September when I delivered my address would turn out to be a watershed in my life.

As Joanne had predicted, each time I spoke in public my sense of empowerment increased. I was learning more about women, our situation in America and myself. At one point in the spring of 1969 I realized that, with considerable effort, I had managed to read everything then available about the women's liberation movement. Within a year, the proliferation of literature would be such that none of us could say that anymore. For the first time in my life, a lot of the work I was doing, particularly the political work, coincided with the person I was — and wanted to continue to be.

My colleagues in Hispanic Literature had deemed my first year at teaching a success. I had been the only woman — and the only American — in the Spanish department. Once again I was in the right place at the right time, both for the department appointment and the move into administration. The dean recognized my talent for innovation and organization and he knew the women's movement was important. I was visible and much of the campus was interested in what I might do next. As assistant dean, I would have more power than an untenured assistant professor, but the male/female playing field was still not by any means level.

I was the only major female administrator at the University and was often referred to in the press, with the unconscious sexism of the moment, as "the new look in Pitt administrators." Under that banner, I was flooded with requests to speak about the new women's movement. With feminist zeal I spoke in colleagues' classes, all-university forums and to many civic and religious organizations throughout the greater Pittsburgh area. I was also besieged by invitations to speak on radio, television, and local and national colleges and universities. I accepted as many invitations as I possibly could and thoroughly enjoyed all the attention.

I was thrilled to sit in my tiny office next to the dean and, for the first time in my life, have a secretary — although I was not quite sure how to relate to her. Jane was a sweet middle-aged woman who had lived all her life in Pittsburgh and was pleased to be one of the team of four secretaries in the dean's office. The women's liberation movement did not include her. She was very happy, thank you, just as she was. However, since she did as the dean bid, she typed my memos and did whatever else I could think to ask of her. At first I did not understand that secretaries were supposed to answer your phone and make all your appointments, so I must have driven her a bit crazy during the first month. But she was well socialized into the bureaucratic hierarchy of the university, and never questioned anything I did.

I wonder if she considered it a bit humiliating to report to a long-haired, mini-skirted woman the age of her daughter. It never occurred to me to consider what the staff thought of me. I was too busy dashing off memos to the provost questioning the lack of female presence on a plethora of important university committees and working with the dean's wife and female graduate students to organize a university-based daycare center. I also negotiated to have a shelf dedicated to books 'on women' in the university bookstore. Just one shelf! It seems incredible that this accomplishment required many phone calls, memos and personal visits.

Several hundred people showed up for my speech for the opening fall meeting of the Pittsburgh chapter of the National Organization for Women, which was billed as *"New University Dean to Speak on Women's Liberation Movement."* To accommodate an audience expected to be larger than usual, Wilma Scott Heidi arranged to use a big lecture hall in the student union. The room was packed with women mostly in their thirties or forties and there was a light sprinkling of men, as NOW was open to male membership. It definitely was not a "women's lib" crowd. I was glad I had worn a rather sedate suit most appropriate for a university administrator. Must not alienate anyone tonight, I remember thinking. The press was also there.

An anticipatory buzz ran throughout the audience. As I stepped forward, I offered what I judged to be a warm, welcoming "we are all sisters" smile.

I opened by saying: *"All women's education is geared to produce secretaries instead of professors, to give out programs at a symphony instead of playing the violin, to help Senator Kennedy rather than to be a senator."* The crowd applauded. Good, I thought. They loved that. Take the next step.

*"In 1954 the Supreme Court outlawed racial segregation, but that was only the beginning for black citizens. The next step was – and is – the breaking down of negative, destructive self-conceptions – that sense of inferiority and self-negation accumulated from years of being a second class citizen."* My eyes strayed over the audience. Was anyone black, or non-white in any way? No, all white, as was attendance at almost all NOW meetings in 1969.

I continued: *"And once black citizens shake off crippling ideas of self to function with a new awareness and confidence, they move for additional legislation and further structural changes propelled by this new awareness and confidence. Something similar is happening to American women today"*. Slight shifting of some chairs, a few coughs... women are like blacks? Forge on Roberta, you can bring them along.

*"It is not so much isolated legal improvements that many women seek*

(although movements such as those for legalized abortion are important), but a major change in self conception. Stimulated in part by the civil rights movement and the demands of American blacks, women (and men) are beginning to reevaluate traditional male-female relationships. This idea is threatening and frightening to both females and males, and this explains the frequent hostility of women to these ideas and why indulgent male laughter is often the response to 'feminist' ideas. It's easy to laugh at women and not take them seriously when many women themselves are ready to join in the laughter." A smattering of nodding heads. "Remember all those movies and stories of the traditional southern black man who joined in others' mockery of himself — too afraid even to realize what was going on? The public as a whole has rejected the idea of full citizenship for women because it challenges the structure of marriage, family and society, as we now know it. It challenges timeworn assumptions that have not only been comfortable for men but convenient for many women too." Careful. Don't push too far; lighten up a bit.

"Thanks to the brilliant manipulation of mass media, females are obsessed with an ideal of femininity as the guarantee of happiness. Be thin, smart, sexy, and soft-spoken. Get new slipcovers, learn new recipes, have bright children, further your man's career, help the community, drive the car and smile. And if you can write a novel or two in your spare time, that's great. Nobody objects to a woman's being a good writer or sculptor or geneticist if at the same time she manages to be a good wife, a good mother, good-looking, good-tempered, well dressed, well groomed and unaggressive. These are the requirements for the approval of other men and women." Okay. We were bonding again. Now move into women's studies and elicit help, advice. This is a Movement you are trying to build, not just a platform for extracting applause.

"Right now we are working to institute an interdisciplinary course on women in history, literature and sociology in the university curriculum. This is as important to women as black studies are to blacks — to empower women and to create new knowledge about women."

My carefully crafted position regarding the women's liberation movement was clear: "I feel very strongly that women's rights cannot be separated from the whole social context. We have to be aware all the time that we're members of a society and any female movement can't be separated from it." I ended with a call for unity that was enthusiastically received: "We have to all work together, in the university and in the community. Let's have a brain-storming session and see what everyone thinks about the next steps to be taken."

This talk, like most of my other public speaking that year, was designed for across-the-political-spectrum female consciousness-raising, along with a call for moderate social reform. I was an academic administrator and the envelope could be pushed just so far. But that night I realized for the first time that I could sway an audience. I could move them to believe in what I said if I ascertained what most concerned them and plugged into it. The numbness I had experienced at Allegheny College never returned. For the rest of my life, I have been an effective public speaker, especially when faced with the opportunity to persuade a lot of people to support something I deeply believe in.

Then came my appearance on *"The Phil Donahue Show,"* a daily half hour TV talk show based in Dayton, Ohio and broadcast in the morning. I liked Donahue from the moment we shook hands. His eyes were those of an intelligent man, and his sensitive reactions and thoughtful demeanor pleasantly surprised me. I had been prepared for an encounter with one of the somewhat coarse "man on the way up" types common on the daytime TV shows that were aimed at women. Phil Donahue was different. Of medium height, jovial and "beefy," he could have been a friendly Irish movie star. Not overly handsome, but intense, he had a big smile whose constant use deeply creased his cheeks. Sandy haired, in his mid-thirties, Donahue knew he was charming, and part of the charm was his interest in listening to others — and at that time in his life, especially to women. While gradually increasing in popularity, it was some years before Donahue moved to New York, reached the pinnacle of success, married Marlo Thomas and publicly prided himself on being a feminist.

The company had sent a little white helicopter to pick me up in Pittsburgh. The wingless aircraft plopped down on the lawn below the deans' suite in the Cathedral of Learning, the unique church-like edifice that housed the College of Liberal Arts. Everyone from the office watched as the pilot helped me into the only passenger seat in what seemed to me to be an overgrown toy airplane. As we lifted straight up into the air, I waved goodbye as my acolytes huddled on the lawn gradually receded from view. I was having a grand time.

I was the only guest on the show that morning and the topic was the women's liberation movement and the emerging field of women's studies. Although I had been a guest several times on *"On Equal Terms,"* a daytime show on KDKA, the local CBS outlet, this felt different. Phil *("Dr. Salper, please call me Phil")* asked penetrating questions directed at my strengths both as an academic and feminist activist. Donahue (or someone on his staff) had done his homework. His astute questions allowed me to articulate my thoughts on the needs for a new women's movement and for university courses dealing with the situation of women in society. From what I could see, the live audience consisted of white, non-professional women, mostly between 30 and 50 years old. Some asked questions that I answered satisfactorily: *"Do you think a woman can raise children and work?" "Won't daycare harm our children?"* The women seemed to be a bit timid, perhaps slightly intimidated. Call-ins from several people were more aggressive: *"Everybody knows women run the world through their men; what more do you want?" "Aren't you afraid of ruining all marriages with your so-called equality?"*

Some days later, Donahue sent me a thank you note and several dozen letters the show had received about my appearance. Those letters from women watching at home jolted me into thinking about how a population different from the university, the educated membership of NOW and the world of young activists would react to the women's movement. They put me in contact with an audience heretofore unknown to me. I saved two of letters; both handwritten on white lined notebook paper—now aged, but still intact.

The first, dated October 5, 1969 is from "J.C.R." a resident of a small rural town in Pennsylvania. This letter typifies the viewpoint of about a quarter of the responses:

"Doctor,

*You are very interesting and very proud. I am watching you on TV. You are not a fair person.... You turn all arguments against those giving them to you. You are very interesting in that you are so wrong and yet so outspoken.*

*When the day comes that you see your mistake of rebelling and not searching out the truth, I hope you think something like this: 'So that's why I was hitting my head against a stone-wall-disorder....' Anyone who is as hating as you is very insecure in the love of others and the fact of a supreme being."*[57]

The second letter I saved consists of three pages addressed to "Dear Roberta Salper," and signed *"Respectfully yours, Vernny Boyd, (thirty-five-year-old gogo girl)."* It begins like this:

*"You were 'out of sight' today on TV—logical, lucid and palatable above all (and sexy to top it off)!"* Further on, Vernny offered a three-point program for women:

*"1. We need radicals and revolutionaries to make the reformists look good.*

*2. We need to use sex to sell our ideas on TV and we must create a new image of the contemporary feminist and not be afraid to call ourselves that name.*

3. *We must be willing to sweat to organize a 'Focus' for enlargement of our group."*

She ended her letter with: *"You with your PHD surrounded with a ruffled dress, long hair, soft voice and a set of legs that won't quit are my new idol and probably the same for many others."*

Those letters registered two extremes of the reactions that I elicited in regard to the incipient women's movement from Middle America in 1969-70. J.C.R. (I assume it was a woman) was the most vociferous of the women who were outraged at what they considered my lack of respect for what god and religious texts had ordained to be the role of women. I kept hers because I wanted to be able to retrigger the emotions I felt when I first read it. I felt a little sick to my stomach. It reminded me of how I felt when Bobby Eschenbach taunted me for being a "Jew Girl" in fifth grade. But that familiar paralyzing nausea only lasted a few minutes and I was able to focus on the difference between anti-Semitism and anti-feminism. I did not choose to be Jewish; I was born into it, and family and society ensured that I remained in this preordained niche. I learned to defend myself from anti-Semitic attacks not because I wanted to but because I had to. Feminism was a personal and political vision that I had consciously made my own. No one had imposed it on me. When I realized J.C.R. was attacking what I believed and not condemning me for something completely out of my control, the waves in my stomach calmed down and I got angry. How could she think these things? This was what we feminists had to combat! *Aux armes!*

Vernny, of course, was a different case entirely. She was from Pittsburgh, so I contacted her and invited her to come to my office. She was strong and direct and itching to help change the world for women. I have never again met anyone like Vernny, although accounts have been written of reactions to feminism by all kinds of sex workers. Vernny's roots were in the working class; she had no education beyond high school and at 35, no family to support her. I have no idea how she became a feminist, but when I met her, she had scorn for men in general and knew something about the history of feminism in the United States. Divorced with a child and completely on her own, she was fiercely independent and adventurous. Vernny had been a maid and a waitress, then found go-go dancing more lucrative. In addition, this was a night job that allowed her to spend days with her child. According to Vernny, no contradiction existed between being a feminist and using male appreciation of her large breasts and well formed long legs to earn a living. In fact, Vernny believed the first feminist movement had gotten us the vote but nothing else because the suffragists *"didn't care about their looks and didn't know how to turn sex into an advantage to win more rights and equality."*

Vernny and I got along very well. We saw each other now and then for coffee or a glass of wine, and I introduced her to some of the movement activists in and out of the university. She became a valuable contributor to the Pittsburgh Women's Movement and continued her night job as a go-go dancer.

Throughout my heady first months as Assistant Dean, a new discipline that would be called women's studies was beginning to coalesce on some campuses, and in Pittsburgh, the moment for such an innovation was ripe. With the collaboration of two female graduate students, one from the English Department, the other History, we successfully lobbied to create the first women's studies course to be offered at the university. It was one of the first in the country. The three of us were jointly to teach *"The History and Social Role of Women in the United States."* It was scheduled for offering in January 1970.

But first I was booked to go to the annual Modern Language Association convention Dec. 26-30 in Denver. The day after Christmas I was on a plane, looking forward to the prominent role the New University Conference would play in making progressive changes in the MLA. A lot had changed in my life, too, since the rebellious convention in New York a year before. I was beginning to feel more comfortable with who I was and what I was becoming. I also understood more about how radical politics operated in the United States.

It was snowing and cold when I arrived late on a Friday afternoon. I rushed off to the NUC planning meeting at the Cosmopolitan Hotel in downtown Denver. I was looking forward to a reunion with alumni of our summer trip to Cuba and to meeting local Latino activists to learn more about a movement for social justice among the Chicano people that had an important base in Denver.

Despite my ties with the Hispanic world, I did not know very much about the emerging Chicano movement. Movement publications occasionally mentioned a Mexican American Civil Rights Movement that represented a broad cross section of issues—from restoration of land grants to farm workers' rights, enhanced education, and voting and political rights. Although the overwhelmingly middle class white membership of NUC had a sense that there was growing unrest within the Mexican American community, then based almost entirely in the Southwest, its activities were not part of our agenda. However, particularly after the month I had spent in Cuba in July, I wanted to learn more about Spanish speaking communities in the United States and enthusiastically signed on to the group that was to meet with the Chicanos.

Corky González and members of his Crusade for Justice,[58] had convened the first Chicano Youth Liberation Conference in Denver in March 1969, making the city the nation-wide focus of Chicano organizational activity. Corky was a poet as well as a social activist. He understood the powerful relationship between literature, particularly poetry, and social change. His long, ringing poem, *Yo soy Joaquín*/I am Joaquin, was a powerful tribute to the historical, social and psychological realities of being Chicano in the United States. It was familiar to Chicanos throughout the country, even those who did not read poetry for pleasure. This reminded me of Spain, where unschooled peasants were able to recite verses from Federico García Lorca's poems because he spoke directly to them.

A group of us went to a working class part of Denver to meet with Corky González and other activists. The meeting was held in a large, sparsely furnished basement room. It was dimly lit, with open folding chairs scattered on its wooden floor. I realized it was the empty gym of a somewhat rundown school. No one was in the huge building except the seven or eight Chicanos who had come to meet with about a dozen of us. That evening I learned first hand about the process that radicalized many Mexican Americans. I had never realized the hurt that remained in the Mexican American community, after over a hundred years, of land lost to the United States in 1848. Nor had I ever heard raw accounts of the brutal treatment Chicano farm workers routinely received from Anglo bosses. Several Chicana women were present, but I have no recollection of their ever speaking.

Corky was an intense, mesmerizing conversationalist. He wanted progressives in the MLA to use our institutional contacts to help make the Chicano vision and culture, particularly literature, available to a broad audience. That was part of the plan to advance the Chicano Civil Rights Movement in the United States. We agreed to try to learn more about their situation and help in any way we could.[59] One obvious way would be to lobby for a major forum on Chicano studies at a future MLA meeting.

I was struck by the clarity of Corky's political reasoning and his understanding of what could be achieved by a relationship between his mass-based social movement and an establishment institution like the MLA. I was impressed because as Corky and his colleagues were explaining their views to us, I became aware of the many areas left undefined, unexamined and therefore unclear about "boundaries" in the women's movement as it, too, began to forge liaisons with organizations such as the MLA. Corky had helped build a large grassroots organization with a small academic component whose role everyone understood. The women's movement was more diffuse, and it blurred class lines without recognizing it; we did not have one unified national program. As women, we were a much larger component of the population, less uniformly organized and not able to rally around precise, short-term goals. The situation was difficult to sort out.

As the Denver meeting concluded, I thought about the past months and my encounters with different points on the continuum of social activism; my appointments to the Commission on the Status of Women and the following year, the MLA Executive Council indicated validation of the New University Conference and the women's movement. While I was pleased with having been granted access to these two bodies, the subsequent reality of belonging to them was more complicated. I liked being offered a piece of the establishment pie, but after several bites, indigestion would invariably set in. I would get frustrated at having to watch and measure everything I said at official meetings. I understood the goal was to convince, persuade and try to effect change by winning over a few more people to a progressive viewpoint. The point was to work for change "from the inside." Sometimes I enjoyed the jousting — curbing my thoughts, self-censoring my ideas — to achieve a small victory, but it was exhausting.

My work with the mechanisms that had to be manipulated to institutionalize aspects of the women's movement made clear that I had a certain ability to function within the establishment. I knew how to behave, to dress, to persuade at that level. It was important to be able to work "from within" as well as from the margins. And I enjoyed the perks that went with "establishment collaboration" — the luxury meals and trips, cocktail parties with cultural icons, major opportunities for career advancement. Yet I missed the comradeship, support and emotional strength that come from exclusive commitment to like-minded people who share a political mission. Solidarity is life affirming in a way donning a social mask to politely persuade can never be. I had worn various social masks too long in Madrid not to be wary of putting them on again.

While I was functioning in the upper echelons of academic bureaucracy, I was also devoting considerable energy to "grassroots" organizing of students in academe. My encounter with the Chicanos reminded me of people in NUC who insisted that "true grassroots organizing" could be only done in a working class community. Although I understood certain colleagues' desire to leave the university and work in factories or do other organizing in working class communities, I knew my skills were more suited to working within academia. My class, ethnic roots and sybaritic proclivities would forever brand me as an outsider in an American working class environment.

Over the years I have learned to live with a basic contradiction in my life: my dedication to building new institutions by being at the center of activities versus my commitment to change that may entail stepping back and not being in a leadership position. Never an expert at putting together the contradictions of my existence, I opted to recognize them as part of my life and avoid brooding about them. When I returned from Denver, I was on the threshold of playing central roles in establishing women's studies in two of the country's earliest programs—first in Pittsburgh and then in San Diego. As long as the New University Conference existed, I never wanted to leave the academic world to organize in any other environment.

On January 12, 1970, the first women's studies course at the University of Pittsburgh was about to begin. Ninety-eight women and two men filled the room to capacity, although the class limit had originally been set at 60 and even though its availability had only been announced at the very end of the fall semester.

Judy Rosenthal, a graduate teaching assistant in the English Department, and Susan Kleinberg, a graduate teaching assistant in the History Department, and I greeted the students as they walked in and handed out copies of our syllabus. We had designed an interdisciplinary course that included history, sociology, and current politics, the study of literature by and about American women, and an examination of the origins and current status of the women's liberation movement. We had no models, no one to consult. I wanted my contribution to be an examination of women within a larger social and political context, not "just literature." At the time I saw no relationship between Hispanic literature and the history and social role of women in the United States (that understanding would not come until some years later). I had no training as a historian, sociologist or political scientist, but not for a moment did that deter me.

The syllabus reflected our individual areas of knowledge, accessibility of texts and in my case, the conviction that this course should be an academic extension of the women's liberation movement. I believed, as I would articulate in various publications some months later, that *"Women's studies, like third world studies, is the academic arm of a broader movement that is challenging time-worn assumptions about North American political and cultural standards – standards determined almost exclusively by Western European culture."*[60] I was also committed to NOT setting up a division between academic women's studies and our social movement, the women's liberation movement. *"Setting up this kind of dichotomy between a social movement 'out there' and some courses safely nestled within the ivy halls is a very effective way to insure both that the courses do not radically change anyone, and that the women's movement does not benefit from the acquisition of skills and other benefits available in the university."*[61]

From the beginning, I did not find the female/male dichotomy to be society's most fundamental; class and race were indispensable elements for any comprehensive analysis. The prevailing culture of male supremacy – not individual males – was what we had to investigate, struggle against and remake. My part of the course concentrated on political aspects of our women's movement and its theoretical underpinnings, starting with Fredrick Engels' *Origins of the Family* and John Stuart Mill's *On the Subjection of Women*. Engels' classic 19th century Marxist text situated women's oppression in the economic oppression generated by capitalism. John Stuart Mill, the most influential English-speaking political philosopher of the 19th century, defended the emancipation of women on ethical grounds. Among other texts, I included excerpts from Simone de Beauvoir's *The Second Sex* and Betty Friedan's *Feminine Mystique*. Robin Morgan's anthology *Sisterhood is Powerful* was published after the course started, but I incorporated many of the articles in the second half of my course.

I worked hard trying to devise the most effective ways to merge activism, political vision and the study of texts, past and present. It was endlessly stimulating. I ran on adrenaline throughout the semester and pondered many things: Did I make the right connections between Engels and John Stuart Mill? Was I unfair to Susan B. Anthony? Did I present a fair introduction to Second Wave feminism?

Almost all the students underwent transformations during the 14-week semester. At the time, the Weathermen were bombing selected establishment targets, and in April, as our class was nearing completion, the accidental explosion of Weatherwoman Cathy Wilkerson's family home in Manhattan took place. Several Weathermen died.[62] As far as I know, "*The History and Social Role of Women*" did not propel any of the students to violent action in the name of taking state power. It did, however, engender life transforming changes. Some walked out angry and opposed; others with more confidence to continue exploration. Some became activists in the movement, and at least one went on to become a distinguished scholar in the field of women's studies.[63]

The class met Monday afternoons for two hours. We devised an innovative format: For the first several weeks, one of the three of us would lecture for about twenty minutes. Then the students would divide into small groups of ten to fifteen to discuss the lecture and the reading for that day. Susan, Judy and I would circulate among the groups, helping here and there. During the last ten minutes of the class one woman (selected by her group) would relate the workings and insights of the group to the whole class. However, we found we did not have enough time, so we tried having the class meet as a whole for the two hours, and on a rotating basis, one of the instructors prepared an informal lecture which students were encouraged to interrupt with questions. This was followed by a class discussion monitored by the instructor. The three of us always attended all classes. We each scheduled an extra hour, and the class was divided into three sections for an additional hour of small group interaction. There was never an objection. On the contrary, most of the students would have come to more than one additional hour.

The impact of "*The History and Social Role of Women in the US*" reverberated campus-wide and throughout the Pittsburgh area. It was one of the early deliberately interdisciplinary courses in women's studies. During the semester, the *Pittsburgh Press* (the region's major newspaper) ran a full-page report with pictures. I kept the clipping because I found the spontaneous, honest reactions of the interviewees (one man and the rest women) to the reporters' questions memorable. I did not want to forget the female student who took the course because her father "is the epitome of male chauvinism," or the tiny eighteen-year old woman with an angelic face who said she wanted to learn how to get revenge "when men treat me like a simple sex object." It was one of the male undergraduates who said he was interested in women as an "untapped source of political power because women's liberation is a growing part of the youth movement."[64] I knew this was just the beginning.

Meetings of the small sections had elements of consciousness-raising, so much part of the women's liberation movement at the time. We sat in a circle, most of the women sharing thoughts on the readings and the lecture and often adding their experiences of growing up female. Gradual awakening to the profound personal dimensions of feminism took place. Denial came first: "This does not apply to me; I am not really ever put down by men, although I do recognize that it happens to other women..." "My father treated me miserably, but now that I know he was wrong, I am fine..." "I know it is very hard for women to succeed professionally, but it's all up to me; if I really work hard, I am sure I can be an exception and make it on my own..." "I just like wearing make-up; it has nothing to do with being influenced by commercials and the media or with pleasing men. It is my own decision, I am old enough to think independently and know what I want." Then defenses would begin to crack; slowly, layers of socialization and unconscious strategies of self-preservation would start to melt away. Women talked in new ways about being vulnerable and frightened. Tense moments stalled narratives; on occasion there were tears.

The first stage of discovery usually took about three weeks. Then, as women attempted to explain their new awareness to boyfriends—and they reported that most of the boys made fun of them—the young women became irate. What to do with the fury? They had to invent strategies to manage that rage, and this is where the movement played a pivotal role. The students needed both new knowledge from the classroom and support from other women undergoing the same process. Our class became an introductory passage to both. Because I was the one faculty member involved in the undertaking, I opted to remain on the margins of the personal, confessional aspect of the small groups. I told the students and myself that because of our unequal status I felt I should not participate. The truth, however, was that I was terrified of being asked to talk about my personal situation, of exposing myself to potential hurt in front of everyone. My emotional vulnerability drove me to seek sanctuary in the dubious comfort of hierarchy—a recourse that I would use again during those early years of the women's movement.

I had been carefully educated to believe that one needed higher degrees in the specific discipline that one was hired to teach. The knowledge that other women across the country were also plunging into the burgeoning world of feminism in the classroom was somewhat reassuring, but I fluctuated between insecurity about what I was teaching, and zealous enthusiasm for the opportunity to teach it. I had no faculty model; women with PhDs and tenure track appointments did not leave the success route to merge activism and scholarship. The three of us, aware that we were a focus of attention throughout the university, were determined to make the experiment a success, and we worked well together. I had the heaviest responsibility as a university administrator. If the experiment were to fail, I would get the blame, not the two graduate students. But the possibility of failure did not occur to me. How could we fail?

The mere existence of the class provoked reactions around the campus. Many faculty were skeptical: did the course meet "true academic standards"? Were the instructors "qualified" to offer this course? Predictably, Pittsburgh feminists from every point on the political spectrum were delighted that such a course existed and asked for copies of the syllabus. Students started talking about requesting additional courses on women for the fall. From the spring of 1970 to this day, the University of Pittsburgh has never been without course offerings in women's studies. Susan and Judy continued to work with the burgeoning program and helped develop it into a full-blown women's studies program. As it turned out, I would not. I was to head west, to a new frontier in women's studies.

# CHAPTER 8

# THE SAN DIEGO STATE WOMEN'S STUDIES PROGRAM

Toward the end of May, Marlene Dixon called to tell me that the San Diego State women's liberation activists had won approval for the first autonomous ten-course women's studies program in the country—in the world! The women themselves would run the program! The one full-time faculty line, a Visiting Distinguished Professorship for a year, had been offered to her, but Marlene was in a struggle to keep her job at the University of Chicago and could not accept. She had suggested me to Carol Rowell, the undergraduate student who had led the process of getting the program approved. Carol called me and urged me to come to San Diego and meet the women.

Members of the New University Conference Women's caucus in southern California had been supporting the efforts of the activists at San Diego State, so in those pre-internet days, we in NUC had been among the first academics to learn of what, in the ensuing months, *Newsweek* would dub *"one of the newest wrinkles in higher education."*[65] In the late 1960s, when the pioneers of women's studies took their first teaching jobs, many were the sole female in any department, and there were very few women among the tenured faculty to serve as either role models or allies. The academic curriculum was determined by and for men; women's accomplishments in all fields—scientists, writers, artists, historians, politicians and activists—were ignored. The female experience had been erased.

Many of these pioneers came to the university as seasoned political organizers with experience in the civil rights and New Left movements, and their initial foray into academia coincided with the rise of the women's liberation movement. Despite the widespread resistance—often nasty but rarely successful— by almost all male academics on the grounds that courses about women were not "academically sound," by 1970 courses in women's studies proliferated across the country. Hundreds of colleges and universities offered courses on *"Women in America," "Women in American History," "Sociology of Literature: Women," "Contemporary American Women Writers," "The Sexual Order," "Women and the Novel," "The*

*Psychology of Women," "Current Issues in the Women's Liberation Movement."* Initially, courses in the humanities and social sciences predominated. "Girls" became "women," and a new academic discipline that would permanently alter higher education in America, and later around the world, was born.

The San Diego program had emerged from a small women's liberation rap group of students, young faculty and community women in fall 1969.[66] The rap group created a loosely organized committee coordinated by Carol Rowell of 6 to 8 students and untenured faculty members Jackie Wertz and Joyce Nower to explore creating a women's studies program at San Diego State. Over 600 students signed petitions indicating interest in taking courses in the program.

The women worked resolutely during the fall semester and most of spring 1970 to guide a formal proposal through the prescribed academic committees and channels. On May 22, 1970, the Faculty Senate approved the first integrated ten-course women's studies program in the country for the following fall term. It began with five courses, mostly already existing liberal arts courses (e.g. literature, psychology) with content changed to emphasize the role, status, identity and potential of women. The instructors were already employed by the college in other departments, or, in at least one case, taught without remuneration. All of these courses had full enrollment. For the first time, women would control an entire program within a major university, and have direct access to institutional power.

Three days after my conversation with Carol, I was on a plane to San Diego to meet the students and faculty who were on the verge of starting this historic enterprise.

From the moment I spoke with Marlene Dixon about the possibility of going to San Diego State, I had started keeping a diary because I knew I was on the cusp of a transformative moment. One of my first entries addressed the issue of clothes:

*May 1970. What should I wear to San Diego? Not sure how to present myself — socially committed academic? Intellectual activist? Some outfit that signifies a smooth merging of the two is what I need.*

*Maybe navy slacks and a white blouse are a safe bet for the plane trip. It'll be much warmer in southern California, so I can wear sandals. I wonder if I can use eyeliner. Better not. But what do I do when I meet male faculty members and administrators? I suppose I could duck into the ladies room to put eyeliner on as well as a touch of eye shadow before I meet the* dean. We'll see. I'll take the three-piece beige suit (the slacks and the skirt) and a beige blouse just in case. Black pumps and stockings too. I want to look serious, but I don't want to alienate movement women.

Now, as I re-read my wardrobe dilemma, it seems as if I were playing a role in a situation comedy. But for me, and I imagine for other women at that time, the issue of dressing for specific occasions was serious business. In 1970 not many women were prominent in the professions, and I found no models in academia for how a female assistant professor, assistant dean and radical activist should dress. Between 1968 and 1970, I had moved from being married, financially secure and a member of the Spanish upper middle class (with its clear, non-negotiable standards for suitable female attire) to being a single, independent woman on a university campus in the United States at a moment of tumultuous social and personal revolt. My understanding of who I was and what I wanted to do was constantly evolving and my clothing choices made public statements about the changes taking place in my life and professional goals.

For my 1968 fall début as a professional intellectual, I had worn one of the two tailored three piece woolen suits (jacket, skirt, slacks) my mother-in-law's seamstress had made for me in Madrid — at the then considerable cost of $30 each. It would have to be the skirt and jacket, not the pants. If I wore a skirt with a hemline that just covered the knee, there was a better chance that the men would take me seriously, but I wasn't sure. Would tailored suits be "female" enough? It would not do for any of my Latin male colleagues to think my attire was not appropriately "feminine." A recent Harvard PhD starting up the ladder of academic success had a certain image to maintain. I just wasn't sure what it was. So I experimented. On an occasional intrepid morning, I would abandon the suits, don a moderately discreet mini skirt and set out to brave the sexist comments of my colleagues: *"¡Qué guapa! ¡ Qué lindo tener una mujer bonita en el departamento!"* [How cute you look! It is so nice to have a pretty woman in the department.] I smiled sweetly and thought *"Qué gilipollas son."* [What assholes they are.]

As Assistant dean and activist in the women's liberation movement on campus, I developed what I now consider to be a thoroughly schizophrenic wardrobe. One day I would wear a slim little sleeveless, scooped neck red jersey minidress with horizontal white and blue pinstripes, several inches above the knee (the fashion in 1969). I also had a navy version of the same dress. These dresses proclaimed rebellion and independence. Why should I conform to stodgy academic standards for how women should dress? Did frumpiness insure intellectual excellence? Wasn't I forging new ground? However, the next day I would wear one of my two suits: either the hunter green wool with small black checks or the beige with a thin rust pinstripe. The suits came out of the closet when I needed to reassure myself that I was a serious professional, not just a "radical." I wore black low-heeled pumps because someone had told me black "went with everything." Once in a while I exchanged the sedate pumps for skintight white leather boots that almost reached the knee; the boots usually went with the mini-skirts. If the dean suddenly announced a meeting with the provost on one of my mini skirt days, I would rush home and change clothes.

I always wore make-up: foundation, rouge, eyebrow pencil, eyeliner and lipstick. My personal vanity, a product of years of unconscious socialization, was more powerful than movement peer pressure to resist ideals of female beauty that I knew perfectly well were created by men and fomented by the beauty industry to please males and extract money from females. I had two hair options: loose, down to my shoulders (to accompany mini skirts) or folded up into a chignon for the suited look.

When I arrived in San Diego for the interview, Carol Rowell, already a skilled organizer, hosted my visit together with Joyce Nower, a faculty member in the English Department, and Jackie Wertz, a young instructor from the psychology faculty. As they drove me around the campus, the sun was setting and the weather was warm and welcoming. Palm trees and pastels dotted the landscape, so different from the gritty industrial environment of Pittsburgh. The smell of orange blossoms, honeysuckle and jasmine permeated the air — a gentle California afternoon of enticing sensuality. The environment was captivating.

Carol gave me copies of the proposed structure of the women's studies program and the Proposal for a Center for Women's Studies and Services. The program was meant to be upper division electives offered within the College of Arts and Letters and directly responsible to the dean and Committees of the College of Arts and Letters. A Faculty Advisory Committee composed of tenured faculty from existing departments would serve for administrative purposes as the senior faculty of the women's studies program, and make recommendations to the College of Arts and Letters concerning recruitment, retention, promotion and tenure decisions for that program.[67]

That Faculty Advisory Committee set off warning bells. After my year in the University of Pittsburgh administration, I knew that committees like that could have enormous power over a new program that had no tenured faculty of its own. I asked who had the power to name the members of the advisory committee. The dean had accepted the women's suggestions that it be comprised of two tenured women and one male, faculty, who, they assured me had supported them all year and understood how important self-determination and control of the program was for them. So the Women's Studies Committee viewed the dean and the advisory committee as rubber stamps for their program. Self-determination and autonomy were paramount. The issue of power—who had the authority to make crucial decisions—would be a defining feature of the first year of the program.

The proposed Center for Women's Studies and Services was meant to be an umbrella organization with seven components. In addition to the women's studies program, which already existed, future modules would include a storefront in the community to provide information and services such as birth control information, abortion counseling, library facilities; a publications center; a research center; a recruitment and tutorial center; a client-controlled, non-profit day-care center staffed by both males and females; and a cultural center to provide the facilities for the artistic expression of women's oppression and liberation.[68] All seven components would be responsible to an overall Center Coordinating Committee chaired by the Coordinator for the Center, who would also be responsible for fund raising.[69] The women's studies program was actually the only part of the plan in existence; the other six were future projections for which a coordinator would seek funding.

The ambitious vision coincided in many ways with my belief that progressive educators should use the resources of universities to make fundamental change in the educational system in the United States, and work with other sectors of the society, such as trade unions and progressive minority organizations, to change the centers of power in our country. Establishing women's studies could be a vehicle for change, not the end in itself.

The next day I met some of the students who had been involved in creating the program. They were all from California. Carla Kirkwood told me that many of the women had been very active in the Students for a Democratic Society student strike on campus in spring 1970, when they had "boycotted classes and organized community and campus teach-ins. Sherry Smith, Cynthia Burdyshaw, Elaine Askari, Elaine Budzinski, Pam Cole, Judy Fry and myself (all the San Diego townies) had been organizers of the events on campus. Many of us had fathers and brothers in the military and family members working in the local shipyards and factories in town. Our politics developed 'at home' so to speak, and we all remained connected to these friends and families. We stayed home to go to school. It was an interesting political canvas for those of us from here. When we talked about community it was a material reality that we were in touch with everyday. And to have these ideas that we held placed all of us in a pretty unusual political situation." [70]

These young women had more political experience than most of the students in Pittsburgh and were generally less affluent. They understood women's subordination in a coherent and systematic way that integrated class and race; they were anti-imperialists. The biggest difference, however, was that the San Diego students had struggled for over a year to win approval for an entire program from an initially hostile administration. When I met them, they had taken ownership of the program; they had fought for it and it was theirs. At the University of Pittsburgh, starting women's studies was not a grassroots effort, it was a top down effort. The dean had approved and funded a request to offer a women's studies course that came from the assistant dean and two graduate students.

My wardrobe choice for San Diego had apparently worked. After the three-day visit, I received the official job offer from the dean for a one-year contract as a Visiting Distinguished Associate Professor of Women's Studies, a full-time appointment with all benefits. Dean Warren Carrier had agreed I would teach three courses a semester (instead of the usual four) and play a leading role in building the program. He said he was impressed by my academic credentials and looked forward to working with me.

The success of the program was contingent on one fundamental question: can women run their own independent program within an institutional setting? I was not sure, but I was willing to take the gamble.

I did not want to continue as assistant dean at the University of Pittsburgh. Being an administrator hindered my relationships with students—and with activists in the women's movement, which was my primary interest. Since arriving at Pittsburgh, I had played the role of the "charming exception" to the traditional mold of the young, promising Ivy League scholar in my academic and public life. On campus I was considered unique—a newly independent female intellectual striking out on her own and involved in groundbreaking work as a feminist scholar-activist. Aware of the contentious nature of my politics and vision, I worked hard to get along with just about everyone, in spite of gender and political differences. For a while I enjoyed all the attention. Then I began to feel lonely. I sensed a quality of insincerity, of play-acting in many of my interactions with colleagues. I knew that as soon as I stopped smiling, flirting a little, and playing all those games designated by our society as "inherently female," my daily life would become a real hassle. In other words, the judgment by my male colleagues of my worth as an academic professional was heavily contingent on my being suitably feminine. Being a token in an academic establishment that represented the interests of those who created and maintained a male supremacist society was exhausting and debilitating. It was not a situation unique to the University of Pittsburgh; it was the traditional academic assumptions of the US system of higher education that I was rejecting.

I had spent several years learning that a token woman can do little by herself. Often she is used as a vehicle by her employers to parade their own social consciousness, and as a consequence, is resented by those very groups she seeks to help. If I had stopped to think about it in a way I was not capable of doing in 1969, I would have realized I really did not even like, let alone admire, most of the men, particularly those in the Hispanic department. They had found their academic niches, and there they would remain for the rest of their professional lives. The isolated life of a scholar did not satisfy me.

I went about arranging my exit from Pittsburgh professionally. I asked the Chair of Hispanic Literature and Languages for an unpaid leave of absence for a year. Rudi Cardona cautioned me that it could hurt my chances for tenure and reminded me that I had a very good career ahead as a Hispanist. Jerry Schneewind, the Dean of Arts and Sciences, warned, "If you leave, I can't promise to hold the assistant dean position for you."

It never occurred to me to take their advice. I wanted to implement a vision. Curiously enough, I also received two other job offers at the same time. One was to become associate provost to study and advance the status of women at Wesleyan University, a major institutional statement, carrying a generous salary. The second offer was for a tenured position at the College of Old Westbury, a new experimental branch of the State University of New York, where New University Conference colleagues were involved in its creation and had accepted jobs. Before I left for San Diego, I signed a contract to be Associate Professor of Humanities at Old Westbury, with the stipulation that they would wait a year for me to arrive.

Before leaving Pittsburgh to drive to San Diego, I attended the third annual New University Conference convention at the University of Michigan at Ann Arbor. Following the convention, the national office (Rich Rothstein was in charge) arranged a retreat in Marlboro, Vermont for about 30 of us to learn how to become more effective movement organizers. My salient memory of the Marlboro retreat is the epidemic of crabs (pelvic lice) that infected most of us. Sex and drugs took precedence over the carefully planned curriculum. When, to write this in 2013, I re-read the NUC newsletters covering the retreat, I recall that it took place, but I cannot conjure up a coherent picture of what transpired during those days—and nights. All I remember is a musical chairs of sexual partners and everything enveloped in clouds of marijuana. It was pleasant but meaningless.

Defining myself a "socialist feminist" and finding new friends in the New University Conference, female and male, who shared my convictions, did not carry as a corollary an automatic guide how to deal with sexual relations as a single woman. I had just come out of a monogamous marriage (on my part, at least) and I had no idea how declaring myself a socialist feminist would affect my daily life. I knew I never wanted to marry again, and I knew I was heterosexual. And that is about as far as I got. I did not allow myself to delve deeper. After my father's death, my mother and my husband—the two people in my life who said they loved me—had hurt me and I was afraid to let down my guard again. Emotional intimacy scared me. I linked it with pain. For me, to love meant, sooner or later, I would be hurt. But sex was fun, so I did what most everyone else was doing in the New University Conference and other New Left organizations: promiscuity with no commitments was the order of the day. Supposedly it was "liberating" for women and men. But it was not for me and I knew it then. First of all, I craved the warmth and tenderness that emotional intimacy brings—I enjoyed the warm "cuddly" part of sex but that was rarely included in the spontaneous, and certainly not secret, coupling that characterized life on the New Left. If, on occasion, a temporary partner attempted to get close to me, I backed off completely. I remember that one very nice man called me "warm but distant". "As soon as I ask you about yourself," he said, "you back away." He was right, but I didn't care.

The paradox of the part of the "sexual revolution" I participated in was that I never found the sex satisfying. The New University Conference did not delve into the practice of sex, but we had good politics: Sexual politics in the organization centered on sexism and the women's caucus' attempt to eradicate it. Buttressed by the strong women's liberation movement, we had enough power of unity to force a change of behavior among the men, in some cases permanent and life changing.

Jackie Wertz's letter from San Diego arrived just as I was leaving to drive to California.[71] Widespread growing resentment against Carol Rowell's "self-appointed, dictatorial leadership" of the program was leading to an open revolt. Would I arrive in time for an emergency meeting in 4 days? I did. I arrived in San Diego and rushed to the meeting of the Women's Studies Committee and other interested students. I entered a bit late. The gathering was held in a large beige stucco classroom, filled to the brim by more than 50 young women. Most were dressed in shorts and t-shirts, sandals or flip-flops. No jewelry, no make-up. I was greeted by a blast of angry voices. Everyone was screaming at two women crammed together in a corner:

> *"Who gave you the authority to be coordinator?"*
> *"You don't represent the women's movement!"*
> *"We haven't approved the program structure!"*
> *"You don't represent Real Women!"*
> *"You have sold out to the establishment!"*

It was even hard to distinguish individual faces. The heavily charged atmosphere functioned like a fog. What next? Physical violence? I remained standing—frozen and mute.

Then slowly, like an old-fashioned camera moving into focus, the faces of Carol Rowell and Joyce Nower, the women who had interviewed me in May, became recognizable, with hordes of women yelling at them.

I was no stranger to heated, impassioned political debate. But this was different. The fury was raw; it represented more than an argument about political differences. This was personal; a verbal exchange infused with individual anger and pain and fraught with danger. The situation was analogous to walking a tightrope over a field strewn with land mines.

Over the summer and unbeknownst to just about everyone else on the Women's Studies Committee beyond Carol Rowell and Joyce Nower, the San Diego State College Foundation[72] had granted $12,000 to the new women's studies program and hired Carol for one year. She had convinced the administration that the women backed her as their leader. With the dean's support, she was to receive $6,000 of the grant to coordinate the Center for Women's Studies and Services and to raise funds to bring the other six components into existence.[73] Carol saw this as seed money. The rest of the women's studies supporters felt it was "tainted money." The fury of the women at the emergency meeting was due to Carol's initial announcement of the foundation grant and her new appointment as a done deal.

The first year, the program was supported by "soft money," temporary funds allocated by the largesse of Warren Carrier, the Dean of the College of Arts and Sciences. However, we needed secure financial support, and the provenance of funding became a critical issue. The dean wanted me to play a leading role in the search for outside funding so he could get administrative credit for building the program and not take money from his permanent budget. Carol Rowell wanted me to take the administrative lead for her agenda, seeking outside foundation money and supporting her as coordinator of the Center. She was one of the few to favor seeking corporate funding at a time when campus activists were extremely wary of corporate influence on universities.

Typical of the moment, the rank and file were deeply distrustful of all power, whether from the dean, Carol or myself. I knew that I could not meet the demands of Carol and the dean and retain credibility and the trust of almost everyone else. Attempting to meet the ever-changing demands of a constantly evolving constituency who so deeply distrusted power and any form of accountability was exasperating, at times infuriating. I constantly felt events were swirling around me, out of control.

Because almost all of the student activists and involved faculty believed that taking corporate money of any kind was illegitimate, Barbara Kessel and I crafted a proposal for a new governance structure that would make the program free-standing, responsible to a Women's Studies Board consisting of the faculty and staff of the program, the Faculty Advisory Committee, and ten student representatives elected by the women students in the women's studies classes. After wide distribution to all interested women and protracted discussion in our classes, the proposal was accepted by majority vote of the Women's Studies Committee. A general election was held from the women's studies' classes and ten student representatives were elected to serve as board members. The informally constituted Women's Studies Committee was now defunct and the democratically elected Women's Studies Board came into being. This was in mid-October.

Carol continued to function as Coordinator of the Center, a job defined primarily as that of fundraiser. She was being paid with San Diego State Foundation money on a contract that ran until August 1971. The board maintained that the foundation's $12,000 grant had been given to the women's studies program and not to Carol. The conflict over who should have the power to spend that money and determine the course of the academically approved women's studies program, hinged on whether or not Carol would agree to renounce key elements of the power she had delegated to herself and be accountable to the Women's Studies Board. She refused.

The board met and overwhelmingly voted that if Carol would not report to the board, we would find a coordinator who would. Since we were convinced that the grant had been given to the program, the board was, therefore, in control of the coordinator's salary.

I started worrying about the legal aspects of what we were doing, so the board voted to send a delegation to talk to the administration. In accord with our collective mode of operating, four of us were elected to attend the meeting (Barbara, myself, and two students). Apart from the most intimate needs of our private lives, we never did anything alone. We refused to break the ranks of solidarity or to give authority to a sole representative, however duly elected, and allow the administration to meet with us one by one.

We asked the administrators to back our firing of Carol if she would not be responsible to the board. Dean Carrier and Ernest O'Byrne, Vice-President of the San Diego State College Foundation, refused: "Can't you just settle the difficulties between you and get on with the program building?"

Then O'Byrne condescendingly suggested, "Carol will represent the (yet to be created) center on your board and you can send someone to sit on the board of her center." We declined.

It was clear that the real reason the dean and the foundation vice-president were so ardently attached to Carol's leadership and her role as liaison with the San Diego Foundation, the Women's Studies Board and the proposed seven-component center, was that this arrangement (combination of academic base with community outreach) was necessary for competing for big time money from the Ford Foundation. Without the academic component, Ford was not interested because, as its 1968 Annual Report, exposed by *Ramparts* magazine, had made clear, issues of women's self-determination and democratic governing structures were irrelevant. The Foundation's main goal was to address student unrest across the nation:

"...There are three groups of students, those who will not stop agitating until the Vietnam War is ended and must be dealt with as security problems (Ford is the main provider of university police training and criminology justice problems), those who demand reform but are impatient for perfection: responsive universities can hope to reduce this group, but not to zero. They [the universities] should assume that a vigilant and reproachful remnant will survive every actual reform, to inveigh against the renewal of complacency which its adoption has induced and to contrast its superficiality with what must still be done. Finally there are those students who are not too visionary to be met halfway, the majority hopefully, and the ones that the university can deal with through educational reforms."[74]

We were not "crazy radicals" in San Diego in 1970. The Ford Foundation, like the Rockefeller and Carnegie Foundations, was largely funded by tax write-offs by the major US based multinational corporations such as Standard Oil. It had a big stake in maintaining the status quo of the American educational system. At that time, this meant the corporate power sought to drive a wedge between student rebellion within the university and external support for that rebellion from the society at large. This was the wedge many of us were fighting to prevent.

I agreed that we had to maintain our financial independence from the US corporate system. This meant that either Carol reported to the board (and not to the foundation) and we controlled how the foundation money was spent and choose if and when to refuse it, or we make a definitive break with Carol. We were headed to a showdown.

Fearful that a seemingly unavoidable internal conflict would tear the program apart permanently, I was miserable and felt powerless to resolve the situation. I recalled my first tumultuous meeting with the Women's Studies Committee in September when I had just arrived. What had we accomplished in these two months? Were we going to self-destruct? How can I help with this mess? I wasn't feeling very confident and my head hurt from too much coffee and too many cigarettes.

I had started smoking Marlboros in April 1969, during the final stages of disintegration of my marriage, and I used to classify problems by how many packs of cigarettes it took to come up with a solution. Generating the idea for a Women's Studies Board was a one-packer: not too difficult. Getting the proposal approved by all the women was a two-packer: challenging but doable. Attempting to resolve the power/money struggles between the center and the program probably did irreparable harm to my lungs.

The Women's Studies Board voted to disassociate the women's studies program from Carol's center in December. The dean lost all patience with what he saw as petty female quarrels and, in a show of power, reorganized the Faculty Advisory Committee without consulting us.[75] He appointed two additional tenured men: Richard Wright, associate professor of geography and Richard Ruetten, professor of history, who joined Clint Jencks (economics), Hilda Nelson (French) and Shelly Chandler (sociology) to create a five-person committee

A male majority in charge of the first women's studies program in the country! Utterly unacceptable. The dean said there were no more tenured female faculty qualified for board membership, and he threatened to fire me (and Barbara and Jackie) if we didn't "shape up." I seethed at his "macho strutting."

And so did the women in the program, who sent out a mimeographed missive "To our sisters around the country." The letter opened melodramatically: "The self-determination of the first Women's Studies Program in the nation is in dire jeopardy... Dean Warren Carrier... appointed two men faculty to the then existing three- member Women Studies Program tenure board... and spelled out the powers granted them by the Faculty Senate to shape the program, should they so desire."[76]

The student newspaper, *Daily Aztec*, ran front-page stories about the conflict for several weeks. Our struggle received national and international coverage: I gave a phone interview to the *New York Herald Tribune International* and the *Los Angeles Times* sent down a reporter to interview me. *The Gainesville Sun* (Gainesville, Florida) ran an article titled, *"Women's Studies Program Hang-Up: Who'll run it?"*

Authorized by a board decision, I invited the newly empowered five-member Faculty Advisory Committee to attend one of our meetings. I urged the board members not to confront or accuse the two new male advisory committee members, but to try to convince them to trust us and our ability to make this new venture a success. We were all on our best behavior as the meeting began. All of us were professional and charming throughout the 90-minute meeting. Perhaps not unexpectedly, the new faculty members shrewdly recognized the situation and agreed that the Women's Studies Board should run their own program, and that they would stay in the background.

But the financial issues remained unresolved. Distrust of Carol had been confirmed, but we had not won the battle for financial independence.

"We believed in a sort of idealism," Carla Kirkwood recalled. "We saw the university as an organizing force. It had been a cultural center for organizing against the war, and for civil rights, so we thought the university would be the same as a bastion of resistance against corporations and imperialism. Radical activity seemed to belong in the university. We believed that we could do what we believed in. After all, we came directly from anti-war organizing in the university. With the idealism that I had about a liberation movement being in a university, why wouldn't it be logical to see the university as a haven to develop socialist feminism? We saw women's studies as a component of this larger picture, but we were suspicious of the foundation from the beginning. That was a red flag for a lot of us."[77]

Although the struggle for control of the program subsided after the first semester, discord surfaced throughout the second semester. Three issues played out simultaneously. The growth of sectarianism characteristic of the political climate on the Left in 1970, and the struggle against corporate influence on higher education—were shaped by a third issue, how we treated each other. Factionalism among women involved in the women's liberation movement and the women's studies program swallowed up any effective response to the economic or political issues our ideology had raised. I was naïve in expecting that we could effectively respond to these issues within an educational institution and with the growing internal personal issues that we faced.

The conflicts that riddled our program reflected much of the women's liberation movement in the 1970s. The basic tenet was female unity. Global sisterhood, commitment to an egalitarian ethic, to collective forms of action and organization by all women were to be tools to combat the injustices of patriarchal society. Sisterhood was also equally committed to self-exploration and the forging of individual self-identities that liberated us from socially conditioned oppression and restriction. But agreement on how to redefine oneself was never easy, and often it was not sisterly.

"You people are also telling me who I am; I don't want to be what you have defined," Kirkwood recalls saying to Carol and Joyce. "They were all about psychological liberty," she told me. "It pissed a lot of us off; even though I was going through my own problems—I had been abused as a child—we didn't care that 'women are psychologically oppressed' as we built the program. We wanted to focus on race and class."[78]

Clashes arose, inevitably, between a commitment to absolute equality (no one woman should lead or direct another woman) and the anger of women who, having been accustomed to being at the bottom of society's hierarchy, suddenly glimpsed an opportunity to challenge oppressive social conventions and aspire to more fulfilling lives if only other women did not restrain them in pursuit of a transcendent sisterhood. Does sisterhood, they asked, mean you can insist that I thwart my development? When, for example, the press sought interviews about the new program, they requested to speak with the "Visiting Distinguished Professor." After *The Los Angeles Times, The London Times,* and *The Chronicle of Higher Education* published good, lengthy articles on the program and took pictures of me, the board voted that I should not be allowed to speak to reporters anymore. I was monopolizing the spotlight and other board members deserved a chance. I acceded to the majority vote. It irritated me, but it was part of the challenge of dealing with the raw human emotions and new kind of female personal development that sprang from the movement's pursuit of women's liberation.

Although I had valuable administrative experience to contribute, I had some shortcomings. I understand now that all of us felt and acted like we had for the first time been "unleashed," and freed to grow and explore in ways that had been previously closed to us in both public and private spheres. I was more certain of what I was against than what I was for. I was a young woman who, in certain circumstances, attempted to make up for her ignorance with militancy. To lead and inspire I would make statements that rang of "absolute truth." If someone had asked me to justify certain declarations historically or even rationally, I might have stumbled a bit. But we were on the march, and didn't want to dally.

There was an intense, frantic quality about our daily lives, an urge to redefine ourselves as quickly as possible so as to be positioned to grasp the ring when it came around. Often, too often, we defined ourselves by whom we rejected: "She is only a reformer"; "She is a crazy ideologue"; "She is too male-oriented"; "She is a careerist;" "She is too political and doesn't primarily care about women." "She is a power hungry manipulator"; "She only cares about women and doesn't see the larger political picture"; "She is too much of an intellectual." There were many labels. Manichean dualisms provided easy ways to self-identify. Condemning the other by negative name-calling was a mechanism used to affirm and justify one's own position and being. "Ideologue", "careerist" and "intellectual" were the labels most often pinned on me. I am sure I dished them out too, but I have conveniently forgotten. What I vividly remember is that soon after I arrived in San Diego I began to feel like a piece of glass inside a turning kaleidoscope — confined within well defined parameters and bumping around with no direction and no way out.

Sectarianism on the Left was reaching a high point, and the women's movement in San Diego was caught squarely up in it. This occurred at the very juncture at which we were most optimistic about uniting socialism and feminism. A few of the movement's women (often with their male partners) belonged to the Young Socialist Alliance, the youth movement of the Socialist Workers' Party, a Trotskyist organization. Others were involved in the Revolutionary Union.[79] Some women were scornful of the male-dominated left and wanted to work exclusively with and for women. Dean Carrier's condescension was insulting, but that of the male-run Left was even worse because it was ubiquitous and they were our "comrades." A lesbian movement did not exist yet. Other women had never joined any organization but were participants in Vietnam War protests. For many women, the women's liberation movement was their first foray into any kind of politics. Almost everyone subscribed to the reigning New Left distrust of the "establishment" and of any person or activity that could be considered "elitist." As I would find out years later when I read my FBI file, another divisive issue — suspicion and presence of FBI informants — also reared its ugly head in San Diego.[80]

Although internal disputes cast a pall over the first year of the program, we took important steps toward realizing women's studies as an activist/academic project. Teaching was our biggest success. No wrangling over the curriculum took place in San Diego, unlike the process of designing the curriculum in many subsequent women's studies programs. The curriculum was the one major issue we all agreed on! That was fortuitous since teaching was what we were all about.

The lack of conflict over course offerings was due, in large part, to the successful program faculty members had offered in the spring of 1970, before the full program was approved. Psychologist Jackie Wertz taught "Self-actualization of Women," and delved into theories of human behavior as they are applied to women and the development of women's self-concept in American society. From the English Department, Joyce Nower taught "Women in Literature," images, roles and identities of women found in literature and their sociological and political implications. Lois Kessler, a specialist in health education, taught one of the first courses on "Human Sexuality". Her course examined the biological criteria in sex role determination and the relationship of sexual mores to a person's self-concept of sexuality. Two additional courses were, "Women and Education," the educational process and female role socialization, and the "Socialization Process of Women," the effects of formal and informal social, economic and political institutions upon role socialization from infancy to old age.

These courses were the nucleus of the program. Before presenting the program proposal to the Faculty Senate, the Women's Studies Committee added five new courses to be offered in the future: "Women in Comparative Cultures," "Contemporary Issues in the Liberation of Women," "Women in History," and "Status of Women under Various Economic Systems." The tenth course was "Field Experience," which required the consent of the coordinator of women's studies (then understood to be Carol Rowell, also the class instructor). It was a course in fundraising described as exploration and analysis of policy and planning practices of public and private agencies in San Diego as they relate to women.

During my interview at San Diego, Carol Rowell had showed me the list of course offerings and asked if I would be willing to teach "Contemporary Issues in the Liberation of Women" and "Women in History." I said sure. Later on in the summer, Barbara Kessel agreed to teach "Women in Education." And that is how the curriculum was created and staffed for the first women's studies program.

I loved the teaching. My required texts for the fall semester of "Current Issues in the Women's Liberation Movement" were four publications that had not been available for my class in Pittsburgh: Kate Millett's *Sexual Politics; Notes from the Second Year: Women's Liberation* (which included Pat Mainardi's *"Politics of Housework"* and articles on abortion and abortion law ) and the May 1970 issue of *Leviathan* magazine with articles on Cuban Women, Toni Cade's *Double Jeopardy: to be Black and Female,* short studies on Chicana and Chinese women and daycare. The fourth text was Robin Morgan's anthology, *Sisterhood is Powerful.* Although I had a copy of the book, it was so new Vintage Books couldn't get it to our bookstore until November, so my students read xerox copies of *The Politics of Orgasm*, by Susan Lydon and Notes of a *Radical Lesbian*, by Martha Shelly.

I gave two sections of "Current Issues." The class practically taught itself: as soon as I entered the room, I was bombarded with questions based on the readings for the day. That was how we began. Then I filled in the gaps and posed questions for deeper probing. I was so excited that I was running on pure adrenalin. Once in a while I had to smoke a cigarette during class—nobody cared; this was 1970 and sins of the lesser order were still permitted. In the spring semester, I modified the syllabus: in addition to Robin Morgan's anthology, we read Toni Cade's, *The Black Woman*, Celestine Ware's *Woman Power*, Evelyn Reed's *Problems of Women's Liberation*, and Shulamith Firestone's *The Dialectic of Sex: Case for a Feminist Revolution*. Firestone argued for freedom from the "tyranny of [women's] reproductive biology." Pregnancy should be eliminated and reproduction relegated to the test tube. Childbearing and child rearing ought to be shared by the whole society and women and children must have the freedom to do whatever they wish sexually. Many of the students (and the instructor) were impressed by the brilliance of Firestone's arguments. The classes devoted to her theories were intense, intelligent, and impassioned—one of the highlights of my year in San Diego.

I am not a historian by training, so I learned a great deal preparing for my course on *Women in History*. In fact, I was usually just a couple of classes ahead of the students. We started by reading English Marxist E. H. Carr's *What is History* and discussed the need for this course. Thankfully, Allison Kraditor (*Up From the Pedestal*) and Eleanor Flexner (*Century of Struggle*) had already published their books. I also used excerpts from William O'Neill's *Everyone Was Brave: The Rise and Fall of Feminism in America* and articles by Gerda Lerner and Anne Scott. The students were enthusiastic about the class and that helped mitigate my occasional flare-ups of intellectual insecurity. "Women in History' was definitely a student-teacher learning experience.

In addition to the teaching, there were other positive accomplishments. We convinced the university's main library to start buying books for women's studies; we protested the jailing of Cesar Chavez and supported *Huelga*, the farmworkers' strike in California. We attended anti-Vietnam War protests carrying placards announcing "Women's Studies against the War." We supported progressive activities on campus and in the community, participating in programs to win abortion rights, help welfare mothers, and women in prison, and we helped form a committee on campus to explore discrimination against women.

We also started a newsletter, *The Second Revolution*, which, in addition to publishing the minutes from all our board meetings, acted as a clearing-house for program and community activities, information on abortion, women's health, women's history, legislation, new publications, and national developments in the women's liberation movement. A collective of six student members of the board and six other female students who were "staff-in-training" wrote, edited and produced *The Second Revolution*. They had complete editorial control. This experience empowered many of the young women in charting their future lives.

The San Diego State Women's Studies Program did not receive Ford Foundation money in 1970-71. Carol, together with Joyce Nower and Rhetta Alexander, accepted the foundation money for their center and were given an office on campus for a year and a half, with no connection to the women's studies program. In 1972, the Center severed ties with the San Diego State Foundation and moved to downtown San Diego,[81] where it no longer had any ties to the college. Carol remained director of the community-based center for 23 years and succeeded in creating many of the proposed components.

During the academic year, nine of the program's ten courses were offered, all with full enrollment and excellent student evaluations. (We couldn't find anyone to teach "Status of Women under Various Economic Systems.")

When I left San Diego, my greatest achievement was to have been part of the group that established a viable curriculum and demonstrated that the study of women could be a doable academic pursuit. For over 40 years San Diego State University has continuously offered a women's studies program. The program has undergone structural changes as well as considerable expansion. Currently it offers a B.A and a Masters degree in Women's Studies.

The fact that 'revolution was in the air' in 1970 had both helped and hindered us. It empowered us to push for change, but it also imparted a false sense of unlimited possibilities. It tested whether the radical approach could be established within an existing institution. And the answer, as Ellen Messer-Davidow would subsequently point out, is no: *"Feminists could not reconcile the academy's objective of producing and inculcating scholarly knowledge with the movement's objective of making social change."*[82]

What we started in 1970 became, in the ensuing decades, a vast academic-feminist knowledge enterprise—an extraordinary academic discipline, to be sure, but a project quite different from my original vision: in the foreseeable future, women's studies was not going to be part of the academic branch of a new US socialist party.

I was not prepared for the personal price of bringing into practice not only a radically new academic discipline, but also new relations between women and men and among women. Foreign relations, human relations and the very definition of higher education were in turmoil across the country. In San Diego our fierce commitment to remaking ourselves, the system of education and ultimately the country, was exhausting and rife with conflict and tension. In hindsight, I recognize this was to be expected; we were visionaries and had set ourselves a utopian agenda. The pressure to implement it was all consuming. The burn out rate of the pioneers in the early days was high. Some came back, others did not.

I left San Diego State frustrated with the lack of structure and clear strategy in our nascent women's studies program and in our outreach to the community. The broader feminist goals that had once seemed so obvious were far more difficult to enact than I, or others, had anticipated.

# CHAPTER 9

# JOURNEY INTO COMMUNISM: THE PUERTO RICAN SOCIALIST PARTY

Somewhat discouraged, I left San Diego in August 1971 and drove to New York in my new green Datsun, acquired for the princely sum of $1200. With a tenured position at the College of Old Westbury, I would begin the fall semester as part of a collective teaching "Introduction to Women's Studies" with Rosalyn Baxandall, Barbara Ehrenreich, Deirdre English and Florence Howe. In addition, I was to create and teach a new course, "Women in the Caribbean."

John Maguire, the new president of the college, was dedicated to establishing social justice on campus, so, with his support, the core faculty, all hired the first year, committed to having a faculty and student body that was 30% White, 30% Black, 30% Latin and 10% Other. Gender parity on the faculty was also a goal, an anomaly in the academic world.

Teaching those two courses did not satisfy my drive to create a more just world as quickly as possible. After the fall semester, our collective broke into three separate teaching teams: Ros and I taught the history and politics of the women's movement, Barbara and Deirdre worked on health and other aspects of the social sciences, and Florence Howe took charge of women in literature. Florence was most interested in institutionalizing women's studies, which she would successfully do, but after my year in San Diego, this was not my priority.

I'd rented a one bedroom apartment in lower Manhattan around the corner from the Bowery at 65 Second Ave, corner of 4th Street, for $190 a month, heat included. This was a decade before the yuppification of this part of New York began.

Each morning I stepped around the friendly alcoholics who had spent the night outside my door and then moved to toss away the parking ticket on the windshield of my Datsun. It would be years before Albany would catch up with me, I reasoned, and by that time I most likely would be living somewhere else. At any rate, the "State" was suspect. Why obey a silly parking rule when it was such an obstacle to my political activities—and comfort? I needed to park in front of my house, just as I had in San Diego. There was serious work to be done and it was ridiculous to waste time looking for a legal spot.

So I taught my classes several days a week, fulfilled my obligations, but I was stepping back from building women's studies and my intense immersion in the women's movement. I believed that consciousness-raising often left people with no place to go, and lack of structure left them with no way of moving on, even if personally empowered by the women's liberation movement. As I had when I came back from Madrid in 1968, I felt rootless and lonely. Where was I heading? I had lots of friends and comrades, but no satisfying love relationship. The New University Conference was running out of money and disintegrating. I was dissatisfied with the anti-authoritarian and fiercely egalitarian spirit that defined the New Left, particularly the women's movement. I needed a new political home and like many of my peers, I looked again to Cuba and revolution in the third world as a focus for my political attention.

Couldn't my staunch feminist anti-imperialist convictions function in Spanish and on other stages? Was an organizational link to the third world and the building of socialism possible? While I respected the work the New York women's movement was doing, it did not provide the community or the international focus I needed. In addition, although I trusted most women more than most men, I liked working with and relating to men, politically and personally.

Sandy Levinson, whom I had briefly encountered in Cuba in 1969, was starting a Center for Cuban Studies in Greenwich Village. The Cuban government was pleased to have a resource center and library supportive of Fidel Castro and Cuban socialism in the US. Sandy introduced me to diplomats at the New York based Cuban Special Interests Section, the stand-in for the prohibited embassy or consulate. We all agreed that I would help Sandy. She became President (and still is), and for some months, I served as Vice-President, helping her raise money and accumulate books and supporters. But what I really wanted was to belong to a political community, an organization.

As Students for a Democratic Society and most of the radical New Left was faltering, a New Communist Movement was beginning to take shape. Irwin Silber introduced me to it. Irwin, an iconic New Yorker of the Jewish Communist brand, was a small jovial man, usually a bit rotund, possessed a smart, quick wit, his conversation rapid and direct, often combative, but always informed. I liked the warm twinkle in his eye and his uncanny ability to cut through superficiality, human and political, in a flash. I could learn from this man.

Committed to some form of the Marxist Leninist left most of his life, Irwin grew up during the Depression on the Lower East Side of Manhattan amidst grinding poverty and radical ferment. When I met him, he had been the cultural editor and film critic of the New York-based *Guardian*, an independent radical newsweekly with a substantial readership among the unaffiliated and the party-identified left across the country. The paper had been an important voice in fighting McCarthyism. I started reading it in 1963 and published several articles on Francoism in its pages after returning from Spain. Irwin, was about to become the *Guardian's* executive editor.

In our intense conversations in an outdoor café near Sheridan Square in Greenwich Village, we agreed on the primacy of third world revolution, especially the example of Cuba, and the need for party building to put our country on the road to socialism. He concurred on the need for radical feminist changes in order for socialism to be successful, but the concerns of the women's liberation movement were not at the top of his list.

Like many young activists, I was attracted to the uncompromising anti-imperialism, focus on third world revolution, clear structure of accountability and responsibility (the "centralized democracy") that Marxism-Leninism provided. I felt reassured by its cross generational links with a left tradition that had won some victories. My introduction to Marxism in fascist Spain had held such intellectual attraction for me. Marxist theory provided a comprehensible explanation of justice and injustice, of why millions of people around the globe were hungry, illiterate and oppressed because of the insatiable needs of the "first world." I never bought into the idea of the "dictatorship of the proletariat," but I decided to resolve that contradiction later. First we had to deal with the greed of the US-based multinational corporations and other "primary contradictions." A disciplined, experienced Leninist Party, I believed, would be better equipped to take on this task than the loosely structured New Left.

Irwin told me about the pro-Cuban Puerto Rican Socialist Party, committed to Puerto Rican independence and socialism. The Party was island-based, but was about to open a US branch to address the almost 3 million Puerto Ricans (over one third of the entire Puerto Rican nation, all American citizens) who lived on the US mainland, mainly in New York, the East coast and Chicago.[83]

Over half a million islanders had migrated to the US between 1950-1960 in search of a better life as a result of "Operation Bootstrap." This was a powerful publicity campaign to bring US light industries onto the island on a 12-year tax free basis, with low salaries (compared to the mainland) and weakened unions for Puerto Rican workers. Agriculture, particularly the sugar industry, which employed the majority of the island's workers for over 50 years, was decimated to make room for a cement and other mainland determined industries. The result was massive unemployment on the Island and mass immigration to the United States.

The agenda of the *independentistas* in the United States was dependent on island politics, but also on movement politics in the US and the willingness of North Americans to engage in solidarity work. Irwin described it as a Marxist-Leninist party, not nationalist or exclusively composed of Puerto Ricans. "They need someone like you," he said, "educated, progressive, feminist, and with bilingual writing skills." They were about to start a bilingual supplement of *Claridad,* the Party weekly newspaper, and their founding convention for the US branch was about to take place. Did I want to come with him?

I did. And that was the beginning of a new chapter.

Ramón Arbona had been sent from island headquarters to head up the US branch. Today the goal of a socialist transformation in the United States or Puerto Rico seems more distant than ever, but when I met Ramón, we shared a belief in the possibility of forging a road toward socialism and independence in Puerto Rico and socialism in the United States. In his early thirties, Arbona was electric, wiry and witty. His intelligence and prodigious knowledge of Marxism and Caribbean and US politics soon became apparent to me. Of medium height and lean, Arbona had wavy black hair, intense brown eyes and a small mustache; not standard Latin handsome, but his sharp mind and rapid, graceful movements (he was always in motion) commanded attention wherever he was. There was something eager and adventurous about him, a quickness of reaction and an energy that made him seize your attention and hold your eye. Charismatic and warm, he knew how to lead. I liked him immediately.

*"The political and legal status of Puerto Rico has been the fundamental constant in the life of Boricuas*[84] *since we stopped being a colony of Spain in 1898,"*[85] Ramón said over lunch in the now defunct Tad's Steak House, a seedy eating place conveniently located on the ground floor of the Party's central headquarters, Casa Puerto Rico, on Man-

hattan's East 14th Street near Union Square. Animatedly gesturing, Arbona described how the island passed from being a Spanish colony to being a neocolonial creation of the US. *"We never got to be independent like Cuba,"* he said. *"We are neither a state nor an independent nation, but a 'Free Associated State'. ¡Es indignante que no podemos controlar nuestro propio destino ni aquí ni allá!* [It is outrageous that we are not in control of our future, neither here nor there.] *Ay, mi amor,*[86] *estamos jodidos!* [We are fucked.][87] *Washington no nos deja ni una pizca de dignidad, coño."*[88] [Washington doesn't leave us even a drop of dignity.]

On Arbona's recommendation, I joined the Puerto Rican Socialist Party in December 1971. I went to the 14 St. Party headquarters and spoke with the *compañero* in charge of membership. He gave me a little white membership card, and explained that the goal was to do such good work that I would be awarded a red card, indicating promotion to *"militante de vanguardia"* [vanguard militant]. I joined because I saw possibilities for the triumph of a more just world linked to revolutions in the third world and I wanted to be part of it. This meant remaining a socialist feminist, but also undertaking other political actions. I was not sure what I would be called on to do, but I have never shied away from political commitments. I embraced what I believed in and defined what I was doing *sobre la marcha*, as I was doing it. The link between domestic campaigns (alleviating miserable living conditions for the Puerto Ricans in the US) and international struggles in support of socialist goals made sense. Working for the Puerto Rican community in New York, I could imagine results like improvement in housing conditions, educational opportunities and medical care. My utopian impulse was satisfied by the not quite-immediate goal of establishing socialism in the US and Puerto Rico. I and other veterans of the New Left, looked to the inspiration of Cuba for models. Though it was never clear how we would take state power in the United States, we all agreed it had to be "inch by inch."

Starting in the spring of 1972, I worked with Digna Sánchez and Alfredo López, two longtime residents of New York, and other editorial and production assistants, on the bilingual edition of *Claridad*, which debuted in March. Ramón Arbona was the Editor; Alfredo López, the Managing Editor, and I was the General Manager, coordinating production, writing articles, translating Spanish articles from the Island paper and occasionally going into the field to cover a story. We wrote and produced the weekly paper in small offices at 30 East 20th Street, a short walk from Party headquarters.

I went to Lincoln Hospital in the Bronx to report on the atrocities— mostly rape, domestic violence, police brutality—being regularly committed against Puerto Rican and black women. I also wrote about workers' discrimination, inferior housing and education in the Puerto Rican community, and on international issues such as the campaign to free Nelson Mandela. A key issue was the campaign to persuade the United Nations Special Committee on Decolonialization to define Puerto Rico a "colony" of the United States, instead of a Commonwealth governed by the Congress of the United States. If Puerto Rico were reclassified as a colony, the United Nations had the power to "decolonize" and could declare Puerto Rico an independent sovereign state. The question is still pending.

Several times I drove a large truck to deliver bulk packages of *Claridad* to 138th Street in the Bronx and to several other drop points around the city for distribution by party members. I am not a particularly skilled driver, but I do know how to drive a shift car, so that qualified me to drive the truck. Upon greeting the obviously "yankee" truck driver, a surprised, but not unfriendly expression flickered across the face of the party members unloading the truck. With my auburn hair, blue eyes and freckles, I do not look at all Puerto Rican. To compound "differences", I speak Spanish with a Madrid accent, *"Imperialista dos veces"* [a double imperialist], my friends in the Party often joked.

As a part of the US (non-Puerto Rican) left, one of my tasks was to publicize the Party to potentially sympathetic audiences. In order to do that, I had to learn not just details about the Party, but the history and culture of Puerto Rico within the Caribbean and US contexts and the history of the struggle for independence. Casa Puerto Rico had a well-supplied bookstore, but there were no books on Puerto Rican women because in 1972 no such books existed. It wouldn't be until the mid-seventies that Edna Acosta Belén and others began to write about the status and oppression of Puerto Rican women (politically and personally), on the Island and in the States.

I enthusiastically dove into the new body of knowledge and in 4 or 5 months, I was moderately competent and knowledgeable. I frequently checked with Digna and Alfredo, the two people with whom I worked most closely. I was responsible, worked hard and completed assignments to the best of my ability. Digna and Alfredo, long time *independentistas*, valued my contributions and I respected their commitment and intelligence.

With Arbona's consent (I was an exemplary party member and always followed the chain of command) and Irwin Silber's agreement, I asked Alfredo López about the two of us sharing a bi-line for a twice-monthly column in the *Guardian* dedicated to the politics and culture of Puerto Rico and the Caribbean in general. He liked the idea. Alfredo was very much a New Yorker, a Puerto Rican New Yorker, who, when I worked with him, functioned more easily in English than in Spanish. A skilled writer, thinker and gifted politician, Alfredo would go on to achieve national recognition for his many books and leadership positions on behalf of Puerto Rico and the progressive left.

Our column was entitled "The Sling of David." It existed from mid-1972 to mid-1973. I did not save copies of the column, but the FBI did. The last article I wrote appeared in the *Guardian* on March 21, 1973, several weeks before the First Party Congress. The strident Marxist language in the column was much used at the time in the Party and parts of the *Guardian* and the New Communist Movement. It was easy for me to adopt the rhetoric and tone because the premises were given and no critical thought was necessary. I knew this when I wrote this brand of journalism; that was part of being in a Marxist Leninist Party. One did not question the platform or the hierarchy or the fundamental content. At times I felt I was play-acting when I wrote this prose, but it was good for "the cause," and I liked being a member of a community with shared politics.

Digna Sánchez had pale ivory skin and long dark hair. The ten pounds she always thought she should lose gave her a soft sensuality that was very appealing. She attributed her high cheek bones to Taino ancestors. The striking bone structure and slightly almond shaped warm brown eyes endowed her with a unique beauty. But Digna's appearance was not one of her top priorities. She was a 24/7 *independentista* and a socialist feminist.

Being a socialist feminist in a Marxist Leninist Party and being a socialist feminist in the women's liberation movement had little in common beyond the name. The role of women's issues in the Party was similar to what we had seen in Cuba in 1969 and learned from Vilma Espin, Fidel Castro's sister-in-law and head of the Cuban Federation of Women. "The personal is political" and consciousness raising were no more a part of the general Puerto Rican agenda than it was in Revolutionary Cuba. Social issues deemed to be women's concerns, like daycare and reeducation of prostitutes in Cuba and the campaign against the sterilization of Puerto Rican women, were often initiated by and always implemented with the approval of the male leadership. The island-based Party did not support abortion rights for fear of alienating the Catholic Church. Most of the *compañeras* I spoke with shared my pro-choice views, but elected not to express their opinions publicly, and urged me not to. So I didn't.

The New York-raised Puerto Rican women were keenly aware of the sexism and *machismo* in their daily lives and throughout the Puerto Rican movement but, it seemed, were biding their time to make a move. However, from the beginning, Vivian Rivera, tall, thin and feisty with a warm smile and somewhat serious demeanor, was one prominent party member who made her feminism public. She believed, as I did, that if women couldn't have a role in carving out a place in the public sphere, no one could be serious about social justice, let alone socialism.

Years after leaving the Party, she wrote about gender relations in the Puerto Rican community: "My experience has taught me something about the persistence of inequitable gender relations. Although I won't minimize the ideological differences between the experiences of Left and electoral politics, both are embedded in a male-dominant structure, one that ultimately leads to the same failures. We have a long way to go before we transform these relations. But of one thing I am sure: until men accept women as their peers and leaders, neither strategy — radical nor electoral — will succeed in changing conditions in our community."[89]

Members of the Island-based leadership, including Juan Mari Brás, the Secretary General, frequently visited New York. They were middle-class men, university educated and older than their New York counterparts. I met professors, cosmopolitan politicians, cultured doctors and lawyers. Spanish was their language and English very much a second, usually imperfect tool of communication that most preferred not to use. As an outsider, I was particularly sensitive to differences between the mainland and Island-based Puerto Ricans. Socializing with the Party veterans was like being back in Madrid, except the Puerto Ricans were more spontaneous and sensual and not impeccably dressed in suits and ties; they wore the loose, lightweight men's shirt called *guayabera*. However, their patriarchal condescension, unconscious sexism wrapped in charm and wit, and proclivity to infantilize women and flirt with the *gringa* echoed my Spanish experience.

My English-dominant New York *compañeros* deferred to the Islanders for two reasons: because of their seniority in the Party and because the Islanders functioned more confidently, culturally and linguistically, in a Spanish speaking world. Speaking impeccable Spanish was considered "first class"; the patch-work bilingualism of New Yorkers was not. This opinion was shared by both Island and mainland Party members, although never publicly acknowledged. I cringed when I witnessed linguistic and educational inequalities create feelings of personal inadequacy, but it was not my place to intervene.

Many of the New Yorkers, almost all working class and first-generation immigrants, were uncomfortable with their imperfect Spanish or gaps in their knowledge of Puerto Rico, the Caribbean and left wing politics. They mainly came from the mass of uprooted islanders whose parents had migrated to the States in the 1950s and 1960s to become part of the large community of poor Puerto Rican families in the Bronx, East Harlem and the Lower East Side. "Newyoricans" grew up and lived in communities plagued by high school drop out rates due to shaky English, drugs, deteriorating living conditions, unending financial insecurity, and bad medical care. Many families were headed by single women and even if two parents were present, both were dependent on irregular menial labor and multiple part time jobs as domestics, janitors, dishwashers. Millions lived one step ahead of the rent collector and the street gangs. The young members of the Party were often the first in their family to graduate from high school, let alone go to college and speak fluent English. The tension this created in the Party was a tension created by class differences. Puerto Ricans come in all sizes, shapes, colors and classes, but in the early 1970s there were very few middle class Puerto Rican professionals in New York. This would not happen for several more decades.[90]

I formed no part of this equation because I was different from everyone else—at times this isolated me and at times it was a protective carapace. I spoke, read or wrote whichever language was needed, but with an accent and a background no one else shared.

An easy *compañerismo* characterized relationships between men and women. We did a lot of things together, in small or large groups: Meals, recreation, meetings, demonstrations. We enjoyed being with each other, and shared a pleasure in comradeship similar to what I had enjoyed in New University Conference conventions and large regional meetings. However, NUC members had been scattered across the country, whereas the bulk of the US-based Party membership was rooted in one of the boroughs of New York. Therefore, we saw each other constantly. Working in the Party was a daily, disciplined commitment which was not the case with the

New University Conference, except for the full time paid staff.

In the pre-AIDS era of the 1970s, easy sexual encounters were part of Party life as they were in the New University Conference. The modus operandi, however, was slightly different among the Puerto Ricans. If a woman transgressed with the married (or unmarried, long term) partner of a party member, it was primarily the woman's fault; she had wrongly intruded on another woman's property, and what was a man to do? I knew this code from years in Spain. In the US Latin community in the 1970s it still operated pretty much ubiquitously. Outside the Latin communities, the women's liberation movement sought to change this and progress was achieved in not automatically assigning all culpability to the "other woman." It was always messy, but we confronted each other and discussed the situation. Or, as some members of NUC did, made a commitment to "trash monogamy." The Party considered this type of discussion a ridiculous waste of time.

I had numerous assignations with numerous *compañeros*. They were physically pleasant, rarely lasted more than several nights and no one ever spoke of commitment, just pleasure. Some of the more sexually adventurous party members reminded me of what superb lovers the Cubans had been with the attention they devoted to satisfying a woman. Once in a while I was approached by a married man or a comrade everyone knew was linked with a female party member. I declined these encounters. However, I slipped up once, with disastrous consequences.

Carlos was handsome in a gruff and sensual way that, in hindsight, reminds me of the popular Mexican actor Gael García Bernal with a touch of the Spaniard Javier Bardem. Carlos, a product of African and European heritage, exuded sexuality. A product of the tough Puerto Rican streets, his body was buff and he had layers of street smarts and charm. Carlos once told me of his brief time in prison and how he had been frequently raped. "Of course I went along with it, otherwise they would have killed me," he explained.

Carlos had been dating María, a party member, with whom I worked. When Carlos and I chatted about the possibility of getting together, he assured me he and María were no longer a couple, and the truth was, I had not seen them together for a time. I chose to believe him, and we went about our trysts, pleasant but not long lasting.

A little over a month later, Ramón Arbona said he needed to have a meeting with me, and María would be there. I imagined it was a project or an article he wanted the two of us to work on. In a booth at Tad's Steak House, Ramón was slightly uncomfortable and María was silent, with a noncommital expression on her round, honey colored pretty face.

Ramón cut to the quick: "Several weeks ago, María brought her concerns over your possible connection to the CIA to me and to the Political Bureau. We took her accusation seriously because, as you know, she has been an exemplary Party member for a long time, both in Puerto Rico and here."

I was stunned. María did not say anything and the expression on her face did not change.

"I have spoken with Juan Mari Brás, Ramón said, "and we have conducted a thorough investigation and are satisfied that you are not a CIA agent. I hope we can all continue working together as we have over the past year."

I was flabbergasted. Was an apology in order? Apparently not. "*Bueno*," concluded Ramón, and his characteristic smile returned "*¿Volvamos al trabajo?*" [Shall we go back to work?]

When I returned to the *Claridad* office, Alfredo looked at me and raised both his eyebrows. I understood the gesture. As a member of the Political Bureau, he knew of the conversation that had just transpired, but preferred not to discuss it. Fine, I knew the rules. The Party was always right. No more discussion.

The next weekend Carlos and María were dancing together at a party at the Casa Puerto Rico.

My assignations continued, but I vetted them more carefully.

The first Party Congress was held on April 8, 1973 at New York City's Manhattan Center and attracted over 2000 people. By then I had been a member of the Party for a year and a half and had received the coveted "red card" promoting me to status of "*militante de vanguardia.*" I attended the Congress[91] as a member of the US Zone Committee, the leadership of the Party. As a Leninist party, it had a clear structure of power. The US Zone Committee was composed of a 7-member Political Bureau: 6 men (among them Ramón Arbona, Alfredo López and José "Che" Velázquez) and 1 woman (Digna Sánchez). Right below the Political Bureau was the 9-member Secretariat, 3 of them women. Arbona was Secretary of the Zone, Digna was Press Secretary and Ché was Secretary of Student Affairs. Ranked below the Secretariat were 19 Additional Members of the Zone Committee. Seven out of the 19 members were women, and I was one of them. The issue of parity in gender representation was never discussed. There were two non-Puerto Ricans on the Zone Committee: Jeff Perry and myself. On the New England

Regional Committee, Denis Berger was Secretary of Finance. We three were the only non-Puerto Ricans in the Party at the time and I was the only non-Puerto Rican woman. The entire US branch was ultimately responsible to Party headquarters in Puerto Rico, and to Juan Mari Brás, the Secretary General.

The officially adopted political position presented at the Congress written by the leadership and discussed and approved in all Party *núcleos* [cells] over the course of many months, was entitled *Desde Las Entrañas* [From the Belly of the Beast]. The document affirmed that Puerto Ricans in the United States were part of the Puerto Rican nation, not a "national minority" in the United States as the Young Lords[92] maintained.

*Desde Las Entrañas* declared that the Puerto Rican Socialist Party would seek to take state power on the Island, and direct the working class in the construction of a socialist and revolutionary society on the Cuban model. Regarding work in the United States, its role "is to unleash that national Liberation struggle, in all its fury, in the very hearts of North American cities to which a significant portion of our colonized population was forced, and to link that struggle to the struggle for revolutionary transformation of North American society."[93]

I, along with all other Party members, enthusiastically voted to accept party strategy. We never disagreed with the leadership. Written in the incendiary prose in vogue at that time, the hortatory invocation reaffirmed and nurtured our anger and frustrations and energized revolutionary zeal. I allowed myself to believe or to hope that the discipline that a Leninist party offered, would equip us to deal with anti-imperialist actions domestically and revolutionary opportunites in the third world. My commitment to women's liberation was simmering on the back burner.

At the conclusion of the Congress, some party members went to Puerto Rico for a respite. I received permission to spend a week in San Juan conducting interviews with Party Island leaders and other key Puerto Ricans for an article on the Independence movement I was writing for *Ramparts*, where I had already published several pieces.

In San Juan, many of the young, single members of the Party lived in small units that were part of a large area of apartments that extended over many blocks in a working class section of the city. The buildings were all alike; two stories high, made of cement and painted white. Some units had one room with a bath and kitchenette and others had a separate bedroom. I never knew to whom the units belonged nor what it cost to live there.

When I arrived in San Juan, it had already been arranged for me to sleep on the couch in an apartment shared by Mayra, an attractive Afro-Puerto Rican and Carmen, a lively, roundish honey colored Islander. Both were in their early twenties. They welcomed me warmly and extended immediate hospitality. They gave me an apartment key, explained how to get around the city, what buses to take to Party headquarters, to *Claridad*, and to other bench marks of independence activity. We then shared a delicious cup of coffee. It all seemed so simple and automatic, like the hospitality we had offered each other in the New University Conference.

I had a list of persons in and out of the Party I wanted to interview for the article. I had managed to arrange access to almost all of them, some with the help of the *compañeros*, some by simply contacting them on my own, via personal contacts. The most significant of my personal bridges to the intelligentsia in San Juan was New York-based Iris Zavala, one of the few distinguished Puerto Rican scholars in the US academic system in the 1970s. She was pro-independence but not involved directly in politics. A literary critic and a historian, Iris was prolific, dynamic, warm and generous — and very smart.

Nilita Ventós Gascón, the founder and editor of *Sin Nombre* [Without Name], a highly respected literary journal, was, in the words of Ramón Arbona, "the most cultured person on the Island." She and Iris were friends and I spent wonderful hours in Nilita's house overrun with books in a plethora of languages, as she introduced me to the current cultural landscape on the Island. She was tiny, energetic with a strident voice and wit that more than compensated for her doll-like status.

Rubén Berrios was the leader of the Puerto Rican Independence Party, which existed exclusively on the Island, and was a social democratic party opposed to the Marxist-Leninist politics of the Puerto Rican Socialist Party. A handsome, clearly well nourished and confident middle class Puerto Rican in his mid-thirties, with green eyes and blond hair, Berrios was anti-Marxist and anti-Party. He enjoyed his international contacts with European social democrats and regarded the possibility of a socialist Puerto Rico as absurd and unrealistic. In hindsight, he was right, but I admit his confident dismissal of the socialist alternative irritated me at the time.

Late one afternoon, as I was winding my way back to the apartment from the bus stop, I saw Mayra, Carmen and several other women from the Party huddled together in intense conversation across the way. As I approached them, their conversation hushed and it was clear they did not want me to stop and chat. I thought that was strange, but continued on home. Half an hour later, Mayra came into the apartment and informed me "Juan Mari wants you to leave the Island immediately, right now." I was dumbfounded. I asked why, but was told they had nothing more to say. I had to leave the apartment right now and return to New York where everything would be explained to me. I had no alternative.

Numb from the shock, I went to the airport and got on one of the Eastern Airline flights that flew many times a day between New York and San Juan. When I got I home, I called Ramón and he asked me to meet the following day with the Political Bureau.

We met at Party Headquarters on 14th Street. Ramón was there, as were Jesús López, Secretry of Finance; Ché Velázquez, Secretary of Student Affairs; José Alberto Alvarez Febles, Secretary of Organization (who some years later would become Digna's second husband) and Alfredo López. As soon as I saw Alfredo's obvious discomfort, I was ready for anything. What could they possibly accuse me of now? They had already confirmed that I was not a CIA spy.

As befitting his status, Ramón opened the meeting. "Roberta, Juan Mari Brás has informed us that you disobeyed party orders about how long to remain in San Juan and asks that you be expelled from the Party immediately."

Total silence.

Alfredo cut through the oppressive quiet, "There is a procedure in the Party to challenge this action," he said, in as friendly a tone as he could manage. This time I had had it.

"No," I replied, "I don't think I will bother."

I picked up my purse, walked down the stairs and out to 14th Street and out of the Party.

I was stunned and very upset as I crossed Second Ave on that sunny summer day. Then I said, "fuck them," outloud, and decided to stop at the Second Ave Deli and have a pastrami sandwich and a Dr. Peppers. I chuckled wryly as I recalled the Stalinist purges of the Communist Party in Moscow in 1937. Well, at least here jail, torture or death were not options!

I never heard from or saw anyone from the Puerto Rican Socialist Party again. As far as they were concerned, I became a non-person—vanished from the face of the earth. That hurt, and I missed many of my "good friends." I have no idea why I was expelled. Pride kept me from asking members of the Party, or even outsiders who were close friends and supporters of the Party. Perhaps they thought I was an FBI agent.

The expulsion was so ridiculous that I decided the most dignified course to follow was to put the Party and the Puerto Ricans out of my mind and move on. To this day, the expulsion remains shrouded in mystery.

Why had I been so willing to suspend my critical thought and inquiring mind so carefully developed during most of my adult life? The strategy and tactics of the Party's struggle for social justice were clearly spelled out and the deep conviction of working toward a Marxist Leninist goal was a powerful, and, for a while, a deeply satisfying force. I was fulfilling the desire I had nurtured since my days in Madrid to be part of an internationally linked political party with a mission I admired. From my time in Cuba, I knew I could not live without freedom of the press and freedom of mobility, but even though the Puerto Rican Socialist Party was modeled on Cuba (and both, to a large extent, on the Soviet Union), I was an American citizen living in New York. I think I always knew that if I really found Party discipline impossible, I could simply leave and return to my previous world. I imagine this also occurred to my Puerto Rican *compañeros*.

I liked being part of a Spanish speaking Latin community. I enjoyed their humor, capacity to enjoy life, and the food and dancing—not very political, any of these reasons, I admit, but it was fun and humanly satisfying. My not being Puerto Rican was, for the most part, subsumed in the mutual solidarity and support that results when a mélange of people—of different class, race and educational backgrounds—come together in pursuit of a political goal that transcends individual interests. I did not feel the need to contradict the rigid Leninist operational principles. I was relieved to be away from the debilitating personal confrontations that had been so much a part of my work in San Diego. Shared goals provided a short cut to friendships in the Party that I valued enormously, and were not part of the route my Harvard PhD had laid out for me. I don't think most of the Party members knew I had Harvard degrees or that I was Jewish. But neither piece of information would have been relevant to their opinion of me. That was the nice part.

I do not regret the time I devoted to the Party. Although the independence of Puerto Rico is probably not a viable goal, over the years the Puerto Rican socialists have improved the lives of some Puerto Ricans in the United States. More important, my yearning to be part of a Marxist-Leninist Party disappeared. Centralized "democracy" was not for me.

I did not know then to what extent the disappointments, frustration and failures of the 1960s would lead part of the New Left, myself included, to excessive sectarianism and to rigid, dead-end notions of hierarchy and centralism in the 1970s. I now share Nelson Mandela's gentle observation in his autobiography that, as one matures, it is hard not to regard some of the views of one's youth as undeveloped and too impulsive.

# CHAPTER 10

# THE DEATH OF ORLANDO LETELIER

Everyone at the Institute for Policy Studies[94] knew that on Tuesdays, I took my 22 month old daughter, Ana Simone, for swimming lessons at the downtown YMCA in the morning and didn't come in to the office until noon. On September 21, 1976 when I dropped Ana off at home shortly after 11:15, Mercedes, the 20-year-old Dominican woman who lived with me and took care of my daughter, said that the office had been frantically trying to reach me all morning. They wanted me to call immediately. Why bother I thought? I'll be there in ten minutes.

I drove down R St. and made a left at Q St, mildly irritated—What could be so urgent?

When I turned into Sheridan Square, I saw several police cars. Part of the circle was roped off. One of the embassies must be having a special event; I took a detour and drove past the Institute at 1901 Q St. to park.

Some 50 people stood in front of the building. The silence was heavy and frightening. I glanced at my watch: 11:35. "There has not been time for something to have happened to Ana and for everyone to have already gathered at the Institute" — a moment of temporary maternal insanity. What was wrong? What had happened?

Richard Barnet, an IPS co-director, came to the door and took my arm: "Orlando!" he said, "They've killed Orlando! Orlando and Ronnie were in the car and it blew up."

Orlando Letelier, previously Chilean Foreign and Defense Minister and Ambassador to the United States, was the leader and single most effective organizer in the international struggle against Augusto Pinochet's military dictatorship in Chile. That dictatorship had begun on September 11, 1973 when Pinochet and his junta led a military coup against President Salvador Allende and the first democratically elected Marxist government in the Hemisphere. The Pinochet dictatorship would rule Chile until 1990, almost two decades.

Orlando's single-minded determination and enormous courage, together with his unique political skills and knowledge of the Washington power structure –he had worked at the Inter American

Development Bank in the 1960s—made him a giant in the resistance. No risk was too great, as he threw himself heart and soul into this high stakes fight. Ronnie Karpen Moffitt, a 25-year-old IPS fundraiser, and her husband of 4 months, Michael Moffitt (Dick Barnet's associate), were in the car too. When the bomb went off, Ronnie, sitting in the front seat, was killed almost instantly, along with Orlando. Michael, in the back seat, escaped unharmed.

Orlando and Ronnie's deaths would be recognized as the first act of foreign terrorism on domestic soil. Relations between Chile and the United States would be strained for almost two decades. September 1976 would also change my life.

In November 1973, some months after I was expelled from the Puerto Rican Socialist Party, as I was about to finish teaching the fall semester at Old Westbury, Saul Landau called and suggested we get together. Nixon had given his "I am not a crook" speech on November 17 and Watergate, the dangerous political soap opera that became a national obsession, mesmerized the country.

A few years older than I, Saul was a well-known activist, political filmmaker and writer with links to the Old and New Left and a particular commitment to Cuba and Latin America. His film *Fidel*, released in 1969, was the first time a North American filmmaker had sufficient access to Fidel Castro to make a full-length movie based on personal interviews. It was fascinating and hagiographic; that was the only way Saul could or would make it.

An articulate New Yorker, Saul had a wry sense of humor that could be wicked if you were an unwilling recipient of his razor sharp wit. He had been immersed in left politics all his life, and a particular combination of intelligence, knowledge and charm allowed him to operate in many political circles, often simultaneously. Saul had been an associate at the Institute for several years. When we sat down to talk that November afternoon, Saul brought up the subject of Chile immediately.

It was barely three months since the coup, in which Salvador Allende had died. Pinochet was continuing to kill, incarcerate or drive into exile tens of thousands of Chileans, among them most of the leaders of the Popular Unity Government. As the extent of the atrocities committed in the name of "saving our *patria* from Communism," became known beyond Chile, anti-Pinochet activity started coalescing throughout Latin America, Europe and the United States. The major role of the Nixon-Kissinger government in the overthrow of Allende would not be fully documented until years later.

"Chile is a bloodbath," he said. "The Institute has to do something."

Praising my organizational skills, knowledge of Spanish and the Spanish-speaking world and experience with Puerto Rico and Cuba, he asked if I would be interested in helping build a Latin American unit. The Institute didn't have any female Resident Fellows and they knew they should, so that could help them. It would mean giving up academic tenure and moving to Washington. Saul assured me the salaries and perks for the Resident Fellows were attractive and the job security, traditionally, had been good. The idea of helping to create a Latin American Unit based in the most well known progressive think tank in the nation's capital made sense. I knew that being part of a new group focused on Latin America within the successfully functioning Institute was something I could be good at. I was ready to use my hybrid experience on the left to further the cause of democracy, feminism and socialism in Latin America and the Caribbean.

Three weeks before I moved to Washington, Nixon had resigned and Gerald Ford was President. I rented a lovely townhouse at 3605 R St, just down the street from Dumbarton Oaks. I started familiarizing myself with Washington and the Institute, positioning myself to have contacts in the parts of Washington officialdom and non-officialdom that dealt with Latin America and the Caribbean.

On November 7, Congressional elections ushered in 6 new Democratic senators and 49 young Democratic representatives, known as the "Watergate Babies." The country was sick of the Republicans and the slime of Watergate. The buzz at IPS was that we were on our way to a Teddy Kennedy presidency in 1976!

I wanted to have a child. A daughter. And I knew that I did not want to marry again. My experience had convinced me that love did not go hand in hand with marriage. I found the institutionalization of love humiliating, but I did believe in love. In 1973-74, I was in love with a man, but neither of us wanted to marry. I decided to get pregnant, hope for a girl, and go my way. The prospect of loving and molding a little piece of female humanity—my second chance, so to speak—thrilled me. I would do this while at the Institute. The salary was generous, I could have a live-in nanny and the progressive ambiance at the Institute would be supportive.

The idea of having a baby by myself was so empowering that I actually believed that because I wanted a daughter, I would get one. I did not think I was being courageous; it was simply being me, authentically. I was developing an ideology of female independence and wanted to live it out. Not only my politics but also my personal life was transgressive, I now realize, but that was not a problem. I knew that I could carry it off.

Thrilled with the prospect of motherhood, I set about enjoying the pregnancy and arranging the birth. I took care to dress professionally and elegantly throughout the nine months and worked productively at the Institute until a day before Ana was born. I always conducted myself with the assurance that what I was doing was perfectly "normal," and did not permit anyone to question my decision.

Since I lived close to Georgetown Hospital, I went to visit the obstetrics department and asked to be given a tour and a description of their procedures. It was a sobering experience: as soon as a woman arrived at the hospital, I was told, she was put in a wheelchair, whether she needed it not. Her pubic hair was shaved (more sanitary, the nurse explained) and while giving birth her feet were placed in stirrups. One could choose between local or total anesthesia. Episiotomies were normal procedure. All the obstetricians I saw were male. As I walked through the corridors of the hospital, I felt diminished and controlled by hostile forces.

Utterly unacceptable, I thought. They are not telling me how to have a baby. I am going to do it myself. So I set about learning about home birthing, which some young women usually called "hippies," were doing in the early seventies. Although I didn't know anyone who had had a home birth—it was usually done in the communal, "back to nature" culture prevalent in the 1970s, not in a townhouse in Georgetown. But, why not?

I learned that Dr. James Brew, one of the obstetricians at Yater Clinic in Dupont Circle, near the Institute, did home births and used a midwife. Good. That was what I would do. When I signed up for home birthing classes in the Lamaze method, I wrote my name as Dr. Roberta Salper. More respect that way, I reasoned. When the receptionist asked the name of my "class partner," I summoned my most professional posture and smiled pleasantly, "I will be coming alone." "Alone?" Her eyebrows arched a bit. "Yes, alone" I replied, wishing I was wearing a sandwich board that said "I am a Harvard PhD."

There were 19 of us in the class; I was the only single woman. The classes were fun and helpful. I became friendly with a couple who lived in a commune and thought it was "cool" that an "older" woman was doing this by herself. I was 35, they were 23.

My close friends and my sister Martha were supportive. My mother and her husband lived near Philadelphia and I did not tell them about my pregnancy and Ana's birth. My mother had never approved of what she considered my risk-taking transgressive decisions, and I was afraid of her hurtful condemnation. More than anyone else, she knew exactly what to say to make me feel worthless. She was not going to ruin this experience for me. I would deal with her later on. During my adult life I had modeled myself on the negation of my mother and would continue to do so as a mother.

The morning of November 8, my water broke. I was on my way to going into labor. I left the Institute and went home. Martha had come to pick me up and Mercedes, the young woman I had hired as a live-in nanny was at home, anxiously awaiting the birth of the baby she would care for five days a week.

Dr. Brew and Megan, the midwife, arrived at my house just as the birthing cramps started. They sat by my side during the 9 hours of labor until Ana was born at 4:01 in the morning. I had no medication except for a glass of red wine half way through the labor. The doctor and midwife strongly disapproved of my little libation, but I reminded them it was my house and I would do as I wished. And I did. The labor was not painful, just very uncomfortable—like having terrible cramps while caught in a Manhattan traffic jam on a blistering August day with no air conditioning and with no way out. When I saw the longed-for tiny vagina, I was ecstatic. My little girl! I nursed Ana briefly and then Dr. Brew cut the umbilical cord and used a clothes pin to clip the remaining portion. The adrenalin flowed and I felt wonderful! After giving Dr. Brew a check for $400, I started calling up my friends and the flow of visitors began. It was a glorious day.

Ten days later, I met Orlando Letelier. It was in the Dupont Plaza Hotel, around the corner from the Institute. He was an elegant, handsome man, a tall, broad-shouldered redhead with intense brown eyes and a warm smile. Orlando carried himself with the knowledge that he was a major personality and very attractive to women. As he stood to greet me, I felt his energy and charisma. He graciously complimented me on my *"español excelente"* and I noted that he had a pleasantly deep baritone voice. Later on, I learned he sang very well.

Orlando had been the first of the high-level prisoners to be released by the junta, after 364 days in Pinochet's prisons, particularly the infamous Dawson Island.[95] His release on September 9, 1974 was directly due to the intervention of Diego Arias, the powerful governor of Caracas, Venezuela and friend of the Leteliers. Arias flew to Chile, met with Pinochet and the next day flew back to Caracas with Orlando on his plane. Some weeks later, Orlando received a call from Saul Landau, offering him a fellowship at the Institute of Policy Studies.

Orlando came to Washington to discuss the details of his appointment at the Institute and Saul brought me to meet "the man you'll be working with in the Latin American Unit." Letelier would be an associate fellow, developing a study of United States-Chilean relations during the Allende years. Although it was never acknowledged publicly, many of us knew that the Institute would be Orlando's base for organizing anti-Pinochet activities and gathering aid for his incarcerated or exiled comrades.

Orlando agreed to organize a major intellectual and policy conference on United States-Latin American affairs, which turned into a five-day international event, with Latin American and US academics, political figures, and parliamentarians on "The Present and Future of US-Latin American Economic and Political Relations." I co-directed the conference, scheduled for Thanksgiving, 1975 in Oaxtepec, Mexico and co-sponsored by CIDE, a Mexican think tank.[96]

The year before a presidential election is a time that electrifies Washington DC. Players and potential players begin the scramble for power in a new administration. It is high stakes poker. Casting one's lot early on with the eventual winner could result in a life-enhancing move. 1975 was an optimistic moment at the Institute because Nixon's resignation and the Democratic sweep of Congress in 1974 had created some political space for progressives. There was much to confront. Repressive dictatorships reigned in major countries in Latin America: Alfredo Stroessner in Paraguay, Hugo Banzer in Bolivia, Ernesto Geisel in Brazil, Isabel Perón in Argentina, Guillermo Rodríguez in Ecuador, Juan María Bordaberry in Uruguay and of course, Pinochet in Chile. All had dependent capitalist economies and junta style models of political repression. But post-Allende Chile was a target for special attention.

Although the political panorama in Latin America in 1974 and 1975 was dominated by repressive right wing dictatorships, there were mitigating factors. Peru [Juan Velasco], Venezuela [Carlos Andrés Pérez], Colombia [López Michelsen] and Mexico, maintained moderate regimes. In Jamaica, Prime Minister Michael Manley was experimenting with "democratic socialism" (a "mixed economy", with features of socialism and capitalism), and had established diplomatic relations with Cuba. Jamaica was a hub of progressive activity, together with Cuba. In addition, opposition to the repressive dictatorships was mobilizing among exile groups in Europe, the United States and Latin America.

This could be a pivotal moment to influence US policy toward the southern hemisphere. Why not create a forum to explore developments in Latin America and the Caribbean and present the full reality of the region to the Washington community?

Nothing like this existed. The Institute would be an excellent base for inviting influential voices from the north and south to an event whose goal was the formulation of an alternate, more progressive US policy. The Democrats would surely capture the Presidency in 1976 and there would be opportunities for change.

Aided by a team of "Chicago boys," (American advisors and Chicago-educated Chilean economists), Chile had become a testing ground for the application of the theories of Milton Friedman and his unfettered, relentless "free market capitalism". Pinochet's economists claimed to be establishing a new model of 'economic freedom' as they ruthlessly destroyed progressive public and private sector reforms that the Popular Unity government had created to alleviate widespread poverty. Their goal was rapid privatization controlled by a small oligarchy.

Writing in *The Nation* magazine three years after the coup (and less than two weeks before his assassination), Letelier lambasted the Chilean junta for its failure to control inflation (their principal monetary goal) and their success in decimating Allende's social services, benefits, subsidies and new employment. Orlando described the 'inner harmony' between the terror of the Pinochet regime and its free market politics. Pinochet and his Chicago-schooled economists had secured *"the economic and political power of a small dominant class by effecting a massive transfer of wealth from the lower and middle classes to a select group of monopolists and financial spectators."*[97] Orlando's article reverberated worldwide.

The Latin American Round Table at the Institute came into being in July 1975, a monthly forum hosting an impressive cross section of policy-makers from the region and from the U.S. Among our first speakers were Ernesto Cardenal, Nicaraguan poet, priest and political activist; Sergio Bitar, former Minister of Mining in the Chilean Popular Unity government; Cheddi Jagan, Secretary General of the People's Progressive Party in Guyana; Fernando Henrique Cardoso, future president of Brazil; and William M. Dyal, Jr., President, Inter-American Foundation as well as Richard Fagan;

Stanford University Professor; Julian Rizo, First Secretary of the Cuban Mission to the United Nations; Honorable Dudley Thompson, Foreign Minister of Jamaica, James Petras, Latin Americanist at State University of New York, Binghamton, Moy Morales de Toha, Founder and Director of the Women's National Secretariat, Popular Unity government, Chile, and Rev. Joseph Eldridge, Director of the Washington Office on Latin America.

LART achieved recognition in the policy community in the capital and as a result, I was often invited to participate in events and debates in government and non-government events. This was beneficial for the Institute and for me. Before long I knew my way around town. I was the only female Resident Fellow and more often than not, the only woman (or one of only several) in the policy seminars and discussions that I attended around Washington. The Institute was a boy's club, as was the nation's capital. I rarely discussed gender issues with colleagues because it would not have served any purpose other than to consciously alienate myself. None of the men at the Institute thought I was the victim of any kind of discrimination. It was all so subtle: small cabals I was not invited to; decisions quietly made behind closed doors; key meetings that took place after work at 5:00, when I went home to be with Ana for two hours before she went to sleep.

Once I decided to protest the 5:00 meetings by an action, not words. It was difficult to win any kind of argument that was not strictly intellectual or political with my male colleagues. So, on a day that such a meeting was convened, I asked Mercedes to bring Ana to the Café Rondo across the street from the Institute at 4:50 and not to feed her beforehand. At 5:00 the IPS fellows were convened around the large round meeting table on the first floor, waiting for me. I entered with Ana. I sat down with her on my lap. Several of my colleagues offered weak smiles and murmured how cute she was. Marc Raskin began the meeting and Ana started to whine and then to wail. I gently explained that 5 to 7 was our time together, but I did not want to miss either seeing my daughter or the meeting. Of course, they said, we completely understand. They tried to carry on with the afternoon's business, but Ana would not let up because she was hungry. Dick Barnet suggested that it might be better if they scheduled these meetings during the work day so I could get home by 5:00.

I considered Operation Ana a success.

During most of 1975, I collaborated on an almost daily basis with Orlando, planning the Oaxtepec conference. Orlando had the clout to invite over 50 Latin American and Caribbean heads of state, prime ministers and significant parliamentarians and intellectuals, and insure their enthusiastic acceptance. He and I worked together on the US list and we agreed on individuals such as Mark Schneider, Legislative Aid to Senator Kennedy, Riordan Roett, Richard Fagan and Abe Lowenthal, all well known US based Latin Americanists. It is hard to convey what a lasting imprint Orlando's unflinching bravery made on the then ongoing struggle against the dictators reigning throughout the hemisphere in the 1970s. For Latin American youth and progressives, Orlando was a powerful symbol that empowered their own struggles.

Orlando and I became good friends. I got to know his family, and his wife Isabel and I socialized together. Many times Orlando and I would eat lunch together, often at elegant restaurants. One of our early lunches was at a small French restaurant on Connecticut Ave. That day, for the first time, we exchanged personal life stories. Orlando was an inveterate, albeit discreet womanizer and on occasion enjoyed chatting about that aspect of life. I also shared personal tales with him; he was a superb listener and commentator. When the bill arrived, I insisted on paying for myself, and on establishing this as a precedent for future shared meals. Initially, he acted like my decision wounded not only his definition of "the masculine," but also his vision of a proper world. Eventually he accepted my little attempt at gender equality as one of the *"cosas de Roberta"* [Roberta's things] he thought a bit silly but not particularly harmful.

I had one more "gender encounter" with Orlando and then I gave up. One morning early on in our collaboration, Orlando and I were in his office on New Hampshire Ave, outlining the Oaxtepec program. His secretary Lilian, a middle-aged Chilean woman who had known Orlando for many years, had made a pot of coffee and left it on a tray near Orlando's desk. As Orlando and I sat down to work, he asked, me to pour him a cup of coffee with a little sugar.

The coffee tray was much closer to Orlando than it was to me. I was surprised; it had been quite some time since a man expected me to wait on him.

*"Pero Orlando, el café está a tu lado, ¿por qué no te sirves tu solo?"* [Orlando, the coffee is right next to you. Why don't you serve yourself?]

In truth, he was more surprised at my comment than I had been by his request. He stared at me for a moment and then said "Of course, that makes much more sense, doesn't it?"

Other women continued to wait on him, and he accepted it as

his due, but I didn't, and that was okay with him as well.

One of the episodes of his complicated personal life that Orlando shared with me was his affair with Consuelo,[98] a wealthy Venezuelan woman he had met in Caracas soon after being released from jail. His wife, Isabel, and her teenage sons had remained in Santiago to pack up their house before moving to Caracas to join him. After securing his release from Pinochet's prison, Arias had given Orlando a convenient office in the heart of the city and attempted to make Orlando's convalescence as pleasant as possible while he awaited his family.

I tried not to grimace as I listened to a Chilean version of a time worn story. He hadn't meant to fall in love with Consuelo. "I thought it would be a night or two, *pero no. Me he enamorado profundamente y quiero estar con Consuelo. Sufro cuando no estamos juntos.* [This turned out to be much more than a one-night stand. I have fallen deeply in love and I want to be with Consuelo all the time.]

I countered gently. "What about Isabel?"

"*Pero yo la sigo queriendo, claro, pero es distinto. Es la madre de mis hijos. Ahora yo quiero pasar mi vida con Consuelo.*" [I still love her, of course, but it is different. She is the mother of my sons. Now I want to spend my life with Consuelo.]

My role was that of a friend, listening. By my standards, I found Orlando's way of relating to women he loved and was intimately involved with duplicitous and unfair to all the women involved. I didn't say anything more. I knew perfectly well he would not take any feminist discussion seriously. I respected his political work and personal courage, so I kept my criticism of his personal life mostly to myself.

Orlando and I flew to Mexico City Tuesday on November 25, several days before the beginning of the Oaxtepec conference to settle last minute details. On the plane Orlando told me that Consuelo was coming to Oaxtepec to be with him. She would be staying at a hotel not far from the conference site. He was sure his time with her would not interfere with his commitments at the conference.

"However", he added, "just in case something unforeseen occurs, ¿*Puedo contar contigo?*" [Can I count on you for help?]

"*Claro*" [of course], I replied.

I was uncomfortable agreeing to "cover" for Orlando's embroilments. In fact, I felt like the living embodiment of a maximum contradiction between socialism and feminism, and friendship. Yet I felt I had to stand by Orlando. So I would help him out, if need be. I could not, however, resist a pungent comment: "¿*Sabes una cosa*

Orlando? Si alguna vez tu y yo hubiéramos sido una pareja, yo me habría salido en dos semanas."* [You know something Orlando? If you and I were ever a couple, I would have left after two weeks.]

Orlando did not miss a beat: *"No te preocupes mi hijita, ¡yo me habría salido en una semana!"* [Don't worry, my dear. I would have left after one week!]

The five-day conference transpired without a hitch, the bilingual presentations and discussions were well prepared and intellectually stimulating. The atmosphere was cordial and frequently jovial. As expected, political positions differed widely — participants advocated policies ranging from socialist, left liberal to lukewarm liberal. And in accord with traditional procedures in this kind of international gathering, considerable (often important) business was conducted in the corridors outside the conference rooms. When I spotted Oscar Pino Santos, among the most distinguished of Cuba's economists and intellectuals, chatting with several of the North Americans, I thought, "Terrific. This is just the sort of communication we hoped would take place."

The reports, roundtables and colloquia received extensive exposure in much of the Mexican press and throughout Latin America. One of Mexico City's leading papers, *El Sol de Mexico*, gave daily coverage to the conference and published large colored pictures of many of us, particularly the North Americans, along with substantial quotes from our speeches. Orlando and I were delighted at the outcome and we made plans to collaborate with CIDE to publish the proceedings.

Some months later, in early spring of 1976, Orlando moved out of his home at Ogden Court in Bethesda and rented an apartment near Dupont Circle. He had decided to leave Isabel and make a life with Consuelo. Many of us at IPS were aware of the Leteliers' marital troubles, but nobody 'took sides', at least publicly.

Soon after he moved into his own apartment, during a lunch on the patio of the lovely Tabard Inn on N St., Orlando informed me Consuelo was coming to live with him in Washington. I just listened. As we were sipping our expressos and smoking a last cigarette before returning to work, he asked me to hold a dinner where Consuelo could meet his Institute colleagues and feel welcomed in Washington.

*"Esas cosas las haces tan bien, seguro que te gustará Consuelo. Es una persona muy especial."* [You do these things so well and I'm sure you will like Consuelo. She is a very special person.]

My response was spontaneous and immediate:

"¡Pero Orlando, yo no puedo hacer eso! ¿Cómo puedo invitar a toda la gente de IPS siendo yo amiga de Isabel? ¿No crees que sería un poco insultante para ella?" [But Orlando, I can't do that! How can I invite everyone from the Institute to meet Consuelo when I am a friend of Isabel's? Don't you think it would be a little insulting for her?]

"Bueno, bueno, pero ya no estoy viviendo en casa... ¿por qué no pensamos en una cena más reducida, quizá solamente con los directores?" [Okay, okay, but I am no longer living at home... why don't we think about a smaller dinner, perhaps just with the directors?]

I agreed to do a smaller dinner only after calling Isabel to see if she objected. The next day I explained the situation to Isabel. She was gracious as always and said she understood and of course, I should go ahead with the dinner. What else could she say? I would have done the same thing in her place.

We ended up being four for an informal dinner at my home: Orlando, Consuelo, Dick Barnet and myself. Orlando was ebullient, smiling constantly and a bit nervous. Consuelo, a slim, attractive woman of Orlando's age, was reserved and pleasant. A brunette with high cheekbones that hinted at Indian ancestry, she was dressed in designer jeans, a white silk blouse and slim strands of gold chains. She had flawless, creamy white skin. Altogether the impression she conveyed was one of refinement and wealth.

We spoke English because Dick was not fluent in Spanish. Consuelo made appropriate comments but it was hard to get a sense of what kind of person she was. She must have felt like she was on parade in front of a panel of judges. The several hours we spent together were agreeable. However, the atmosphere was subtly inauthentic. For Barnet and myself, the absence of Isabel was a constant presence that one could not acknowledge. Orlando just wanted to make everyone happy and Consuelo (I imagine) wanted to leave a favorable impression of the 'new couple' together. So no one really relaxed.

Minutes after the guests left, Mercedes, who had prepared and served the dinner, made a pronouncement, as she was frequently wont to do. Her non-negotiable declarations, which I had come to appreciate, dealt with both international and individual relations. "Señora Roberta, Orlando nunca va a dejar a Isabel por esa mujer. Los hombres siempre prometen mucho luego no cumplen." [Orlando is never going to leave Isabel for that woman. Men always promise a lot and then they never come through.]

Mercedes was prescient. In mid July, Orlando returned to Ogden Court to live with his family. Orlando never mentioned the return home to me, but I gathered he resumed the various threads of his complicated personal life during the months that were remaining to him to live.

On September 15, 1976 I was in Orlando's office. He told me that the Chilean Junta had stripped him of his nationality and that on September 10 in a speech at Madison Square Garden, New York, he had given his reply: "I was born a Chilean, I am a Chilean and I will die a Chilean. They, the Fascists, were born traitors, live as traitors, and will be remembered forever as Fascist traitors."

I was deeply moved and was almost successful in suppressing the tears welling up in my eyes. We went on to discuss the reactions to his recent article in *The Nation*.[99] Suddenly he stopped in the middle of a sentence and said, "*Roberta, sabes que me van a matar.*" [You know, they are going to kill me.] I smiled and replied, "Orlando, don't be silly. This is America. They can't kill you here."

I remember the date of that conversation because my birthday was the following day, September 16, and at the end of the afternoon Orlando walked over to my office to give me a present: Yves St. Laurent's "Y" perfume. It was the last time I saw him alive.

The bombing was fatal. Orlando died en route to George Washington Hospital and Ronnie shortly afterward, mid-morning, September 21, 1976. Moments after Dick Barnet gave me details, Saul Landau told me Isabel was still at the hospital with her family and Chilean colleagues from the Institute. I immediately caught a cab. I told myself my motive was to be with Isabel, but mostly I needed to keep in motion.

As I walked into the hospital I saw Isabel, ashen, statue-like, and strong. When I hugged her, I realized her body was stiff from the effort to control herself. Standing next to Isabel were Waldo Fortín and Juan Gabriel Valdés, two young veterans of the Chilean struggle whom Orlando had brought to the Institute. I had worked closely with Waldo, and Ana had often played with Juan Gabriel's two young sons. The three of us exchanged intense glances for what seemed like a long minute, but no one could speak. I saw fear and sadness on Waldo Fortín's expressive face; Juan Gabriel Valdés just stared ahead with grim, firm resolution.

I don't remember how and when I came back from 23rd St to the Institute, but that afternoon it was decided I would go to the morgue early next morning to identify Ronnie Moffit's corpse. Her parents lived in New Jersey and her husband Michael Moffit was unable to go. Sue, Dick Barnet's administrative assistant, said she would come with me.

I called Mercedes and said everything was under control at the Institute, but to stay inside with Ana until I got home later that afternoon. She told me over 30 people had called to ask if anything had happened to me. Fortunately, Mercedes' English was adequate to the task of calming down my mother in Pennsylvania.

A flurry of events filled the afternoon. The FBI came to interview all of us. Saul and Ralph Stavins, another Institute fellow who would play an important role in the post-assassination investigation, took charge of gathering the staff for interviewing. Since I knew Orlando well, I told Saul I wanted to be one of the first on the list while the FBI still didn't know enough to delve into his personal life. My interrogation was superficial and brief; it took place around our large, round conference table on the first floor of the Institute. Two FBI officials were present and Ralph Stavins, acting temporarily as Institute counsel, sat near me. I said little more than, "Orlando was my colleague at the Institute and yes, I knew he was an enemy of the Pinochet regime."

Fortunately, the officials appeared to be unaware of my existing extensive FBI file, as I was too, until 1980.[100] After my interview, I went upstairs to my office on the second floor. Waldo Fortín and Marcia Grandon, our Chilean administrative assistant, shared an office. Neither was there and many of the offices were empty. I didn't want to be alone, so I went back to the ground floor. Tension, restlessness and a fog laden with sadness permeated the Institute. It was claustrophobic inside the building. Alyce, the receptionist— still sobbing but aware that I was too stunned to know what to do— told me to go join the demonstration outside the Chilean Embassy, around the corner on Massachusetts Ave. So I did.

A constantly swelling mass of demonstrators was marching in front of the Embassy. In addition to many from the Institute, I recognized members of the Washington policy community who had nothing to do with the Institute—Riordan Roett from the School of Advanced International Studies at Johns Hopkins and some of his colleagues and students; Guy Erb from the Overseas Development Council, Joe Grunwald from Brookings Institution and other 'main stream' folks who did not even know Orlando. The bombing had outraged decent citizens. Soon hundreds had congregated. The indignation would become worldwide.

This was just the beginning of the "fight back" to avenge Orlando's and Ronnie's murder.

The next morning I awoke earlier than usual, confused. Something was wrong. Was Ana crying? No, that was not it. Then reality hit: the morgue. Ronnie's corpse. I mechanically went through the preparations to get myself presentable and drove to identify Ronnie's body.

At the morgue, a middle-aged male attendant led me into a small, sparkling clean, medium size grayish room. A circular stairway in the middle of the room was enclosed by glass. The attendant instructed me to watch for the appearance of the body. The corpses, he explained, were refrigerated on the floors below and then brought up for viewing from outside the glass enclosure on the main floor. I leaned over a wrought iron railing and saw what appeared to be a downward spiraling staircase. Suddenly the staircase started to move upward and when it flattened out, I saw the peaceful reposing face of Ronnie Karpen Moffit. The rest of her body was covered. The official asked both Sue (who had just arrived) and me to identify the body. Each of us, in turn, stated the full name of our dead friend and colleague. The experienced attendant repeated what he had previously told hundreds of grieving individuals: "Thank you, that is all. Will you please sign the forms as you leave." What a quick, lifeless moment it was—so quick, so simple, so efficient, so utterly horrible. I went home and played with Ana for several hours before rejoining the reality of the deaths hovering over IPS.

Over thirty-five years have passed since I watched Ronnie's dead body being propelled up the down staircase and pronounced her name out loud, as if to confirm her murderous end for all humanity. I will remember the tiny smile on the lips of her already pale face and the gentle expression trying to break through the closed eyes as long as I live.

Isabel chose to bury Orlando on Latin American soil. Venezuelan President Carlos Andrés Pérez and Caracas Governor Diego Arias made the arrangements in Caracas, and flew Isabel, Orlando and their four sons there. I accompanied them, as the representative of the Institute.

I had been asked to speak at the funeral and since I would be the only North American to do so, I put considerable thought into the politics as well as the emotions of what I would say. I discussed part of the speech with Mark Schneider, legislative aide to Senator Edward Kennedy and a skilled speechwriter.

As I stepped off the plane with Isabel and her sons, the first person I saw was Isabel Allende, the dead Chilean President's daughter. She and Isabel embraced and then we were all driven to the town hall, where Orlando's body would remain overnight. During the trip from the airport, throngs of Latin Americans, mostly Venezuelans and exiled Chileans, lined the streets ten or more abreast to express solidarity. I was very moved by the dense mass of people holding posters and shouting slogans of support: *"Orlando hoy presente para siempre"* [Orlando, present today and forever] became a loud, unified chorus as we slowly made our way from the airport to the meeting room of the Concejo del Distrito Federal (town hall of the federal district) where the President of the Republic would welcome Orlando's coffin.

The small reception area was crammed with family, close friends, dignitaries, the press and photographers. Isabel and her sons stood close to the coffin. It was so crowded everyone was almost stuck together. I was at one end of the imposing box that held Orlando's body when President Carlos Andrés Pérez walked confidently into the room. As the President began to speak, standing inches away from me, he moved his feet slightly and the heel of one of his brightly shined heavy black shoes landed firmly on my left toe (I was wearing low-heeled open toe black sandals). The pain was excruciating, but I dared not move. I do not remember a word of what he said; all of my attention was consumed in controlling my reaction to the large heel grinding into my bare toe. I don't think anyone in the room was aware of the unfortunate placement of the President's heel; any pained expression on my faced was surely attributed to the solemn occasion. Later, at the hotel, I bandaged my toe and selected another pair of shoes for the march the following morning at 11:30 to accompany first the coffin, and then the hearse to the Cementerio del Este. Thousands walked with us.

As I stepped to the microphone, I was aware that not only was I the sole North American among the speakers, but also the only woman. I was glad the Institute had asked me to be part of a eulogy to a valiant, grand human being. It was one of my proudest moments as an American citizen. I swallowed hard, raised my voice and began: [101]

"I am here today as a representative of the Institute for Policy Studies where Orlando worked during the last two years of his life. But I am also part of the North American people who have seen that believing in democratic values and human rights makes us soldiers and the battleground can be Washington, DC.

We are here to pay tribute to Orlando, to Chile, and I, particularly, to the representatives of the people of Latin America.

We are present to say that this act of horrible violence—to kill this noble human being—does not belong in a civilized world.

We are here to say that men and women who are committed to liberty will not rest until liberty exists in Chile.

But we are also here to ask questions.

Who assassinated Orlando Letelier and why?

Why was he imprisoned for a year with no charges against him?

Who bestowed and who bestows the authority to define the Chilean nationality to a group of puppets?

Why does a military junta exist that forces men and women to flee their homeland because they believe in justice, equality and liberty?

The answers to these questions are what I and thousands of other North Americans are going to demand.

It was the United States government that violated the democratic traditions of Chile, as well as those of its own country, with an economic boycott against the Popular Unity government—as well as other actions that I do not need to repeat here.

It was a Secretary of State who sent weapons to keep the junta in power, in spite of the torture, in spite of the assassination, in spite of the terror that exists in Chile today.

We come here today to express our condemnation, together with Orlando's, of those persons who govern Chile today, and those that govern in any other land, who support the terror and violence of the junta. They will be regarded by history as traitors.

Some day soon the current situation will change because the force of history has to be—is—oriented toward liberty.

Let us pledge now, together with Orlando, to do everything possible so that this day comes soon."

The following day I flew back to Washington, DC.

I knew Orlando's murder would precipitate changes in the Institute—probably cause a re-examination of its program and goals. I was not sure how the Latin American Unit would fare. By 1976 the New Left had all but disappeared, but had bequeathed a lasting legacy, especially the women's movement. I was proud to look around the country and see how much mainstream America was benefitting from our feminist struggles, but it was clear I would not be part of a socialist revolution in my lifetime.

Ana would soon be two years old. I felt I had run the gamut of a politically active life for the time being. Although I liked the work at the Institute and felt it was worthwhile, it was time for a new chapter for my daughter and myself.

Figure 11. Karen Spaulding, Roberta, Martin Diskin with Cuban comrades in Santiago de Cuba in Oriente Province, near Sierra Cristal where I drank the best "buchito" [tiny cup of Cuban coffee] I have ever had. July 1969. Personal archive.

Figure 12. Roberta sitting on "el malecón" in Havana, Cuba. July 1969. Courtesy Elizabeth Diggs archive.

Figure 13. Roberta and John McDermott on the "guaguita" [little bus] traveling with the NUC group across Cuba. July 1969. Courtesy John McDermott archives.

Figure 14. Roberta pregnant in Washington, DC. September 1974. Personal archive.

Figure 15. Nursing Ana Simone. Washington, DC. November 1974. Personal archive.

## EU Saca de Iberoamérica 23 mil Millones al año

**Viene de la Página 15**

861 a 16 mil 220 millones de dólares (de 73 mil 262 y medio a 202 mil 750 millones de pesos) de 1966 a 1973, pero el 94 por ciento de esos totales fue vendido a los mercados locales quedando en la exportación sólo el 6 por ciento restante.

Comentó sobre el comercio exterior que en tanto en 1950 las exportaciones latinoamericanas representaban el 11 por ciento del total mundial, para 1970 cayó al 5 por ciento. Finalmente dijo que en los últimos 15 años, los países latinoamericanos obtuvieron un saldo comercial favorable superior a los 21 mil millones de dólares ($262 mil 500 millones), sin embargo, los pagos netos por utilidades e intereses de capital extranjero superaron los 43 mil millones ($537 mil 500 millones), los que al añadírseles los gastos de fletes y servicios relacionados, por casi 17 mil millones ($212 mil 500 millones), determinan saldos desfavorables cuyo monto alcanzó los 37 mil 240 millones ($465 mil 500 millones).

Figure 16. Conference on "Present and Future of U.S.-Latin American Economic and Political Relations" held in Oaxtepec, Mexico, co-sponsored by Institute for Policy Studies and CIDE, a Mexican think tank. El Sol de México, November 26, 1975.

Figure 17. The assassination of Orlando Letelier. Washington, DC. September 21, 1976. Personal archive.

Figure 18. Roberta with daughter Ana Simone on her wedding day. NYC, November 2, 2002. Personal archive.

Figure 19. Jason Cowart, my son-in-law. Personal archive.

Figure 20. Roberta in Cambridge, MA. Fall, 2011. Personal archive.

# EPILOGUE

I never married again. By choice. I wanted Ana Simone to be the sole emotional focus of my life, and the rewards have been immeasurable.

After I left the Institute for Policy Studies in 1979, I taught Caribbean issues at the Johns Hopkins School of International Studies, around the corner from IPS, off Dupont Circle. I was an adjunct for several years, but I needed to make more money. Unable to get a job in Washington that would allow me to support my daughter, I soon understood my left wing political resumé had closed all doors to me. Ronald Reagan was President and the nascent far right was galloping to power.

By 1982, I had backed myself into a corner professionally and financially. Reinsertion into the academic world was impossible. I had not published scholarly work in a decade and the American university was in crisis; tenure track positions dried up during the second half of the 70's and never returned to the fulsome years of post World War II.

So, in August 1982, Ana and I went to live in Israel. I had cousins in Tel Aviv that I was fond of, having gotten to know them during their frequent stays in the United States. During my five years teaching at Tel Aviv University, I experienced a new type of marginalization. I found Israel a conservative, tradition-bound society. Adherence to Jewish ritual, family and religion (even though in the 1980s most Jews I met in Tel Aviv considered themselves secular) was the glue that bound together Jewish Israelis. Beyond the family, I had no close Israeli friends. Even though I was welcomed as an American Jew, I soon realized I had little in common with my peers. It wasn't their fault: I was not a Zionist; hadn't served in the army, felt overwhelmed by the constant reminders of the Holocaust. The inward looking sameness was claustrophobic. Initially I made an effort to learn Hebrew, but soon gave up. Why learn such a difficult language that was only spoken in Israel, especially when English was the widely used second language?

I never met another single mother. My situation was not condemned on moral grounds — Ana and I were Jewish and that was paramount. However, it became obvious that I did not fit into any niche in this hierarchical society. Here I was, free from the kind of anti-Semitism I experienced in the United States and I felt utterly marginalized! The American Women's movement was largely regarded as a frivolity; Israeli men and women had more "serious" goals, like defending themselves from hostile neighbors. Because of the importance of the military, a new phenotype appeared: the *macho Israeli man*. Israel no longer admired the stereotypical sensitive Jewish intellectual man who disliked physical violence. These new Jews, men and women, were strong and tough, physically and emotionally. No one was going to do them in again.

As an adolescent, I had been cowed, intimidated and scarred by the anti-Semitism in Caldwell. Being different was a curse. All I wanted to do was to belong and feel accepted.

On the other hand, Ana, in Israel between the age of 7 and 12, was strengthened by the sameness of her peers: the families of her friends came from Turkey, Iraq, France, England, Australia, North and South America, but they were all Jews and belonged together in Israel. Ana learned Hebrew, joined the Young Pioneers along with her classmates, and excelled in physical undertakings. She, like her friends, was proud to be a Jew and loved life in the sun and sea of Tel Aviv. No one was excluded on the grounds of being different. I watched as Ana became a strong, confident teenager and was grateful to Israel for her experience.

We returned to the United States in 1987 and lived in various places. I reconstructed my academic life both as a feminist scholar and administrator, and returned to live in Cambridge, MA ten years ago.

The feminist journey is ongoing. Be it Europe, Latin America, the Caribbean or in my own country, I have never faltered in my commitment to socialist/radical feminism. It has been the constant anchor in my life for over half a century. I am so grateful to have had the privilege to be a young activist during 1960-1976.

***

Years ago, when Ana was an undergraduate at Columbia University in the 1990s, I asked her why she never took a women's studies course. Her answer was brief and to the point: *"Mom I've been in a women's studies course since I was two years old!"* My journey had many positive outcomes, perhaps none as satisfying as my daughter.

# ACKNOWLEDGEMENTS

Among the many people who helped me in the process of writing this book, one heads the list: Ana Simone Salper. My daughter Ana Simone was with me from the first sentence to the last word. Her unconditional love and incisive mind helped at every stage of my writing.

Dan Frankforter, Professor Emeritus of History at Pennsylvania State University-Erie and my former colleague and close friend, meticulously and skillfully copy edited an early draft of my manuscript. I am indebted to him for his intelligent, relentless improvement of the clarity of my prose.

Martha Vicinus, formidable intellectual and dear friend, ordered my thoughts and prose in essential ways, patiently reading draft after draft.

Louis Kampf, Elizabeth Diggs, Emily Arnold McCully, Roxanne Dunbar-Ortiz, Rosalyn Baxandall, Claire Bruyere, Marilyn Kriney, Linda Dittmar, Victor Wallis and Susan Fainstein, friends and skilled professionals, provided help and encouragement whenever needed. I fondly thank each of them.

Paul Lauter and Barbara Kessel generously gave me complete access to their personal files for my research on the New University Conference. Clara Kirkwood graciously participated in several telephone interviews, Jane Kenealy, archivist at the San Diego Historical Society, helped me locate copies of "The Carla Kirkwood Papers" for my chapter on the first year of the women's studies program at San Diego State. Archivists at San Diego State University also provided me with essential documents for this chapter. The archivists at the Charles McCormick Library of Special Collections at Northwestern University helped locate useful material from the Jenny Knauss Collection. James Lesar of Washington, D.C., my Freedom of Information lawyer, patiently dealt with the FBI to obtain as much of my file as possible.

I want to thank Shulamit Reinharz, Founder and Director of the Women's Studies Research Center (WSRC) at Brandeis University, for her help and unremitting optimism. Thanks also to Sarah Hough-Napierata, Assistant Director of the WSRC, for her humor and technical help. I am grateful, also, for the space provided to me by the Women's Studies Research Center as a Resident Scholar, and for the encouragement and friendship of many of the scholars.

Finally, Louise Bernikow, New York editor extraordinaire, did her magic during the final, crucial months of producing this manuscript. Without her incisive intelligence and breadth of knowledge, *Domestic Subversive* would not exist.

# ENDNOTES

1   File document SD100-14670, page 13 of 21 page administrative report from San Diego field office to FBI headquarters, 18 Feb. 1972.

2   Or the ADEX — Administrative Index — to which the name was changed in 1971. There have been a series of names the FBI has used for the Security Index, since the 1920s and the "Red Scares," to mean the same thing: a list of persons who the FBI thinks are potentially dangerous to the public safety or internal security of the United States and who should be interned in case of "national emergency." ADEX was computerized in 1972 and discontinued, in this form, in January 1976.

3   Sara Evans, op.cit., See also Rosalyn Baxandall and Linda Gordon, *Dear Sisters, Dispatches from the Women's Liberation Movement* (New York: Basic Books, 2000) 41-66.

4   A four sided spinning top with a Hebrew letter written on each side. The four letters together mean "A great miracle happened there" (meaning the creation of a Jewish homeland). The player spins the *dreidel* and when it stops, the letter that is facing up decides the fate. The letter NUN means nothing happens, next player spins the *dreidel*; GIMEL - player takes all money in the pot; HEY - player takes half of the pot; SHIN - player must put one coin into the pot. During the holiday, children 'gamble' with Hanukah *gelt* (real or candy). The game ends when all but two top players have run out of money. The winners often get presents in addition to everyone else's "money."

5   The Fulbright exchange did not exist with Spain at that time.

6   In 1957, British literary critic Ian Watts published *The Rise of the Novel: Studies in Defoe, Richardson and Fielding*, which explored the connections between social change in 18th-century England and the emergence of the novel as a distinct genre. It helped shift the attention of literary criticism from New Criticism, which em-

phasized poetry, to a focus on sociological and cultural criticism..

7    In 1987, Tod Gitlin wrote, "In my sophomore year, 1960, I was swept up in a Harvard-Radcliffe peace group called Tocsin. I identified with a scatter of campus organizer-intellectuals who called themselves the New Left. In 1963, at twenty, I was elected president of their organizational center, Students for a Democratic Society, SDS, which numbered a grand total of six hundred paid members and harbored the modest ambition of shaking America to its roots." Tod Gitlin, *The Sixties: Years of Hope, Days of Rage* (New York: Bantam Books, 1987) 3.

8    Pozuelo de Alarcón is now an affluent city of 80, 000 with the highest per capita income in the country.

9    The US government feared the growth of a strong Communist movement in Spain if they withdrew their unconditional support for General Franco.

10    The *"Sección Feminina"* or Women's Branch of the Spanish Fascist Party was a powerful government tool in the national redefinition of 'femininity' that took place under Franco.

11    *Ramón María del Valle-Inclán: Questions of Gender*, eds. Carol Maier and Roberta L. Salper. (London and Toronto: Bucknell University Press, 1994). Valle-Inclán (1866-1936), dramatist, novelist, poet and essayist, was one of the leading turn-of-the-20$^{th}$ century Spanish writers. Esteemed both for their aesthetics and social criticism, most of Valle-Inclán's works (there are more than forty) were banned in Spain during the Franco era. It was impossible to locate a complete edition of Valle-Inclán's texts in Spain until some years after Franco's death.

12    Gilman was married to Teresa Guillén, the daughter of renowned Spanish poet Jorge Guillén, who had been exiled from Spain in 1938. Guillén was a member of Spain's "Generation of 1927" along with Federico García Lorca, Luis Buñuel, Salvador Dali, Pedro Salinas and others. This small group of poets, painters and playwrights rebelled against the conservative romanticism dominant in Spain. Inspired by the cubist work of Picasso, they began experimenting and collaborating with surrealist techniques. Guillén taught at Wellesley College in Massachusetts from 1941 to

1967 and died in Spain in 1984. Many of this generation (including Ortega y Gasset and his descendants) and their families remained in close contact after the Civil War and continue to have strong links to this day.

13   *Writing a Woman's Life.* (New York: Ballantine Books, 1989), 18.

14   However, in spite of Prime Minister José Luis Zapatero's social democracy, all is still not entirely rosy for women in Spain where, as the London-based *Guardian Weekly* reported on April 25, 2008, "one woman a week dies as a result of domestic violence" (p.7).

15   Marlene gave me statistics on the exploitation of women in the workplace—particularly black women. This was 1968 and those of us who wanted to argue for reform needed statistics to confirm the existence of gender inequality. The percentage of black working women in the labor force had always been proportionately greater than that of white women. In 1900, 41% of black women were employed as compared to 17% of white women. In 1960, 44% of black married women with children under six worked outside the home in contrast to 29% of white women. Black women did not need just "equal opportunity to work"—forty years ago their need was more basic. A huge segment of the black female population needed access to education in order to move out of domestic service and other forms of menial labor at the bottom of society where most were trapped.

16   *NUC Papers* 3 (fall 1970) 1. Quoted statements were agreed upon by the membership at NUC's first annual convention in June 1969 in Iowa City.

17   For analyses of the roots of WLM in the civil rights movement of the early 1960s, see Salper, "The Development of the American Women's Liberation Movement, 1967-1971," in *Female Liberation, History and Current Politics.* R Salper, ed. (NY: Alfred A. Knopf, 1972) 169-183; Sara Evans, *Personal Politics: The Roots of Women's Liberation in the Civil Rights Movement and the New Left* (NY: Vintage, 1980), and Rosalyn Baxandall and Linda Gordon, eds, *Dear Sisters, Dispatches from the Women's Liberation Movement* (NY: Basic Books, 2000).

18   Subsequently Roxanne Dunbar changed her name to Roxanne Dunbar-Ortiz.

19   "Female Liberation as the Basis for Social Revolution," published in the journal Dunbar and others started at that time in Boston, *No More Fun and Games*. Issue 2, Spring 1969.

20   "Bread and Roses," published in *Leviathan* (June 1969).

21   A year later, Marge Piercy published her now classic article on sexism in the radical movement, "The Grand Coolie Dam," *Leviathan* (May 1970).

22   Within a year NUC had identified itself as "a national organization of radicals who work in and around institutions of higher education." Its mission was two-fold: We, the members of NUC, critiqued the hierarchical teaching methods used in primary schools to accustom students to obedience, we opposed the grading system used to instill the spirit of competition, and we objected to the system of tracking in secondary schools that channeled students into college preparatory or vocational programs based principally on their social and economic backgrounds. But the force of our work was aimed at higher education. American universities received money from and were partnered with private industry and the government. This resulted in a symbiotic, but unbalanced exchange of goals, intellectual and human capital. Corporate money too often directed and controlled the university. We aimed to transform education so that it would furnish students with the critical knowledge and skills needed to understand (and when necessary, change) the relationship of power between a corporate State and its educational system.

At its height in 1970-71, NUC had a paid membership of approximately 2,000 members on 60 campuses. In addition several thousand more were local members or fellow travelers. About half the members were junior faculty and half were graduate students, with a sprinkling of senior faculty and other members of the college community. Importantly, NUC provided a new organizational framework for continued mobilization around an issue that had torn SDS apart during 1967-68: the relationship between the women's movement and male-run radical organizations.

23    Ramón María del Valle-Inclán (1866-1936) was a dramatist, novelist, poet and one of the most innovative stylists of Spanish literature. He attacked the hypocrisy, moralism and sentimentality of bourgeois playwrights while satirizing the views of the ruling classes. In particular, he targeted concepts such as masculinity, militarism, patriotism and hegemonic attitudes about the Crown and the Catholic Church. Valle-Inclán was the subject of my doctoral dissertation and subsequently, two books and numerous articles.

24    Over two years later, in a *NUC Newsletter* (Vol. 4, No. 17, July 4, 1971: 4), the Coordinator of the NUC Women's caucus summarized the issue this way: "Our relationship to the rest of the women's movement is still very ambiguous... I think as NUC women work on our program those relationships will be strengthened... As long as [male] chauvinism is still rampant in NUC, women have good reasons for not joining and we should not cut ourselves off from these women..."

25    Saul Slapikoff, Professor Emeritus, Tufts University, and a member of NUC from its inception, told me the daycare center at Tufts University that NUC members struggled to start in 1969 is still functioning. "Without the initiative of NUC members," Saul explained, "day care would never have been established that early at Tufts." Conversation with Slapikoff, December 27, 2007, Cambridge, MA.

26    Nicolás Sánchez Albornoz, a historian then based at New York University, and Antonio Sánchez Barbudo, a literary critic then at the University of Wisconsin, were exiled from Francoist Spain after the Spanish Civil War. Clara Lida, an Argentinean historian, and Iris Zavala, a literary critic and writer from Puerto Rico, belong to the next generation, but by the late 1960s already had solid reputations in the world of Hispanism.

27    The following quotes attributed to Louis Kampf took place in a November 30, 2007 chat in Cambridge, MA.

28    Kampf and Lauter, p. 34.

29    File document from Security Agent in Charge, Pittsburgh (100-16075) to Director FBI, 2 April 1969.

30     Robinson's *Sex, Class, and Culture* (New York: Methuen, 1978) was a groundbreaking book of feminist critical theory.

31     The constitution stated that "The National Committee (NC) shall have ultimate authority over the operation of the National Office... membership shall be as follows:

> the fourteen national officers, seven of whom shall be women and seven of whom shall be men, elected by the convention, and serving as the Executive Committee.
> up to two representatives, one male and one female, from each chapter with members not exceeding 25 members. Each chapter shall have additionally one representative for each group of 25 persons after the first 25."

The constitution also mandated that the National Committee meet four times a year and that there be a membership convention once each year which any member could attend. Constitution reprinted in *NUC Newsletter* (Chicago, IL), Vol. III, No. I (August 15, 1969).

32     Conversation with Lauter, May 2, 2007, Trinity College, Hartford, CT.

33     "What Has the Power?" published by WOMEN from the New University Conference, 1970. This is a thrity-one page document with no page numbers; it is valuable both because of its content and because it became the first of ten newsletters from the NUC women's caucus issued during 1970-71. Starting with the second issue, the publication was called *NUC Women's caucus Newsletter*. This quote and the following are from an article entitled "History of the Women's caucus."

34     Ibid.

35     Members: Beth Cagan, Elizabeth Diggs, Lucy Gadlin, Diana Horwitz, Barbara Joye, Rosario Levins, Ruth Mahaney, Inez Martinez, Lucy Moore, Allyne Rosenthal, Michele Russell, Carol Sheehan, Rue Wallace, Rinda West, Priscilla Zirker and Terry Radinsky.

36     "What Has The Power?" published by WOMEN from the New University Conference, 1970. This is a 31 page document with

no page numbers; it is valuable both because of its content and because it became the first of ten newsletters from the NUC women's caucus issued during 1970-71. The above quote is from the third page. Starting with the second issue, the publication was called *NUC Women's caucus Newsletter*.

37      Many NUC women wrote articles for the *Women's caucus Newsletter*, as it was called, starting with the second issue. A significant number would distinguish themselves in a plethora of ways in the years to come: Maurine Greenwald, Martha Vicinus, Heather Booth, Ann Kaplan, Ellen Bravo, among others. Ten issues were published, between fall 1970 and the end of 1971.

38      See articles on "Men's Meetings" by Mark Ritchey, Bart Meyers and Len Radinsky in *NUC Newsletter*, Vol. 4, No.17 (July 4, 1971): 12-15.

39      Members of the delegation were: Jim Cockcroft, University of Wisconsin at Milwaukee, Latin American history; Elizabeth Diggs, Queens College, English literature; Martin Diskin, MIT, Latin American anthropology; Alex Georgiadas, University of California, Berkeley, Latin American history; Barbara Kessel, Malcolm X Community College in Chicago, English and American literature; John McDermott, MIT, political journalist; Ruth Misheloff, The New School, American literature; Michael Ornstein, Johns Hopkins, Sociology; Len Radinsky, University of Chicago, Anatomy; Lillian Robinson, MIT, Comparative Literature; Roberta Salper, University of Pittsburgh, Spanish and Latin American literature; Judith Shapiro, University of Washington, Economics; Karen Spalding, Rutgers, Latin American history; Anne-Marie Taylor, University of Wisconsin, Latin American literature; Carl Tunberg, Central State College in Wilberforce, Ohio, playwright. This list was published on the first page of the *NUC Newsletter*, Vol. III, No. 3 (September 15, 1969). Years later when I obtained my FBI file, a list of "NUC delegates to Cuba" was released to me, marked "Confidential," and all names except my own were blacked out.

40      Our trip preceded by about six months the start of the "Venceremos Bridgades," the hundreds of American students who came to Cuba to cut sugar cane, starting in January 1970. In their file on me, the FBI mistakenly gave me credit for going to Cuba to make arrangements for the Venceremos Brigades.

41     One of the most influential figures in Latin American literature, José Lezama Lima, poet and novelist (1912-1976), became world famous with his 1966 novel *Paradiso,* which was instantly acknowledged as a masterpiece in the Spanish-speaking world. It is a linguistic tour de force, written in an elaborate, baroque style, a semi-autobiography with complex homosexual interludes. It has been translated into dozens of languages.

42     In the early 1970s, the first Cuban Congress of Education and Culture, voicing the opinion of its hundreds of thousands of participants representing every segment of the Cuban population, declared homosexuality a "social pathology which reflects leftover bourgeois decadence and [... that] has no place in the formation of the New Man which Cuba is building." This was the prevailing public stance when I was in Cuba. Over thirty years later, radical changes had taken place. In 2003, Mariela Castro, a professional sexologist and the daughter of Raúl Castro, the President of Cuba, and Vilma Espín, the first president of the Federation of Cuban Women, became director of The National Center for Sex Education [Centro Nacional de Educación Sexual, or CENESEX], a government-funded organization that is well known for advocating tolerance of lesbian, gay, transgender and bisexual issues on the island. Since 2008 Cuba has provided free sex change surgery.

43     A new institution created in 1960, the Culture Council was headed in 1969 by novelist Lisandro Otero, who had fought, together with Padilla, against the dictatorship before the triumph of the Revolution in 1959.

44     The controversy over *Fuera de juego* marginalized Padilla, and in 1971, when officials learned he was writing a novel that also would be an affront to the government, he was arrested. Padilla then recanted publicly by reading a statement before the writers' union saying he had been wrong for questioning and challenging the Revolution. He let the world know he was not the author of the statement and that he was acting against his will by letting stand the grammatical mistakes of the state security official who wrote it. The scandal brought international condemnation of the role censorship had begun to play in the Cuban revolutionary process. Thanks to the intervention of Sen. Ted Kennedy, Padilla, who had been held in virtual house arrest since 1971, came to the United States in 1980.

He died here in 2000 at the age of 68.

45     Translated as *The Autobiography of a Runaway Slave, Esteban Montejo*. (NY: Pantheon Books, 1968). With this book, Barnet established a new testimonial narrative tradition and won international recognition.

46     Cuban sense of humor, characterized by frank, quick wit.

47     On July 26, 1953, Fidel Castro and 100 rebels launched an assault on the Moncada barracks, the headquarters of the Batista military in Santiago, and the second most important military garrison in the country. The attack failed, and Fidel and the others escaped to the nearby Sierra Maestra mountains. Over one-third of the rebels were immediately captured, tortured and killed. Fidel was captured later and put on trial, where he defended himself and delivered his "History will absolve me" speech. Upon his release from jail, Fidel returned to the Sierra Maestra on December 2, 1956 and lived in the mountains for two years until the success of the revolutionaries on January 1, 1959. The Moncada barracks are now a school and the Museum of the Revolution.

48     The Communist Party in Cuba is a party of the "vanguard," that is, membership is not automatic for all Cubans. One opts to join and then passes through various stages of acceptance.

49     One of Cuba's important newspapers.

50     Elizabeth Diggs, "The New Women vs. Old Ideas," *Cuba: Essays by NUC members in Cuba during summer 1969*. Chicago: New University Conference, 1970, p. 25.

51     In 1969, household and family relational reforms were not yet on the agenda. It would not be until 4 or 5 years after my summer in Cuba that Cuban women would begin publicly to insist on more equality at home and in the family. Ultimately, many of their demands that men share housework and childrearing would be incorporated in a major piece of legislation, the Family Code of 1975. These demands were, in Cuban style, discussed nation-wide by mass government sponsored organizations (instituted in the early 1960s), such as the Federation of Cuban Women (FMC) and the Women's Front of the Cuban Workers Central (CTC). The CTC,

with over a million members, was the workers' trade union organization, and about a third of its membership was female. Workers at each workplace elected one woman to the "Women's Front," and it was her job to identify and help solve problems that challenged women's productivity, such as daycare centers, school lunches, help for nursing the sick, special work schedules, leaves of absence and other issues that were of special importance to female workers.

52   The term "brigade" — a group of persons organized for a specific purpose — is widely used in Cuba to denote any group of persons in solidarity with the Revolution that is charged with carrying out a specific government-approved task.

53   A phrase in vogue at the time.

54   Personal notes from the meeting with Vilma Espín (Havana, July 1969).

55   Six years later, in 1975, after over a year's discussion by the populace in numerous local and national organizations, a sweeping new Family Code became law in Cuba. It stipulated a new equality between women and men in their social relationships. "Marriage," the text of the newly formulated Cuban civil marriage ceremony stated, "is constituted on the basis of equal rights and duties of both spouses." The clauses in this code that stipulated both parents' equal responsibility for childcare and housework became heated topics for national discussion. In the early years, it was a widely used educational tool for island wide discussion.

Much has changed in the years since the Family Code became Law — and in the Cuba that I first visited over forty years ago. Cuba has instigated new measures to improve the lives of women that would have seemed incredible to us in 1969. In 1997 the FMC created a national organization to combat domestic violence and set up shelters for battered women across the island. Currently women are entitled to eighteen weeks fully-paid maternity leave (six weeks before birth and twelve after), plus an additional forty weeks at sixty percent pay, assured of returning to their same job. Both father and mother have the option to take paid leave at sixty percent of their salaries to care for their infants from the age of twelve weeks up to one year of age. Fathers may take this leave regardless of whether the couple is married or not.

56     National Organization for Women, founded by Betty Friedan in 1966.

57     Original letter in author's personal files.

58     Organization of Chicano activists that González created in 1968; two years later the Crusade would become *La Raza Unida*, the most influential Chicano organization in the country at the time. Subsequently embraced by César Chávez and farm workers, *La Raza Unida* later turned to the struggles of urban youth, and increasingly, to political participation on a national scale, particularly farm workers' strikes.

59     Louis Kampf recalled that during one of the MLA Executive Council meetings in 1969 two professors asked to meet with the EC to request support in the ongoing process of creating a new discipline within the profession: Chicano Studies. One of the professors was Carlos Blanco Aguinaga, a prominent Spanish Hispanist then at the University of California at San Diego and the other, a young Chicano colleague, Arturo Madrid. Madrid would go on to become one of the leaders in the development of Chicano Studies and in later life achieved national prominence as an administrator and bureaucrat working on behalf of Chicanos. *Conversation with Louis Kampf, Cambridge, MA, November 9, 2007.*

60     "Women's Studies: Theory and Practice," *Some Politics of Women's Studies*, (*NUC Women's caucus Newsletter*, #8, 1971), 2.

61     *Ramparts* 10.6 (December 1971): 55.

62     In *Flying Close to the Sun* (NY: Seven Stories Press, 2007), Cathy Wilkerson recounts this episode.

63     Among the many passionately committed undergraduates in "The History and Social Role of Women" was psychology major Gail Hornstein. She took a leadership role from the beginning and has since gone on to become a major figure in Women's Studies. As Professor of Psychology, Dr. Hornstein chaired the Women's Studies Program at Mount Holyoke College for seven years and was the founding director of the Five College Women's Studies Research Center for ten years.

64   *Pittsburgh Press*, March 1, 1970, page unknown.

65   "Women's Studies," *Newsweek*, Oct. 26, 1970, 61.

66   The origins of the San Diego WSP are also recounted in Catherine Orr, "Representing Women/Disciplining Feminism: Activism, Professionalism and Women's Studies," Ph.D. diss. University of Minnesota June 1998; Ellen Messer-Davidow, *Disciplining Feminism, 87-127;* Marilyn Boxer, *When Women Ask the Question, Creating Women's Studies in America* (Baltimore and London: The Johns Hopkins Press, 1998) 7-14.

67   *Author's Personal files.* Dated 1970.

68   "Proposal for a Center," 3. Xerox copy dated spring 1970. *Personal files.*

69   The coordinating committee would hypothetically be composed of two representatives from each of the seven components, plus two staff representatives from San Diego State Women's Liberation and two from the community.

70   Carla Kirkwood, telephone conversation July 28, 2009. I have focused on Carla Kirkwood because she was the only student who was present in the struggle to create the program who served continually as a member of the Women's Studies Board from its inception in fall 1970 to its demise in 1974. A sophomore when she took my course on "Contemporary Issues in the Women's Liberation Movement" in fall 1970, Kirkwood had been active on a women's committee against the Viet-Nam War during the two years she studied at San Diego City College before coming to San Diego State in 1969. Her father was in the military and she has lived in San Diego all her life. An Emmy-winning writer and director, Kirkwood has been a teacher of performance and public art, acting and directing. In 2009, she was Director of International Studies at Southwestern College in Chula Vista, California.

71   Barbara Kessel, a Chicago-based NUC member, accepted a half-time position in the program and accompanied me to San Diego.

72      SDCF (now "San Diego University Foundation") is a nonprofit corporation charted to [provide and augment programs and goals not financially supported by the State of California. It administers funds for grants and contracts and oversees real property development and management for the university. In 1970 Standard Oil was a contributor to the foundation.

73      Carol was also given a quarter-time position in the WSP. She taught the course in Field Experience in the fall semester. This provided the link between the foundation, the proposed CWSS and the university academic program—a link that the foundation insisted on in order to be eligible for funding. The remaining $6,000 paid for two part-time staff in the Women's Studies office.

74      F. Champion Ward, "The Fabric of Universities," *Annual Report of the Ford Foundation*, 1968, pp.19-20.

75      *Women's Studies Board, Minutes of meeting November 19, 1970.* Sherry Smith and Carin Howard were student members of the board. *Carla Kirkwood Papers,* San Diego Historical Society. Collection 208, file 14, p.5.

76      The Dean appointed Richard Wright, associate professor of geography and Richard Ruetten, professor and chair of history. They joined Shelly Chandler, Hilda Nelson and Clint Jencks.

77      Carla Kirkwood, telephone conversation with author, August 11, 2009.

78      Carla Kirkwood, telephone conversation with author, July 28, 2009.

79      The Revolutionary Union (RU), A Marxist-Leninist group formed in 1968, worked with working class youth and community college students. Subsequently RU became the Revolutionary Communist Party and still exists today.

80      According to Kirkwood, the first openly gay faculty member in the WSP was Margaret Small in 1973-74. See Salper, "US

Government Surveillance and the Women's Liberation Movement, 1969-1973: A Case Study," *Feminist Studies* 34 (3), (Fall 2008): 431-455. Marilyn Salzman-Webb suspected that the women who were fracturing women's groups in 1969-71 might be provocateurs intent on magnifying tensions in the groups. She is quoted in Messer-Davidow, *Disciplining Feminism,* 119. See also Ruth Rosen, *The World Split Open: How the Modern Women's Movement Changed America* (NY: Penguin Press, 2000).

81    Mimeo copy dated Dec.11, 1970; Salper personal files.

82    Messer-Davidow, 88.

83    According to the 2010 US census, there are now more Puerto Ricans living in the United States than in Puerto Rico; 4.6 million reside in the United States and and 3.7 on the island.

84    Popular term for Puerto Ricans, derived from "Boríken," name given the island by the indigenous Taino indians.

85    Arbona and I always spoke in Spanish. During my time in the PSP the decision to use Spanish or English depended on what the person with whom I was speaking preferred.

86    "Mi amor", literally "my love" is a casual term of affection widely used in the Spanish speaking Caribbean. "Mi negro" or "negrito" is also a term of endearment for all colors of Caribbeans.

87    For excellent histories of Puerto Rico, see Alfredo López, *Doña Licha's Island.* Boston: South End Press, 1987, and Raymond Carr, *Puerto Rico: A Colonial Experiment.* New York: Vintage Press, 1984. For an understanding of the Puerto Rican social movement of the 1960's and 1970's in the US, see *The Puerto Rican Movement, Voices from the Diaspora,* Andrés Torres and José E. Velázquez, eds. Philadelphia: Temple University Press, 1998. The co-editors were in the PSP Leadership in New York when I was a member of the party. I knew them both and frequently worked with "Che", Velázquez' nickname.

88    "Coño" is literally the word for female genitalia. However, it is widely used as strong way of exclaiming "Damn!"

89     Carmen Vivian Rivera, "Our Movement: One Woman's Story," in Torres and Velázquez, *The Puerto Rican Movement, Voices from the Diaspora*, p. 208.

90     The 2010 census indicates that 848,000 Puerto Ricans now live in Central Florida, especially in the Orlando and Tampa area, second only to the Puerto Rican population in New York. "Many of the Puerto Ricans who have settled in Florida in the past decade hail from the well-educated or professional class, a departure from those who set down roots in New York decades ago," *New York Times*, June 10, 2011, p. A12.

91     As Max Elbaum wrote, "With the prestige of the radical tradition on the Island behind it, a deep bond with Cuba and a base among older workers and intellectuals as well as youth, the PSP was able to spread its message quite broadly. More than 2000 people attended the official founding meeting of the PSP's US branch in the spring of 1973... Leninism was the dominant perspective on the Puerto Rican left.," *Revolution in the Air, Sixties Radicals Turn to Lenin Mao and Che* (New York: Verso, 2002), 76.

92     Formed in 1969 in New York City, the Young Lords consisted principally of US-based Puerto Ricans and its premise was that they were a 'national minority' in the US. They were not a Marxist-Leninist Party. Its strength was community organizing, and service, although they supported independence for Puerto Rico. Juan González, now a prize-winning journalist and co-host (on radio and public television) with Amy Goodman of *Democracy Now!*, was Minister of Education. El Comité was another New York based Puerto Rican Marxist Leninist organization, but was soon eclipsed by the PSP.

93     *Desde las entrañas*. (New York: Puerto Rican Socialist Party, 1973), part 3.

94     Founded in 1963 by former Kennedy administration officials Marcus Raskin and Richard Barnet, the Institute for Policy Studies (IPS) developed critiques of and alternatives to US foreign policy. During the 1960s and early 1970s IPS became a center for radical thought on domestic as well as foreign policy issues, and was an important hub for civil rights activism and anti-Vietnam War organizing. By 1973-74 it housed a dozen scholar/activist

fellows, each devoted to a particular project. At that time it also founded the Transnational Institute with offices in Washington and Amsterdam, to study and remedy disparities between rich and poor countries.

95     A desolate island with a semipolar climate located in the Straits of Magellan, 100 km south of the southernmost city in Chile. Immediately after the coup, the junta incarcerated 50 top officials, ministers and advisors from the Allende government, on the island. For a description of the immediate aftermath of the coup, see, John Dinges and Saul Landau, *Assassination on Embassy Row* (New York: McGraw-Hill, 1980), 68-91.

96     Centro de Invesitagación y Docencia Económicas [Center for Economic Investigation and Teaching]. CIDE was founded and directed by Trinidad Martínez Tarragó in 1974. Luis (Lucho) Maira, a Chilean exile and friend of Orlando's, was in charge of North American Studies at the Mexican think tank.

97     *The Nation*, 28 August, 1976, 140. Many decades later Naomi Klein described Pinochet's economic policies as a prime example of what she calls the "Shock Doctrine" in *The Shock Doctrine. The Rise of Disaster Capitalism*. Metropolitian Books, 2007.

98     Not her real name.

99     "The Chicago Boys in Chile: Economic Freedom's Awful Toll," *The Nation* (August 28, 1976).

100    See Roberta Salper, "US Government Surveillance and the Women's Liberation Movement, 1969-1973: A Case Study," *Feminist Studies* 34 (3), (Fall 2008): 431-455.

101    I wrote and delivered this speech in Spanish. This translation is mine.

# BIBLIOGRAPHY

Albert, Michael. *Remembering Tomorrow. From SDS to Life After Capitalism*. New York: Seven Stories Press, 2006.

Alpert, Jane. *Growing Up Underground*. New York: William Morrow and Company, 1981. Reprinted by Citadel Press in 1990.

Barnet, Miguel. *The Autobiography of a Runaway Slave, Esteban Montejo*. New York: Pantheon Books, 1968.

Baxandall, Rosalyn and Gordon, Linda. *Dear Sisters. Dispatches from the Women's Liberation Movement*. New York: Basic Books, 2000.

Boxer, Marilyn Jacoby. *When Women Ask the Questions. Creating Women's Studies in America*. Baltimore: The Johns Hopkins University Press, 1998.

Breines, Winifred. *The Trouble Between Us. An Uneasy History of White and Black Women in the Feminist Movement*. New York: Oxford University Press, 2006.

Brownmiller, Susan. *In Our Time. Memoir of a Revolution*. New York: The Dial Press, 1999.

Buitrago, Ann Mari and Immerman, Leon Andrew. *Are You Now or Have You Ever Been in the FBI Files?* New York: Grove Press, 1981.

Carr, Raymond. *Puerto Rico: A Colonial Experiment*. New York: Vintage Press, 1984.

Diggs, Elizabeth, "The New Women vs. Old Ideas," *Cuba: Essays by NUC members in Cuba during summer 1969*. Chicago: New University Conference, 1970.

Dinges, John and Landau, Saul. *Assassination on Embassy Row*. New York: McGraw Hill, 1980.

Dixon, Marlene. "Why Women's Liberation," *Ramparts* (December 1969).

Dunbar-Ortiz, Roxanne. *Red Dirt, Growing Up Okie*. London: Verso, 1997.

_____. *Outlaw Woman. A Memoir of the War Years, 1960-1975*. San Francisco: City Lights Books, 2001.

_____. *Blood on the Border. A Memoir of the Contra War*. Boston: South End Press, 2005.

Duplessis, Rachel Blau and Snitow, Ann, eds. *The Feminist Memoir Project. Voices From Women's Liberation*. New York: Three Rivers Press, 1998.

Dworkin, Andrea. *Heartbreak, The Political Memoir of a Feminist Militant*. New York: Basic Books, 2002.

Echols, Alice. *Daring to Be Bad. Radical Feminism in America 1967-1975*. Minneapolis, University of Minnesota Press, 1989.

Eisenstein, Hester. *Feminism Seduced*. Boulder and London: Paradigm, 2009.

Elbaum, Max. *Revolution in the Air. Sixties Radicals turn to Lenin, Mao and Che*. London: Verso, 2002.

Ehrenreich, Barbara and John. "The New Left: A Case Study in Professional-Managerial Class Radicalism," *Radical America* 11/31, 1977.

Evans, Sara. *The Roots of Women's Liberation in the Civil Rights Movement and the New Left*. New York: Vintage, 1980.

Freeman, Jo. *The Politics of Women's Liberation*. New York: David McKay, 1975.

_____. *At Berkeley in the '60s. The Education of an Activist, 1961-1965*. Bloomington: Indiana University Press, 2004.

Gardiner, Judith Kegan. "What Happened to Socialist Feminist Women's Studies Programs? A Case History and Some Speculations," *Feminist Studies* 34/3 (Fall 2008)

Gitlin, Todd. *The Sixties. Years of Hope, Days of Rage*. New York, Bantam Books, 1987.

Gordon, Linda. "A Socialist View of Women's Studies: A Reply to the Editorial, Volume 1, Number 1," *Signs: Journal of Women in Culture and Society* 1/2(1975).

Graves, Lucia. *A Woman Unknown, Voices from a Spanish Life*. Washington, D.C.: Counterpoint, 1999.

Heilbronn, Carolyn G. *Writing A Woman's Life*. New York: Ballantine Books, 1988.

Holmstrom, Nancy, ed. *The Socialist Feminist Project. A Contemporary Reader in Theory and Politics*. New York: Monthly Review Press, 2002.

Howe, Florence. *A Life in Motion*. New York: The Feminist Press, 2011.

_____, and Ahlum, Carol, eds. *Female Studies III*. Pittsburgh: KNOW, Inc., 1971.

Kampf, Louis. "The Humanities and the Inhumanities," *The Nation*, 207/5, September 1968.

Kampf, Louis and Lauter, Paul. Eds. *The Politics of Literature: Dissenting Essays on the Teaching of English*. New York: Pantheon, 1972.

Kerber, Linda, Kessler-Harris, Alice, Sklar, Kathryn Kish eds. *U.S. History as Women's History, New Feminist Essays*. Chapel Hill: University of North Carolina Press, 1995.

Kirkwood, Karla. *Carla Kirkwood Papers*. San Diego Historical Society. Files 12, 13, 14, 15, 16 17,

Krause, Charles A. "What is Left of the New Left? The New University Conference,"
*The New Republic*, March 1971.

Lerner, Gerda. *Fireweed, A Political Autobiography*. Philadelphia:

Temple University Press, 2002.

Letelier, Orlando. "The Chicago Boys in Chile: Economic Freedom's Awful Toll," *The Nation*, August 28, 1976.

López, Alfredo. *Doña Licha's Island*. Boston: South End Press, 1987.

Mandle, Joan D. *Can We Wear Our Pearls and Still be Feminists?* Columbia and London: University of Missouri Press, 2000.

Mangini, Shirley. *Memories of Resistance. Women's Voices from the Spanish Civil War*. New Haven and London: Yale University Press, 1995.

Marwick, Arthur. *The Sixties*. Oxford: Oxford University Press, 1999.

New University Conference (NUC) Papers, Fall, 1970. Personal Files Paul Lauter.

NUC Newsletter., 1/3 October 4, 1968; 3/5, October 20, 1969; 3/3, September 15, 1969. Personal Files Roberta Salper.

NUC Newsletter, 4/17, July 4, 1971; 3/1, August 15, 1969. Personal Files Paul Lauter.

NUC Women's Caucus Newsletters, nos.1-10. Personal Files Roberta Salper and Barbara Kessel.

NUC at the Modern Language Association, Newsletter 1, January 1969. Personal Files Paul Lauter.

McDermott, John. "Notes on the History of the New University Conference," unpublished paper. Boston, 2005.

Messer-Davidow, Ellen. *Disciplining Feminism. From Social Activism to Academic Discourse*. Durham and London: Duke University Press, 2002.

Myers, R. David, ed. *Toward a History of the New Left*. Brooklyn: Carlson Publishing Inc., 1989.

Northwestern University Library, Evanston, Ill. Charles Deering McCormick Library of Special Collections. Jenny Knauss Collection, Series X111

Oglesby, Carl. *Ravens in the Storm. A Personal History of the 1960s Antiwar Movement*. New York: Scribner, 2008.

Ohmann, Richard. *English in America: A Radical View of the Profession*. New York: Oxford University Press, 1976.

Orr, Catherine M. "Representing Women/Disciplining Feminism: Activism, Professionalism and Women's Studies," Ph.D. dissertation University of Minnesota June 1998.

——————. "Telling of our Activist Pasts: Tracing the Emergence of Women's Studies at San Diego State College," *Women's Studies Quarterly* 27, nos. 3-4 (1999).

Piercy, Marge. "The Grand Coolie Dam," *Leviathan* (May 1970).

Pincus, Fred and Erlich, Howard. "The New University Conference: A Study of Former Members," *Critical Sociology* 15 (1998).

Randall, Margaret. *Cuban Women Now: Interviews with Cuban Women*. Toronto: Women's Press Publications, 1974.

Rivera, Carmen V. "Our Movement: One Woman's Story," Torres and Velázquez, *Puerto Rican Movement, Voices from the Diaspora*.

Rosen, Ruth. *The World Split Open. How the Modern Women's Movement Changed America*. New York: Penguin Books, 2000.

Rosenfeld, Seth. *The FBI's War on Student Radicals, and Reagan's Rise to Power*. New York: Farrar, Straus and Giroux, 2012.

Sage, Lorna. *Bad Blood. A Memoir*. New York: William Morrow, 2002.

Salper, Roberta, ed. *Female Liberation: History and Current Politics*. New York: Alfred Knopf, 1972.

_____. "U.S. Government Surveillance and the Women's Liberation Movement, 1968-1973: A Case Study." *Feminist Studies* 34.3 (Fall 2008): 431-55.

_____. FBI File Documents CS100-45069, October 14, 1968; 100-16075-4, October 2, 1970; SD100-14670, February 18, 1972.

_____. "Women's Studies," *Ramparts* 10/6 (December 1971).

_____. "Women's Studies: Theory and Practice," *Some Politics of Women's Studies* (NUC Women's Caucus Newsletter, #8 1971)

Teodori, Massimo, ed. *The New Left: A Documentary History*. New York: Bobbs Merrill, 1969.

Tremlett, Giles. *Ghosts of Spain. Travels Through Spain and its Silent Past*. New York: Walker and Company, 2006.

Tobias, Shelia, ed. *Female Studies I*. Pittsburgh: KNOW, Inc., 1970.

Torres, Andrés and José E. Velázquez, eds. *The Puerto Rican Movement: Voices From The Diaspora*. Philadelphia: Temple University Press, 1998.

Weinbaum, Batya. *The Curious Courtship of Women's Liberation and Socialism*. Boston: South End Press, 1978.

Weisstein, Naomi. "Kinde, Kirche, Kuche: Psychology Constructs the Female , or the Fantasy of the Male Psychologist," in Elsie Adams and Mary Briscoe, eds., *Up Against the Wall Mother: On Women's Liberation*. Beverly Hills, CA: Glencoe Press, 1971.

Wilkerson, Cathy. *Flying Close to the Sun: My Life and Times as a Weatherman*. New York: Seven Stories Press, 2007.

Zimmerman, Bonnie. "In Academic and Out: The Experience of a Lesbian Feminist Literary Critic," in Greene, G and Kahn, eds., *Changing Subjects: The Making of Feminist Criticism*. New York: Routledge, 1993.

# ORAL INTERVIEWS

Diggs, Elizabeth. New York City. May 6, 2007.

Kampf, Louis. Cambridge, Massachusetts. June 21, 2007; November 9, 2007.

Kirkwood, Carla. Telephone interviews, July 28, 2009; August 11, 2009.

Lauter, Paul. Hartford, Connecticut. May 2, 2007.

McDermott, John. Cambridge, Massachusetts April 5, 2007; Boston, MA. October 5, 2009.

Slapikoff, Saul. Cambridge, Massachusetts. December 27, 2007.

# OTHER ANAPHORA LITERARY PRESS TITLES

*PLJ: Interviews with Best-Selling YA Writers*
Editor: Anna Faktorovich

*Inversed*
By: Jason Holt

*Notes on the Road to Now*
By: Paul Bellerive

*Devouring the Artist*
By: Anthony Labriola

*100 Years of the Federal Reserve*
By: Marie Bussing-Burks

*River Bends in Time*
By: Glen A. Mazis

*Interview with Larry Niven*
Editor: Anna Faktorovich

*An Adventurous Life*
By: Robert Hauptman

CPSIA information can be obtained at www.ICGtesting.com
Printed in the USA
BVOW05s0827020914

364595BV00001B/8/P